Edward B. Latch

Indications of the Book of Job

Edward B. Latch

Indications of the Book of Job

ISBN/EAN: 9783337736767

Printed in Europe, USA, Canada, Australia, Japan

Cover: Foto ©Lupo / pixelio.de

More available books at **www.hansebooks.com**

OF THE

BOOK OF JOB:

ALSO,

A PRELIMINARY TO THE INDICATIONS.

BY

EDWARD B. LATCH,
AUTHOR OF
"A REVIEW OF THE HOLY BIBLE."

PRESS OF
J. B. LIPPINCOTT COMPANY,
PHILADELPHIA.
1889.

PREFACE.

This volume takes up the general views as given in the work entitled "A Review of the Holy Bible," and carries with it the system of interpretation therein set forth.

A brief historic line has been prefixed as a preliminary upon which the "Indications" may rest as a base, and from which the interpretative system may radiate.

The Sacred Records clearly call for the existence of man—a chosen instrumentality in God's great Purpose by Election—far beyond the conventional six thousand years from the so-called Adam and progenitor of the human family.

If man did exist back of this Adam, and if the Scriptures are given by inspiration, then the Scriptures will surely harmonize in this particular also by giving man his proper place in the history of the world.

The Ages of Man once established, and the instrumentality of man (see Deut. vii. 6–14) once established, then the wonders of God in his great Purpose will become manifest to hosts that shall be "as the sand which *is* upon the sea shore" for number; hence the indications are that every point that is set or that shall be set upon a sure foundation by the hand of true science will confirm Scriptural truth, and bear fruit that will endure forever in the Kingdom of Righteousness.

The text used is the Holy Bible as issued by the American Bible Society, New York, 1860. (Brevier, 12mo.)

CONTENTS.

	PAGE
Preface	3
Preliminary to the Indications of the Book of Job	17

CHAPTER I.

(1) Who is Job? (3) Job as the Adam and progenitor of the Third Race of Men. (4) Job's children as allegory. (6) Who are the sons of God? Satan. (9–12) The Law enters into Job's Edenic home. (13–22) Satan's aggression upon the Third Race. Job still retains his integrity. 41

CHAPTER II.

(1–6) Job as a free agent under the Law confronted with Satan. (7, 8) Job's fall indicated by his afflictions. (9, 10) Job's hope and faith. (11) Job's three friends . . 49

CHAPTER III.

(1–10) Job laments his fall. (11–17) The subjugation of evil not all of man's mission. (18, 19) The valley of rest. (20–23) Man's mission as a priesthood indicated. (24–26) The priesthood of man further indicated 55

CHAPTER IV.

(1–6) Eliphaz assays to answer Job. Job's righteousness by works. (7) Evil has no hold upon the perfectly upright and righteous. (8–11) Job as a transgressor. (12–21) Man cannot equal the justness and purity of God. With Eliphaz descent into the valley of the shadow of death is annihilation 61

CHAPTER V.

(1, 2) Eliphaz seeks to confirm his view that the shadow of death is annihilation. (3–5) The philosophy of Eliphaz evidently includes the transgressor irrespective of host. (8–16) Eliphaz acknowledges the supremacy of God. The elevation of the creature during natural life. (17, 18) From the stand-point of Eliphaz the chastening of the creature by the Almighty induces the elevation of the creature during natural life. (19-27) The philosophy of Eliphaz consigns the creature to oblivion after the natural life shall have expired. Eliphaz accords Job a full natural life.   64

CHAPTER VI.

(1-3) Job's grief and calamity as weighed in the balance is against the philosophy of Eliphaz. (4, 5) Job's condition indicates his transgressive state. (11) Job reverts to the futility of his free agency that, as a subjugator, his life should be prolonged. (12, 13) Job contrasts his strength with the strength of the Adversary. (14) Job complains of the reasoning of his friend. (24) Job seeks to know wherein he erred. (25) The forcibility of right words. (26, 27) Job confronts Eliphaz as hopelessly condemning the creature under bondage to sin 68

CHAPTER VII.

(1-3) Time as appointed to man. Man's mission. (7-10) Job states "he that goeth down to the grave shall come up no more." Wherein does Job's reasoning differ in result from that of Eliphaz? (11-16) What is the life of the creature under tribulation that he should live forever? (17-19) The predestination and calling of man. (20, 21) Job admits that he is a transgressor . . . 79

CHAPTER VIII.

(1-3) Bildad advances his philosophy. Bildad's philosophy averse to that of Job. (8-10) Bildad calls Job's attention to conditions pertaining to the First and Second Ages of Man. (11-19) Bildad endorses the philosophy of Eliphaz. (20-22) Bildad accords life to a perfect man . . . 87

CHAPTER IX.

(1, 2) Job admits that God will not cast away a perfect man, but he also asks, "How should man be just with God?"

(3) Man cannot be just with God. (4) Man under the
Law cannot contend against God and prosper. (16-18)
The Almighty permits tribulation under the Law. (20, 21)
Why should Job despise his life were he perfect? (24)
The earth as given into the hand of the wicked. (25, 26)
Summary of Job's righteousness under the Law. (30, 31)
Future righteousness cannot take away transgression. (32,
33) Job acknowledges the supremacy of the Almighty,
and, hence, the immutability of the Law also . . . 93

CHAPTER X.

(1-3) Job seeks to know why the Almighty contends with
him. (7) Job's transgression unknown to him; that is,
Job has sinned through ignorance. (8-13) Job's faith in
existence beyond the natural life. (14-17) The confusion
of Job, in that if he sin he will not be acquitted, and if he
be righteous then he will not hold up his head. (18, 19)
Job laments anew his bringing forth into the world. (20-
22) The valley of the shadow of death 101

CHAPTER XI.

(1-4) Zophar defines Job's doctrine as being a multitude of
words, a statement of false issues. Job's doctrine includes
redemption and an existence after the natural life shall
have vanished. Zophar's philosophy condemns the doctrine of future life. (7-9) Wherein does Job derive his
doctrine of the redemption? (10-12) Zophar fails to see
beyond the Law. (13-20) Zophar admits life through a
fulfilment of Law, even to the creature that has transgressed. 108

CHAPTER XII.

(1-3) Job considers Zophar's reasoning as commonplace.
(4) Job's condition apparently unheeded by the Almighty. (5) Tribulation no indication of the true worth
of the sufferer. (6) Prosperity may cover the greater
transgressor. (7-10) Tribulation permitted for a wise
purpose. (12-25) Job defines attributes and powers pertaining to the Infinite Majesty, the Sublime Unity . . 113

CHAPTER XIII.

(1, 2) Job fully comprehends the philosophy of his three friends. (3-5) Job condemns the philosophy of his three friends. (13-16) Job reaffirms his faith in his Redeemer, and positively asserts the soundness of his reasoning. (18) Job expresses his faith in his justification, and, hence, in his glorification. (19) Job feels impelled to declare his position. (23) Job's iniquities 117

CHAPTER XIV.

(1, 2) Man in the hand of the power of Evil. (3) The strength of man, the strength of the Adversary, the strength of God. (4) The improbability of the subjugation of Evil by man. (5, 6) The bounds of time and the instrumentality of man. (7-12) Death and resurrection shadowed through the hope for a tree that is cut down. (13) Job longs for rest in the dark valley from the great trials that are upon him. (14, 15) If a man die shall he live again? (19-22) The Law of Generation and the Law of Iniquity 124

CHAPTER XV.

(1-3) Job's reasoning classified as vain knowledge by Eliphaz the Temanite. The possible soundness of Job's deductions. (5, 6) From Eliphaz's stand-point Job's uttered hope of a future existence is iniquitous. Job looks beyond the Law or First Covenant, with its ministration of death, but Eliphaz does not. (7-10) Eliphaz implies that Job was not the first man that was born. Eliphaz brings to notice the First and Second races of men. (12, 13) By the Law the transgressor shall die, yet Job, although a transgressor, hopes to live. Eliphaz condemns this hope as contrary to the Law. (14-16) The general uncleanness of the creature indicated by Eliphaz. The reasoning of Eliphaz favors the annihilation of the creature, even though it combine both good and evil. (17-19) The philosophy of Eliphaz points to progress from some created atomic or molecular system of life unto which the earth was given as a field of progress. (20-28) Eliphaz pictures the fate of a wicked man. (29, 30) Eliphaz consigns the transgressor to utter annihilation. (31–33) Eliphaz thrusts his barren deductions into Job's bosom 130

CHAPTER XVI.

(1, 2) Job replies, "I have heard many such things: miserable comforters *are* ye all." (3–5) Eliphaz's philosophy irretrievably condemns the transgressor, but Job's doctrine should assuage the transgressor's grief. (6) Tribulation comes from a source beyond Job's control. The inability of man as a subjugator of Evil. (7–10) The wrinkles and leanness of Job. (11–14) Job in the hand of Satan. Transgression does not, of necessity, make the creature a total depravity. (15–17) Job's tribulation due to unrecognized transgression. (18, 19) Job solicits investigation as to why his blood should be shed through transgression. (20–22) Job's belief in the immutability of God . . 141

CHAPTER XVII.

(1) The graves of Job. (3) Who will agree with Job's philosophy? (6–8) Job as the Adam and progenitor of the Third Race. The rigid imputation of sin. (10) Job cannot find one wise man among his friends, in that they provide no way for the abolishment of tribulation. True wisdom will find a means or way for casting down tribulation forever. (11–16) Job's failure as a subjugator. . 148

CHAPTER XVIII.

(1, 2) Job's words are but empty logic from Bildad's standpoint. Why should the philosophy of Eliphaz, Bildad, and Zophar be rejected by Job? (4) Shall the Law be removed out of its place that the creature may live a renewed life beyond the valley of darkness? (5–21) Bildad unequivocally declares his belief in the absolute eternal death of the wicked. No separation of the good from the evil . 153

CHAPTER XIX.

(1–4) Job condemns the arguments of Bildad. (5, 6) Job as a transgressor is overthrown by the Law that was established by the Almighty. This Law reaches to the very heart of the Evil Kingdom. (7) The wrongs of Job are due to the aggression of the Evil Kingdom, in that Job, through transgression, is under bondage to it. (8–10) Job's crowning glory was his mission as the subjugator of Evil. (12–20) The excessive tribulation of Job is due to the aggression of the Evil Kingdom that is superinduced through Job's fall into transgression. (21) Job seeks for pity from his friends. (22) Job's friends, however, persecute him and would chase him out of the world, so that neither root, branch, nor remembrance pertaining to him should evermore remain or be. (23–27) Job utters his immortal postulate, "For I know *that* my Redeemer liveth." Regeneration accomplished through the Communion of the Lord's body 156

CHAPTER XX.

(1–3) Zophar acknowledges his comprehension of Job's theory of redemption. (4–9) Zophar condemns Job to absolute eternal annihilation. (10) The places of the departed, from Zophar's stand-point, to be filled with their children. (22–27) Zophar's philosophy gives no indication of redemption for the transgressor after death. Zophar's philosophy annihilates the transgressor from the day of his death, whether such transgressor be a total depravity or whether he be a creature in which dwells both good and evil . . 163

CHAPTER XXI.

(1–3) Job will not agree with his friends that death seals the sum of existence pertaining to the creature. (4–6) Job troubled because of the apparent disregard of equity on the part of the ruling Power in the compensation for transgression. (7–16) The prosperous wicked man. (17) A man is not prosperous simply because he is wicked. (23–26) All transgressors under the same ban by the Law. Judgment after the natural life of the creature shall have passed away. A Redeemer called for by the judgment of the creature. (27, 28) Where is the house of the Redeemer? (29) The destructions of the creature are foundation-stones in the arguments of Eliphaz, Bildad, and Zophar, that the grave is the final resting-place of the creature. (31–34) Who shall declare the way of the transgressor to his face? Job accuses his friends with distorting the truth 169

CHAPTER XXII.

(1-4) The creature not called as a source of profit or of pleasure to the Almighty. The creature called that it might enter into His pleasure. (5-11) Eliphaz accuses Job of great iniquity, based, in all probability, upon the abundance of Job's afflictions. (15-18) Eliphaz calls Job's attention to the First or Euphratic race of men that fell under the rule of the Adversary. (19) The righteous, from Eliphaz's stand-point, are escaping remnants. (21, 22) Eliphaz indicates that his reasoning is based upon the Law. (23-30) Righteousness by works 178

CHAPTER XXIII.

(1-5) Job groaning under the burden of the Law seeks unto the Almighty for relief. (6) Job does not accredit the Almighty with being the source of his troubles. (7) Job's judge is the Law. The righteous, doubtless, is Job's Redeemer. (8-10) Job as a free agent under the Law. Job's righteous works a proof of faith. (11, 12) Job's transgression unknown to him. Job's postulate that his Redeemer lived marks him as being a transgressor. (13, 14) Purpose on the part of the Almighty and mission on the part of Job 183

CHAPTER XXIV.

(1) The Four Ages of Man. The limits of time. (19, 20) The fate of evil-doers. Absolute death the last link in the chain of labors that separates the good from the evil. (21-25) Who will make Job a liar? 188

CHAPTER XXV.

(1-6) Bildad's philosophy does not grasp any system whereby man can be justified with God, or whereby he can be made clean in the sight of God. Bildad's questions fail to answer Job's rigid construction of the Law, his faith in redemption, and his hope of a life after he shall have passed into the valley of the shadow of death, and even after absolute death 193

CHAPTER XXVI.

(1, 2) Wherein does the philosophy of Bildad help the creature that is taken captive at the will of the Adversary? (3) The foolish, the demented, the blind as transgressors. Bildad's philosophy condemns them also. (5, 6) Every grave contains a known occupant. (7-14) Job calls attention to ways of the Almighty, but how small a portion of them? 194

CHAPTER XXVII.

(1-6) Job positively refuses to justify his friends in their reasoning that there is no redemption for the creature, no life hereafter. (8-10) What is the hope of the hypocrite? (11-17) Job defines the portion of the wicked man. The portion of the wicked man well known to the friends of Job. Job's deductions very different and widely separated from those of his friends. (18-23) The wicked man that is destroyed is the evil element that pervades man. The separation of the good from the evil 198

CHAPTER XXVIII.

(1-3) The separation of the good from the evil indicated by Job. (7, 8) The hidden mystery shadowed. (12-22) Where can wisdom be found? (23-28) God understandeth the way of wisdom and he knoweth the place thereof. 207

CHAPTER XXIX.

(1-7) Job calls attention to the days when, as the Adam and progenitor of the Third Race, he dwelt in Eden free from sin and transgression. (8) The overlap of the Second and Third races shadowed. (9, 10) The respect in which Job was held before he transgressed. (11-13) Job's righteousness by works under the special protection of the Almighty. (14) The Law now enters in to Job as a governing principle whereby Job becomes a free agent under the Law. Satan a free agent under the Law. (15-25) Job's rightcous works under the Law as a free agent. The fall of Job. The transgression of Job 211

CHAPTER XXX.

(1, 2) Job the sport and prey of the Evil Kingdom. Old age perished from Job. (3-14) Job persecuted by the later generations of the Second race, and by his own family. (15-19) The great Hiddekelic Famine indicated. (25-31) Job expresses his righteous actions. When he looked for good evil came 215

CHAPTER XXXI.

(1, 2) Righteousness by works under the Law as a free agent. (3) Destruction to the wicked through the Law. (4) God takes cognizance of all steps, good and bad. (5, 6) Job requests an even balance, a just weight, under the Law. (7-15) The remarkable integrity of Job. Job admits transgression. (16-18) Job as the Adam and progenitor of a race of men. (24-28) Job brings himself into condemnation, in that his mouth hath kissed his hand. (32-34) Who is the Adam spoken of by Job? (35-37) Job expresses a desire that the Almighty would answer him, and that his adversary had written a book. (38-40) Why should Job have been so particular in setting forth his own righteousness under the Law? 220

CHAPTER XXXII.

(1-3) Job's three friends cease to answer him. Elihu's wrath is kindled against Job. Elihu's wrath also against his three friends. Why Elihu's wrath was thus kindled. (4, 5) Who is Elihu? Elihu as Satan transformed as an angel of light. (6-9) Elihu begins to answer Job and his three friends. Elihu briefly defines man. (10-13) Elihu admits that Job's friends failed to answer Job's words. (16-22) Elihu as the Adversary of Job; Job having expressed a desire that his adversary had written a book . 228

CHAPTER XXXIII.

(1-3) Elihu's words to be measured by the character of Satan. (4, 5) Did the Spirit of God make Satan? Satan claims to be a creature. (7-11) Job subject to both good and evil. (14-17) An aggressive power greater than man indicated. (19-22) Elihu points to the grave as a probable finality to the transgressor. (23-26) Elihu advances the righteous works of a transgressor under the Law as a ransom from death. (27, 28) Elihu sets aside the Law through repentance. (29, 30) Elihu still further advocates self-righteousness and repentance as ransoming conditions. No Redeemer called for. The irrevocability of the Law demands fulfilment of the Law. (31-33) Elihu seeks to teach Job wisdom. Will the wisdom of Elihu exceed that of Job? 233

CHAPTER XXXIV.

(1-6) Job's right. What is good? Why Job's wound is incurable without transgression. (10-12) Elihu defines certain attributes of the Almighty,—" Neither will the Almighty pervert judgment." (13-15) Elihu points to no return of the spirit of man after death. (16, 17) Elihu advances the immutability of the Law that condemns the transgressor. Elihu's view does not unsettle Job's position that his Redeemer lives. (18, 19) Elihu sets forth the improbability of any redeemer arising to redeem the transgressor. (20-22) By Elihu's reasoning death is annihilation. Elihu denies the existence of a valley of the shadow of death, but Job holds to the valley of the shadow of death. (23) Compensation through repentance from Elihu's standpoint. (24-28) By Elihu's reasoning the unrepentant are cut off, and others will be set up in their stead. The philosophy of Elihu establishes the Evil Kingdom indefinitely. (29, 30) Elihu's plausibility. (31, 32) Elihu points to a series of rewards and punishments during the natural life of the creature. (33) Elihu asserts that the system of rewards and punishments comes from the Almighty and not from the Evil Kingdom: which is it? (34) Elihu considers that Job spoke without knowledge, and that his words were without wisdom. (36, 37) Elihu as Satan demands that Job be tried unto the end because of his answers for wicked men. Are Job's answers rebellion against God? Are Job's answers a multiplicity of words? 240

CONTENTS. 15

CHAPTER XXXV.

(1–3) Elihu misconstrues Job's words. (4–7) The Sublime Unity. The Three Persons of the Trinity. (8) The Kingdom of Righteousness. The Redeemer. (9–11) The arm of the mighty is the Law. (12) The oppressed can find no relief from the Law in the Law. (13, 14) Elihu enjoins Job to trust in the Almighty that judgment come not upon him. (15, 16) The words of Elihu indicate that tribulation has come upon Job because Job heeds not the system of repentance as set forth by Elihu . . . 252

CHAPTER XXXVI.

(1–4 The words of Elihu as the words of Satan. (5–12) Elihu's position calls for no Redeemer. Self-righteousness and repentance, from Elihu's stand-point, ransoms the transgressor. Job's philosophy the stronger of the two. (16, 17) Elihu argues that Job transgresses in that he goes beyond the Law. (18, 19) Elihu's words imply that, after death, nothing can deliver, not even all the forces of strength. From Elihu's stand-point death is absolute, eternal annihilation 257

CHAPTER XXXVII.

(1–20) Elihu calls Job's attention to the wondrous works of God. (21–24) Elihu continues his record of the attributes of the Most High. Still Elihu points to no Redeemer; still he points to no system whereby the creature may be delivered from the frightful tribulative chain that binds him to the Evil Kingdom. Is this situation the result of far-reaching wisdom? Wherein is essential Evil vitally touched by it? Wherein is the earth and every living thing that moves upon the earth subjugated by it? The deductions of Elihu are at variance with the plans of the Almighty, and fail to answer Job, or throw down his great postulate, "I know *that* my Redeemer liveth" . . 263

CHAPTER XXXVIII.

(1, 2) The words of the Lord evidently condemn the sayings of Elihu. (3, 4) The Lord calls upon Job to answer him.

The foundation of the earth. (5-7) The Chief Corner-Stone. (8-11) The Evil Kingdom. (12, 13) The Dayspring. (16) The Source of Evil. (17) Absolute death. The valley of the Shadow of Death. (18) The earth includes all matter. (19-21) Neither the Source of Good nor the Source of Evil can be traced to the house thereof. (22, 23) The Judgmental Era. (24) The separation of the good from the evil. (25-27) The Plan of Redemption. (28-30) Job's attention is called to the Almighty as the Creator. (31, 32) The Almighty as Governor. (33-35) The Almighty as Master. The Almighty as unerring Judge. (39-41) The Almighty as Provider . . . 268

CHAPTER XXXIX.

(1-4) The Almighty as the watchful Guardian. (5-8) The Almighty as the life-conferring Source. (9-12) The Almighty as the Subjugator 278

CHAPTER XL.

(1, 2) How can man contend with the Almighty? Eternal life through free agency or righteousness by works under the Law. (3-5) Job's transgression meets him face to face. (6-8) Eternal life a free gift of the Almighty. (9-14) The strength of Job as a free agent under the Law compared with the strength of the Almighty. (15-24) The behemoth as shadow 282

CHAPTER XLI.

(1-34) The leviathan as shadow 285

CHAPTER XLII.

(1-3) Job accords the infinite knowledge and perfection of the Almighty as Governor of all things, that he alone should order, subdue, provide, protect, and deliver, whenever and wherever such may or might be called for. (4-6) Job now more fully comprehends the greatness of the one that shall be Subjugator and Ruler. Job repents in dust and ashes. (7-9) Job's three friends commanded to offer a burnt-offering for themselves. Elihu left out. (10-15) The replenishment of Job. The years of Job. . 289

PRELIMINARY

TO THE

INDICATIONS OF THE BOOK OF JOB.

THE INFINITE REACH. | Antecreative Eras, or eras during which no creature exists.

The Infinite Reach combines and includes within itself all eras, ages, periods, and times, from "everlasting to everlasting."

The Antecreative Eras are reaches with only one common finite limit or border, in which but two Existences as Powers have being and place. These two Existences are, first, The Infinite Majesty,—to whom be glory in the highest forever,—and, second, Satan, King of Evil.

The Infinite Majesty is the One God, the True Light, the Source of every good and perfect gift. He is without beginning of days or end of life, and is the Supreme Ruler of, and in, and throughout, the Infinite Reach.

The One God is the Sublime Unity, the Holy Trinity, the Unity of the Power that conceives, the Power that signifies assent, and the Power that fulfils.

The Sublime Unity is the Creator and the King of Righteousness.

The Power that conceives is Thought.
The Power that signifies assent is the Word.
The Power that fulfils is Action.

These three Powers are equal the one with the other; the fulness of the three rests with and dwells in each one as a Person; hence each is positive and perfect as a Power; and they, as the Holy Trinity, combine into the Sublime Unity.

The Sublime Unity, being the One God, is perfect within himself, and needs nothing to complete his happiness; for "known unto God are all his works from the beginning of the world." The Sublime Unity is the Giver of every good and perfect gift.

Satan is the King of Evil, the Power of Darkness, the Source of pain and tribulation. Satan is without beginning of days, yet not, of necessity, without end of life.

Satan is King of Unrighteousness, and is a non-creator.

Satan combines within himself a conceiving power, an assenting power, and a fulfilling power; but, as a unity, he is imperfect; for, although combining these three powers within himself, yet, not being a creator, he is far below the Sublime Unity as a Power; hence these powers in Satan are not positive and perfect, in that he, Satan, cannot carry out or bring to pass all his thoughts and words. The evil, however, that the Infinite Majesty permits, that only can Satan bring to pass.

Satan is aggressive, and, although powerful beyond all human conception (see 1 Kings xix. 11, 12), he is, without the creature, powerless for want of a field of aggression.

Satan in this portion of the Infinite Reach, for want of an aggressive field, is unproved as an Evil Tree, although the Infinite Majesty fully comprehends him and the inherent attributes of which he is a unity.

Satan being aggressive, yet being unproved as an Evil Tree, God's great Purpose by Election is framed.

God's Purpose by Election clearly demands a kingdom filled with intelligences, in which all thought and action will be justified, and be without blemish, through the Word or Assenting Power of the One God, in which Word or Assenting Power "dwelleth all the fulness of the Godhead bodily."

At this point (see margin) let a tag or mark be placed upon the Infinite Reach as a tangible comprehensive beginning to the Creative Eras.

The Kingdom of God now, at or about this point in the Infinite Reach, begins in the ordination of the Word of God as the King and the Messiah. (See Psalm ii. 6, 7.)

A. *The Messiah* is the beginning of the creation of God, and the beginning of the Kingdom of God; hence the creation and preparation of a body for the Word of God, which Word has been ordained as Messiah and King. This body (see Col. i. 15–18; Rev. iii. 14) is the first-born of every creature, the very beginning of the creation of God, and is pure and unblemishable; hence Satan cannot touch this body, for it is created pure, and it ever will be kept pure. This body (see Col. i. 18) has the pre-eminence in all things; wherefore it must be the tangible foundation, base, and building that constitutes the tangible Kingdom of God, as pertaining to the living creature (see Eph. ii. 18, 22), that shall endure forever; hence immortality pertains to this body.

B. *Creation of earth or of matter.* This creation comprehends the material from which, later, a body was prepared for the living creature in the day that the living creature was created. This earthy body is blemishable, and it forms no part of the pure body that was previously prepared for the Word; they are separate and distinct, the one from the other. Mortality pertains to this earthy body; hence, through the earthy body, Satan has a field of operation before him in which to prove the quality of the fruit that inheres to his kingdom.

C. *The spirit of the living creature* (host not being considered) is now brought forth and clothed with or born into its earthy body. This is the first generation of the living creature; hence this body is the first or natural body of the living creature. (See the Infinite Reach at B.) Eternal life may fall to the creature in this body through the fulfilment of a perfectly upright and righteous life.

D. *Satan* now having a field of operation before him, makes aggression upon the living creature thus brought forth, and proves thereby that his kingdom bears bitter fruit.

E. *The power of Satan* is so great that the living creature falls into transgression; but, in this period or age, sin (see Rom. v. 12, 13) is not imputed, for there is no law; hence no penalty is attached to the offence. The adherents of the Evil Kingdom, therefore, through the non-imputation of sin, fearlessly develop their aggressive schemes, but they are undoubtedly proving the deadly quality of the attributes of which they are unities.

THE INFINITE REACH.		B.C. 31863
Creative Eras, or eras in which the creature does exist.	Time, or determinate periods or ages.	The Pre-Euphratic Era, or The First Division of Reuben.

F. *The Son begotten.** At this point in the Infinite Reach time or determinate chronology begins.

In and as the beginning of the creation of God, however (see the Infinite Reach at A), a body was prepared for the Word of God,—the Word of God, before such creation, having been ordained as Messiah and King,—that the Word of God might do the will of God. The will of God is briefly given as follows (Gen. i. 28): "Be fruitful, and multiply, and replenish the earth, and subdue it: and have dominion over the fish of the sea, and over the fowl of the air, and over every living thing that moveth upon the earth;" wherefore the Word of God, "in whom dwelleth all the fulness of the Godhead bodily," now, or about this point in the Infinite Reach, comes forward and invests the body that had been prepared for him in and as the very beginning of the creation of God; that in, by, and with this body he may do the will of God by subjugating all hosts, by driving out evil in all its ramifications, and by replenishing the earth with those of his own choosing; hence with the advent of the Word of God as the begotten Son (for when the Word of God invested the body that had been prepared for the Son or Word, the indication follows that

---

* Advent of the Messiah as the Living Bread.

the Son was begotten at the period or time of such investment) the war against Satan is inaugurated; and with the advent of the Word of God as the begotten Son determinate chronology begins. (See margin.) The indication also follows that when the Word of God invested the body that had been created for it (see the Infinite Reach at A), that such investment endowed it with life, and hence this body became and was, after the investment, the Living Bread which (see St. John vi. 50, 51) shall be eaten that eternal life may, through the eating thereof, pertain to the creature.

G. *The Word of God* is the Messiah, the Messiah is the King, and the King is the Son of God, who now dwells in the body that was prepared for him in the beginning that he might do the will of God; therefore, can Satan bring any tarnish upon the unblemished body of the Son because of the non-imputation of sin? Never; for this body is unblemishable through the power of the Infinite God that created it perfect and without spot; hence the non-imputation of sin possesses no strength as a temptation to the Son of God that he should transgress through the prevailing condition of leniency. The indication is also manifest that the purity of the Kingdom of Righteousness depends upon the perfect unblemishability of the body that was prepared for the Word or the Son; into which body the spirit of the living creature is and will be regenerated or born that it may be clothed upon with this unblemishability. (See, also, 2 Cor. v. 1–4.)

H. *The war against Satan* (see Rev. xii. 1–9) is made manifest after the begetting of the Son. In this war Satan is cast out of heaven into the earth, and his angels are cast out with him. Before this casting out, however, Satan (see Rev. xii. 4) drew a great host after him and cast them into the earth; hence the unsubjugated host of evil, and the host under bondage to it, roam the earth, apparently unchecked, with no penalty attached to their offences; for no law has entered even yet for the imputation of sin.

B.C. 29789

I. *Creation of the First or White Race of Men.* At or about this time in the Infinite Reach, a body was formed for this Race (Adam's, see Gen. v. 2) of the dust of the earth, the breath of life was breathed into it by the Creative Power, and it became a living soul. Thus the spirit of man of Adam's race is, at the first, or at the time of its bringing forth, clothed with an earthy body, and, hence, the earthy body is the first or natural body of man of Adam's race. (For the elementary creation, not formation, of this material body, see the Infinite Reach at B.) Man (see Gen. i. 28) is called as a subjugatory Element.

K. *The Law* enters in with the creation and bringing forth of man of Adam's race; for (see Rom. v. 13–20) "until the law sin was in the world; but sin is not imputed when there is no law;" and (see Gal. iii. 19) the law was added because of transgressions. Inasmuch, however, as death reigned from Adam to Moses, so the ruling of the Law is made manifest from the calling of Adam, whether such Adam be the progenitor of the First Race of men or whether he be the progenitor of the Fourth Race.

The Law entered because of the transgression that existed prior to the advent of man of Adam's Race; hence, from the entering thereof, sin will be imputed to the transgressor irrespective of host, that the offence may abound against the transgressor irrespective of host.

The indication becomes manifest that inasmuch as the Law is a righteous embodiment, that all hosts must come under its rulings, whether such hosts pertain to the heaven or to the earth; hence the Law contains an ordination to life that the one who fulfils the Law may live in it, and it contains a ministration of death that the penalty of transgression may rest over the transgressor irrespective of host. Wherefore the entering in of the Law, with its accruing penalty,—viz., death,—calls for the absolute presence of two or more witnesses that shall offer faithful testimony for and against the transgressor irrespective of host, when, through the imputation of sin and the abounding of the offence, the books shall be opened for the judgment of the transgressor.

L. *Advent of the Messiah* as a Faithful Witness. The two Faithful Witnesses (see Rev. i. 5; Rev. iii. 14) are the Lord Jesus Christ and the Spirit; hence they must have testimony to present from the entering in of the Law until judgment shall have been rendered against the transgressor irrespective of host.

The First Person of the Trinity may also be a Witness, whereby two Witnesses will be found who can testify for and against the transgressor for the period of time,—viz., three days and three nights, during which the Messiah as Jesus Christ lay environed with absolute death.

The indication is also clear that inasmuch as Satan continues from the entering in of the Law until the same shall be ready to vanish away, that the witnesses that shall testify in his case must also endure for the same period of time.

M. *Creation of the Second or Red Race of Men.* This Race of men is created independent of and distinct from the First Race, and is called forth as a subjugatory Element; wherefore the ruling of the Law is over it also; but, like its predecessor (for the First Race fell into transgression), it was too weak to resist the wiles of Satan, king of Evil.

N. *The First Race of Men* having failed in its mission as a subjugatory Element, is swept away from the face of the earth through the agency of earthquake and volcanic eruption.

O. *The Law of Iniquity* calls for the transmission of the iniquity of the fathers upon the children (see Ex. xxxiv. 5–7) unto the third and to the fourth generation; hence, in order that this Law may fulfil, an escaping remnant will always be provided that the destruction of the human family be not total.

P. *The Escaping Remnant* is made manifest in and by the overlap of the First and Second races of men (see the Infinite Reach at M–N), during which, by intermarriage, the iniquity, blood, and characteristics of the First Race are visited upon the Second.

THE INFINITE REACH.	Creative Eras, or eras in which the creature does exist.	Time, or determinate periods or ages.	Overlap of the Second and Third Races of Men.
			B.C. 13465
		The Gihonic Era.	
			B.C. 12098
		Overlap of the Third and Fourth Races of Men.	
			B.C. 3897

Q. *Creation of the Third or Black Race of Men.* This Race is created and brought forth independent of, and distinct from, either of the two preceding races. Moreover the indication is clear that the intermarriage of the White and Red races would not produce a Black race.

This Race, in turn, was called and given a mission comprehending the subjugation of Evil, but it failed to cast down the mighty Power of Evil; and, hence, failed as a subjugatory Element.

R. *Destruction of the Second or Red Race by drought and famine.* This destruction, however, was not total; for by intermarriage during the overlap of the Second and Third races a remnant was made to escape, whereby the iniquity, blood, and characteristics of the Second were visited upon the Third, and (see the Song of Sol. i. 5, 6) not only those of the Second, but, by the operation of the Law of Iniquity, those of the First Race also.

S. *Creation of the Fourth or Pale Race of Men.* This Race was created independent of, and distinct from, the three that preceded it. Inasmuch, however, as a mixed multitude may be produced through the intermarriage of the White, Red, and Black races, the predominating color of which would be pale, so the pale color of the Fourth Race of men serves as a veil to screen the independent creation of the first three races.

After the creation of the Fourth Race of Men the Most High rested from his labors, and He will not take them up again until His great Purpose by Election shall have become established; which Purpose, as already indicated, is the justification of all thought and action, through the Word or Assenting Power of the Infinite Majesty, in a kingdom of which He is the absolute unblemished Monarch.

The Fourth Race also falls into transgression, and fails in its mission as the subjugator of Evil; wherefore the promise is given in the garden of Eden that a subjugator shall arise in the House of Man.

T. *The Second and Third Persons of the Trinity,* now that the whole four races of men have failed in their respective missions as subjugators, evidently must carry out the plans of the Most High for the subjugation of Evil, and for the redemption of the creature that is under bondage to Satan, and, also, to establish God's great Purpose by Election; hence no new creature will be created or brought forth that the futile efforts of such new creature for the establishment of righteousness through free agency, or righteousness by works under the Law, may be still further extended; the indication being clear that, while the creature is on trial, the Second and Third Persons of the Trinity will not, or do not, take up the subjugatory labors; and that they will not now, or do not, take them up until after the complete failure of the creature world shall have been fully demonstrated, whether such creature pertain to the heaven or to the earth.

In the plans of the Most High man (see Ex. xix. 3-6) is pointed to as a possible kingdom of priests and a holy nation, which indication is confirmed by the choosing of the tribe of Levi in the stead of the first-born, that are males, among all the tribes of Israel. As a priesthood and a holy nation man becomes a peculiar people unto the Lord, and a choice instrumentality in the wonders pertaining to the regeneration of the creature.

U. *Destruction of the Third Race of Men by the Deluge of Noah.* Thus the Third Race was swept away; but by the intermarriage of the Third and Fourth races during the overlap or contemporary existence thereof, the iniquity, blood, and characteristics of the First, Second, and Third races were visited upon the Fourth race or generation in full harmony with the Law that governs the transmission of iniquity to the fourth generation.

Side margin table:

THE INFINITE REACH.			
Non-creative Eras, or eras in which the creature does exist, but during which no new creature is or will be created.	Time, or determinate periods or ages.	Overlap of the Third and Fourth Races of Men.	
			B.C. 2241
			The Pisonic Era or Age.

The escaping remnant of the Third race (see Isa. xxi. 16, 17), and that of the overlapping portion of the Fourth (see Gen. vii. 7-13), was very small, consisting of but eight persons in all,—viz., Noah and his wife, his three sons and their three wives. Upon these eight persons, therefore, the iniquity, blood, and characteristics of four independent consecutive races of men rested; and hence, from them are redeveloped the mixed multitude that peoples the Fourth or Pisonic Age.

The indication is now clear that, because of the complete failure of man of Adam's race, the Second and Third Persons of the Trinity must, in themselves, fulfil the plans of the Most High for the subjugation of Evil, and for the redemption of the creature that is under bondage to Satan, and, also, to establish God's Purpose by Election; hence the grand struggle for supremacy will be carried on between the Second and Third Persons of the Trinity on the one part, and Satan, King of Evil, on the other part. (See, also, Jer. xv. 11-21.)

V. *Advent of the Messiah as the Living Bread* that came down from heaven, as the Redeemer, and as the Subjugator. Melchizedek (see Gen. xiv. 18-20), priest of the most high God, brings forth bread and wine. This bread is the pure body, or is of the pure body, that was prepared for the Word in the beginning of the creation of God (see the Infinite Reach at A), suitable for the labors involved in the subjugation of evil, and for the redemption of the fallen creature.

This bread, as already indicated, became the Living Bread in the day when the Word of God invested it (see the Infinite Reach at F); and hence, the Word of God by thus investing the pure body that had been prepared for the Word, invested it with life, and thus the Word became and was begotten as the Son of God that he might do the will of God. This Living Bread, therefore, is the Living Bread that, later (see St. John vi. 51; St. John viii. 54–58; Gen. xiv. 18–20), came down from heaven; and, inasmuch as it was and is created unblemishable, the indication is clear that no evil or unclean thing can become united to it, or even touch it.

Melchizedek is, with little or no doubt, the Third Person of the Trinity, the Fulfilling Power of the Infinite Majesty; the Messiah is the Second Person of the Trinity, the Word or Assenting Power of the Infinite Majesty; hence the Prime Movers in the work for the subjugation of evil and for the redemption of the fallen creature are made manifest as presences.

When Melchizedek, priest of the most high God, brought forth bread and wine he met Abram returning from the slaughter of the kings. At this meeting (see Gen. xiv. 18–20) Melchizedek blessed Abram of the most high God, and called him possessor of heaven and earth. From the greatness of Melchizedek (see Heb. vii. 1–4) and from the magnitude of the blessing wherewith he blessed Abram, the indications are almost positive that Abram ate of the bread brought forth by Melchizedek; and, also, that this bread was the Living Bread that came down from heaven, that it was the body of the begotten Son (see the Infinite Reach at A), that it was the flesh of the Redeemer which (see St. John vi. 51–58) must be eaten that life may ensue; wherefore, when Abraham ate of this Living Bread his spirit was born into it or transferred into it, that, through such transfer, he might obtain life.

At the first, however, where man of Adam's race is concerned, the spirit of man was born into the earthy body (see the Infinite Reach at I) that was prepared or formed out of the dust of the earth for it; but now, by partaking of the Living Bread, the spirit of man is born into the Living Bread also; and, hence, is regenerated or born into the body that was created and prepared for the Word or Son (see the Infinite Reach

[Side marginalia, bottom to top:

THE INFINITE REACH.
Non-creative Eras, or eras in which the creature does exist, but during which no new creature is or will be created.

Time, or determinate periods or ages.

The Pisonic Era or Age.]

at A) prior to the creation of matter or created condition otherwise.

When Abram ate of the Living Bread, the Living Bread, from the time of the eating thereof, took upon itself the flesh of Abram, or of Abraham, as he afterwards was called, whereby the iniquity that rested upon Abraham also rested upon the Living Bread through the operation of the great Law of Iniquity.

The indication follows from these conditions that when the spirit of man is regenerated or born into the Living Bread, the Living Bread or second body with which the spirit of man is thus clothed really is (see 1 Cor. xv. 44-48; St. John vi. 51-58) the flesh of the Lord that came down from heaven, or, in other words, that it really is of the body that was prepared for the Word (see the Infinite Reach at A), in and as the very beginning of the creation of God.

W. *Advent of the Messiah as the Son of Man, and as the Seed of Abraham.* Abraham having eaten of the Living Bread, the Living Bread, as already indicated, became through the operation of physical laws part of his flesh; wherefore, by the power of God, it, the Living Bread, was brought forth into the world a manifest physical presence as the flesh and seed of Abraham; even as woman (see

Gen. ii. 21–23) was brought forth into the world, by the same Power, from the flesh of Adam as a manifest physical presence.

From these conditions indications follow that, at this time (see the Infinite Reach at W), the Living Bread became the seed of Abraham, and that the seed of Abraham (see Gal. iii. 16) is the Messiah as the Son of man (see, also, Gen. iii. 16); hence the Messiah made his advent as the Son of man (see St. John viii. 56–58) in the day of Abraham.

X. *Advent of the Messiah as the Prophet.* (See Deut. xviii. 15.) The Messiah as the Prophet is manifest as a physical presence in and as Elisha the son of Shaphat; the proof being witnessed (see 2 Kings v. 10–14; St. Luke vii. 19–23; St. Luke vi. 44) by Elisha's works; wherefore, from these conditions, indications are evident that the Living Bread descends into the valley of the shadow of death, and that it returns from thence (see Isa. vi. 13) and shall be eaten.

By descent into the valley of the shadow of death the Messiah changes his tabernacle as the Seed of Abraham, the Seed of Isaac, the Seed of Jacob, and as the Seed of Jacob after him; hence it follows that the Messiah (see 1 Chron. xvii. 4, 5) walked in many tabernacles; one of which, as already indicated, is that manifest in Elisha the Prophet.

Y. *Advent of the Messiah as the Seed of Woman.* Through the ministrations of the priesthood of Melchizedek (see St. Luke i. 26–35, in harmony with Gen. xiv. 18–20) the Virgin also ate of the Living Bread; hence the Living Bread was, in due time, born of the Virgin in fulfilment of the promise given in the garden of Eden, and also in fulfilment of the sign given Ahaz, king of Judah. The name of this son of the Virgin was called Jesus, and Jesus (see St. Matt. xxvii. 17) is called Christ.

Z. *Crucifixion and absolute death of the Messiah as Jesus Christ.* In this death the penalty that rested upon the redeemed transgressor (see the Infinite Reach at K) was absolutely paid in strict fulfilment of the Law.

When the Messiah as Jesus Christ thus died he laid down his life in the pure, unblemished body that had been prepared for him (see the Infinite Reach at A) in and as the very beginning of the creation of God; and into which the spirit of the creature, through the communion or eating thereof, had been regenerated prior to this absolute death; hence, through regeneration, the creature died an absolute death (see, also, 2 Cor. iv. 10, 11) in the absolute death of Jesus Christ the Messiah, the Escaping Remnant (see Isa. i. 9; Romans ix. 29), of and for the creature world.

A'. Resurrection of the Messiah as Jesus Christ. When Messiah as Jesus Christ, the manifest Lord and Saviour, arose from the dead on the third day after his death, he arose as the Word of God, clothed with the pure, unblemished, and unblemishable body that was prepared for him in the beginning of the creation; hence, inasmuch as the spirits of the redeemed were regenerated, born into, or transferred from the earthy body that was formed for them in the day they were created and with which they were clothed (see the Infinite Reach at I) in the day they were created into the pure, unblemishable body of the Messiah (see the Infinite Reach at A), so they, the redeemed, will rise with Christ the Redeemer when he returns from the absolute death that environs him after his crucifixion, clothed with this body; and, hence, will partake of eternal, never-ending life through the redemption thus provided.

With the death of Christ the judgment of the creature host commences; and with the resurrection of Christ the Year of Jubilee for the creature host is ushered in.

Now, although the Judgmental Era commences from the time of the absolute death of the Messiah as Jesus Christ, yet, inasmuch as transgression does not come to the full until the seventy weeks of the book of Daniel shall have expired, the indication becomes manifest that the judgment of the Evil Host will not begin until after such fulness shall have been established.

B'. *Transgression comes to the full* at or about this time in the Infinite Reach, according to the seventy weeks of the book of Daniel; hence the judgment of the Evil Host commences with or about the year A.D. 2133. The judgment of all hosts doubtless will have been rendered prior to the advent of the Messiah as King of the Thousand Years Era; although the entire destruction of Evil may not find accomplishment until after this wondrous reign shall have expired.

C'. *Advent of the Messiah as King of the Thousand Years Era.* This wondrous reign will constitute proof of the subjugation of the earth, as called for (Gen. i. 28); and it also reveals the Ruler as the Subjugator Jesus Christ, the Word of God, for whom, as Messiah and King, a body was prepared which is and was the very beginning of the creation of God, and into which body the creature world is regenerated or born.

D'. *The Era of Destruction.* During this Era the fire from God out of heaven shall come down and shall test all things; that which is good will endure, but that

THE INFINITE REACH.			
The Word returns to the Father. Creative labors re-established.	Non-creative Eras in which the creature does exist.	Time (determinate).	The Pisonic Era or Age.
Indeterminate periods or ages.		A. D. 3963	
The Kingdom of Righteousness.			

which is evil will perish forever as an energy and as an active principle. After these great things shall have been fulfilled, then the Word will return to the Father, and the Infinite Three as the Sublime Unity will crown the unfolding future with glories inconceivable for wonder and for magnitude.

E'. *End of Time.* Time was set apart for the overthrow of Evil, and for the establishment of a kingdom in which all thought and action will be justified through the Word or Assenting Power of the Infinite Majesty; hence, with the exit of time, Evil ceases to exist as a vitality; but the Kingdom of Righteousness is enthroned forever upon an indestructible base without any rival to mar the creature or to force development from its perfect path.

INDICATIONS

OF THE

BOOK OF JOB.

I. 1. "There was a man in the land of Uz, whose name *was* Job; and that man was perfect and upright, and one that feared God, and eschewed evil."

Thus the record is given that Job was a perfect and an upright man. Who, therefore, is Job? man of Adam's race, or is he one of the Eternal Three that combine into the Sublime Unity? for of man it is stated (2 Chron. vi. 36), "for *there is* no man that sinneth not," and also (Psalm xiv. 3), "*there is* none that doeth good, no, not one." If the meaning conveyed by these quotations—viz., that there is no man that sinneth not—be absolute truth, how can a man of Adam's race be pointed to as a perfect and an upright man? The indications are clear that such a one can only be found in the progenitor of a race of men, as Adam, who was created perfect and upright by the Creative Power; for Noah, Abraham, Isaac, Jacob, David, Solomon, all were transgressors, while even Enoch, that was translated, by the law bore upon him a burden of iniquity that could only be washed away by death. If, however, Enoch did not transgress, then he would live in the Law independent of the labors of the Messiah; for Death possesses no control over the righteous.

Is, therefore, Job identical with Adam?—that is, is he identical with the Adam of the Fourth Race, that the truth of the text may apply to him as such and thus be considered as established? or is Job identical with a person of the Trinity, that he thus stands before the Lord as a perfect and an upright man? The context states,—

I. 2. "And there were born unto him seven sons and three daughters."

As seven sons and three daughters were born unto Job, the indication is strongly marked that Job is not a person of the Trinity, but, rather, that he is of and after the race of Adam. Indications further follow that if he is a man of and after the race of Adam, to fill the measure of the text (see verse 1) he must be the progenitor of a race of men, and that, as such, he was created perfect and upright.

If Job, in order to fill the measure of the text as a perfect and an upright man, must be the progenitor of a race of men, how is it that (see xxxi. 33) he speaks of an Adam that was a transgressor contemporary with or before him? If Job's reference be to the Adam of the Fourth Race, then, in Job, a man is found that is born of woman who is free from sin,—which, clearly, cannot be; for, as already stated, "*there is* no man that sinneth not;" hence the indications are that Job was created prior to the Adam of the Fourth Race, that he was created subsequent to the Adam of a race preceding him, and that he himself was the Adam or progenitor of a race independently brought forth, and thus was distinct from the others; hence he was not the Adam of the Fourth Race.

I. 3. "His substance also was seven thousand sheep, and three thousand camels, and five hundred yoke of oxen, and five hundred she asses, and a very great household; so that this man was the greatest of all the men of the east."

The very great household pertaining to Job indicates the multiplication of the newly-created race of which Job is the progenitor. The term "east" indicates the Second Age of man; hence, as Job was a perfect and an upright man, and, as such, was the Adam of a new order or race of men, and as he was the greatest of all the men of the east, the indications are that Job was the first man of, or the Adam of, the Third Race; which race, in its mission, must cast out the men of the east or of the Second Age, and, hence, must become greater than the men of the east. Moreover, as Job (see verse 6) lived contemporary with the sons of God, and as the sons of God (see Gen. vi.) were destroyed by the Deluge of Noah, so indications are further given whereby he established the age to which Job belonged; the sons of God called for by the text being with little doubt the people of the Third Age, whose days subsequently ran out at the time of the Deluge.

I. 4. "And his sons went and feasted *in their* houses, every one his day; and sent and called for their three sisters to eat and to drink with them."

It is quite probable, inasmuch as Job pertains to the Third Age, that the three sisters shadow the daughters of

Jerusalem (see the Song of Solomon), that allegorically represent the first three ages of men,—viz., the White or Euphratic, the Red or Heddekelic, and the Black or Gihonic. The feasting of Job's sons, every one his day points to the progress of time from the calling of man.

I. 5. "And it was so, when the days of *their* feasting were gone about, that Job sent and sanctified them, and rose up early in the morning, and offered burnt offerings *according* to the number of them all: for Job said, It may be that my sons have sinned, and cursed God in their hearts. Thus did Job continually."

This verse points to time subsequent to the entering in of the Law, for (see Rom. iii. 20) "by the law *is* the knowledge of sin;" hence sin was round about Job, although he himself was, as yet, perfect and upright; transgression may, however, have overtaken his children, or it may overtake them at any time.

I. 6. "Now there was a day when the sons of God came to present themselves before the Lord, and Satan came also among them."

Who are the sons of God called for by the text? They are evidently (see Gen. vi. 1–7; Song of Sol. i., ii. 1–3; Rev. vi. 5, 6) the people of the Third Age, of which Job is the progenitor; hence the sons of God would be the children of Job.

The day when the sons of God presented themselves before the Lord doubtless was a special occasion for the offering of burnt-offerings, and of expressing their gratitude to their King and Creator; but who is Satan? The answer to this question is given as follows (Rev. xii. 9): "And the great dragon was cast out, that old serpent, called the Devil, and Satan, which deceiveth the whole world: he was cast out into the earth, and his angels were cast out with him."

Did the Lord God create Satan and his angels, or did he not? There appears to be little or no evidence to show that the Lord created them, for it is stated (Gen. i. 31), "And God saw every thing that he had made, and, behold, *it was* very good." If such was the case, how is it possible to call Evil very good? It is not possible, for Evil is evil, and Good is good; the one being diametrically opposed to the other; but the fruit of the two kingdoms may be made manifest in one individuality, as witnessed in the creature, whether such creature be animate or inanimate.

In the allegory of the Creation (see Gen. i. 1, 2), the Power of Evil may be recognized as Darkness, and the Power of Good as Light; hence these two Powers (see also Rom. v. 13) coexisted from infinity; yet (see St. John i. 5) "the light shineth in darkness; and the darkness comprehended it not;" nor will it ever comprehend the magnitude before which it slowly sinks into oblivion.

The bringing forth of the creature by the Creative Power rouses the dormant energy of Evil into a state of sleepless activity; but such activity does not develop comprehension of the Creature Power whose unfolding plans it ruthlessly tramples under foot. The text indicates the presence of Satan in Job's Edenic home.

I. 7. "And the Lord said unto Satan, whence comest thou? Then Satan answered the Lord, and said, From going to and fro in the earth, and from walking up and down in it."

Here again, by the Lord's question, the indication is given that the Lord did not create Satan, while

Satan's reply is confirmatory of independent existence. The Lord, however, comprehended Satan in all his infinity, and read his most secret thoughts; but his question opens out to finite intelligences the improbability of the creation and development of evil by the Creative Power. Had such been the case, the worlds would form but one vast amphitheatre in which man and ravening beasts would prey continually one upon the other, under the skilful guidance of Satan, their evil trainmaster, otherwise called "that old serpent, the devil." The Scriptures, however, from the very first (see Gen. i. 27, 28), call for the subjugation of evil; man having been predestinated and was called as the subjugatory element through which the commandment of the Lord might be fulfilled.

I. 8. "And the Lord said unto Satan, Hast thou considered my servant Job, that *there is* none like him in the earth, a perfect and an upright man, one that feareth God, and escheweth evil?"

The record is again given that Job is a perfect and an upright man; hence, where can such a one be found? The Adam of the Fourth Race fell before a son was born to him, but Job has seven sons and three daughters, and still he is a perfect and an upright man. From these indications it follows that Job cannot be identical with this Adam who also was created perfect, but who fell (see Rom. vii. 9) with the entering in of the Law. What man, then, brought forth since the Adam of the Fourth Race can fill the measure of the text: Enoch? No; for (see Gal. iii. 11, 12) "that no man is justified by the law in the sight of God, *it is* evident: for, The just shall live by faith.

"And the law is not of faith: but, The man that doeth them shall live in them;" moreover (see Rom. iii. 20), " by the deeds of the law there shall no flesh be justified in his sight: for by the law *is* the knowledge of sin," and again (Rom. iii. 23), "for all have sinned, and come short of the glory of God;" hence the perfection and uprightness of Job point to him as one who was created perfect and upright and who had not, as yet, fallen under the devices of Satan.

I. 9–12. "Then Satan answered the Lord, and said, Doth Job fear God for nought?

"Hast not thou made a hedge about him, and about his house, and about all that he hath on every side? thou hast blessed the work of his hands, and his substance is increased in the land.

"But put forth thine hand now, and touch all that he hath, and he will curse thee to thy face.

"And the Lord said unto Satan, Behold, all that he hath *is* in thy power; only upon himself put not forth thine hand. So Satan went forth from the presence of the Lord."

These verses indicate that, up to this time, the law had not entered into Job's Edenic home, but when Job and all that he had were put in the power of Satan, the indication comes forth that the law had entered as a ruling principle to him and to his house, whereby Satan (see Rom. vii. 9–11) could essay his power against them.

I. 13–22. "And there was a day when his sons and his daughters *were* eating and drinking wine in their eldest brother's house:

"And there came a messenger unto Job, and said,

The oxen were ploughing, and the asses feeding beside them :

"And the Sabeans fell *upon them,* and took them away; yea, they have slain the servants with the edge of the sword; and I only am escaped alone to tell thee.

"While he was yet speaking, there came also another, and said, The fire of God is fallen from heaven, and hath burned up the sheep, and the servants, and consumed them; and I only am escaped alone to tell thee.

"While he was yet speaking, there came also another, and said, The Chaldeans made out three bands, and fell upon the camels, and have carried them away, yea, and slain the servants with the edge of the sword; and I only am escaped alone to tell thee.

"While he was yet speaking, there came also another, and said, Thy sons and thy daughters *were* eating and drinking wine in their eldest brother's house:

"And, behold, there came a great wind from the wilderness, and smote the four corners of the house, and it fell upon the young men, and they are dead; and I only am escaped alone to tell thee.

"Then Job arose, and rent his mantle, and shaved his head, and fell down upon the ground, and worshipped.

"And said, Naked came I out of my mother's womb, and naked shall I return thither: the Lord gave, and the Lord hath taken away; blessed be the name of the Lord.

"In all this Job sinned not, nor charged God foolishly."

These verses indicate the success of Satan in his aggression upon the house of Job: they soon fell into transgression, and the penalty thereof came upon them;

still, the record is given that in all this Job sinned not, nor charged God foolishly.

The widespread destruction that came upon Job's household probably shadows or is coincident with the disasters that culminated in the destruction of the people of the Second Age, together with those of the Third Race who lived contemporary with them, the second or Heddekelic Race having been swept away by the great famine that prevailed (see Gen. xli. 54–56) over all the face of the earth. The Second Race of men was created about the year B.C. 23,017, and was destroyed about the year B.C. 12,098; the Third Race was created about the year B.C. 13,465; hence, in the light that Job was the Adam of the Third Race, he would have been thirteen hundred and sixty-seven years old at the time the earth was thus depopulated.

II. 1–6. "Again there was a day when the sons of God came to present themselves before the Lord, and Satan came also among them to present himself before the Lord.

"And the Lord said unto Satan, From whence comest thou? And Satan answered the Lord, and said, From going to and fro in the earth, and from walking up and down in it.

"And the Lord said unto Satan, Hast thou considered my servant Job, that *there is* none like him in the earth, a perfect and an upright man, one that feareth God, and escheweth evil? and still he holdeth fast his integrity, although thou movedst me against him, to destroy him without cause.

"And Satan answered the Lord, and said, Skin for

skin, yea, all that a man hath will he give for his life.

"But put forth thine hand now, and touch his bone and his flesh, and he will curse thee to thy face.

"And the Lord said unto Satan, Behold, he *is* in thine hand; but save his life."

From foregoing indications it is quite evident that, at the time of this presentation, the people of the Third Race are transgressors through the wiles of Satan, and that Satan presents himself before the Lord conscious of the great success that has attended his aggression upon the human family. Job, however, still retains his integrity; but now that the special protection of the Almighty is taken from him, and he stands as a free agent under the ruling of the Law, affliction will take hold of his own flesh, for Satan will surely prevail against him in some particular.

II. 7-8. "So Satan went forth from the presence of the Lord, and smote Job with sore boils from the sole of his foot unto his crown.

"And he took him a potsherd to scrape himself withal; and he sat down among the ashes."

Now, although Job was perfect and upright when he together with the sons of God stood before the Lord upon the second day, yet when Satan went forth from the presence of the Lord upon the second day, the test of strength will be between Satan and Job: for Job, under the Law, will now be a free agent, the Almighty permitting the Law to rule over Job. If, therefore, Job be the stronger he will fulfil the mission of his calling,—viz., the subjugation of Evil or of Satan; in which case Satan (see Ex. xv. 26) cannot bring tribulation upon him; but should Satan be the stronger of the two, then he will certainly cause Job to transgress either in thought or deed; by which he could bring disease upon him. The boils with which Job was smitten are evidence, if not actual proof, that Job fell before Satan, and that he had transgressed either in thought or in deed.

II. 9–10. "Then said his wife unto him, Dost thou still retain thine integrity? curse God, and die.

"But he said unto her, Thou speakest as one of the foolish women speaketh. What? shall we receive good at the hand of God, and shall we not receive evil? In all this did not Job sin with his lips."

Even as Job's wife asks, does Job still retain his integrity? The indications are that he does not; wherefore his wife said, "Curse God, and die." Why? Because the penalty of transgression rests upon him, which penalty is death. Job, however, reproved his wife, and accused her of speaking foolishly. If Job was under the ban of transgression the penalty of which is death, why was his wife's counsel as foolishness to him? Further on (see xix. 25) Job gives his immortal reply to this and to all such questions, "For I know *that* my Redeemer liveth;" hence, although transgressive through the wiles of a power stronger than himself, he proclaims the actual personal existence of his Redeemer, and that through his redemption proof would be manifest that the evils wrought by Satan will be undone forever. Curse God, and die? If all were included in the ruling of the First Covenant, then well might Job despair, and even hearken to his wife's ill-advised counsel; but Job's prophetic vision reaches beyond to a newer and better covenant through the Seed promised by which or of which all families of the earth shall be blessed.

Now, although Job sinned not with his lips, yet that does not prevent him from being a transgressor: for it is stated (St. Math. xv. 19, 20), "For out of the heart proceed evil thoughts, murders, adulteries, fornications, thefts, false witness, blasphemies:

"These are *the things* which defile a man;" hence so perfect is the great plan of the Almighty for the overthrow of evil that not a vestige of it will be left to lurk in the innermost recess of any living creature. Evil thoughts engender aggression; aggression involves pain and tribulation; pain and tribulation wreck the happiness of the creature; whence it follows that evil thoughts spring from the fountain of evil. If evil thoughts spring from the Fountain of Evil, and if Evil shall be overthrown, then it is clear that the evil thinker must be counted as a transgressor that the offence may abound and judgment be rendered against him as a transgressor; hence with the fulfilment of the judgment pronounced against the transgressor (be the transgression great or small, for by the Law the penalty is the same) Evil is met in all its ramifications, both great and small; hence, again, while Evil, root and branch, will be swept away forever, the creature may exclaim with Job (xix. 23–25), "Oh that my words were now written! oh that they were printed in a book!

"That they were graven with an iron pen and lead in the rock forever!

"For I know *that* my Redeemer liveth, and *that* he

shall stand at the latter *day* upon the earth." The faith of Job is sublime; for, as the progenitor of the Third Race, many years must elapse before the advent of the Messiah as the Redeemer of man will be witnessed; nevertheless the Redeemer of man lived (see Psalm xl. 6-8; Heb. x. 5-7) before Job was brought forth as an instrumentality in the great purpose of the Almighty; but the Messiah as the Redeemer of man must, clearly, by the Law, make his advent as the son of man; which advent took place (see Gen. xiv. 18-20; St. John viii. 56-58) in the day of Abraham. The day of Abraham, by the indications of the Scriptures, truly is the "latter day," the latter Time or Age, to Job; hence in the Fourth Age the Messiah, Job's Redeemer, the Redeemer of man, stood upon the earth as witnessed by the records of both the Old Testament and the New.

Faith in the Redeemer stands to-day upon vastly different grounds, or rather upon grounds far more widespread than it did in the day of Job. Why? Because in Job's day the Messiah had not made his advent in the flesh, but to-day, in the Fourth Age, the Sacred records claim that he has made his advent as the Redeemer of man, in the flesh of man, and as the son of man. Job's faith, therefore, rested solely upon promises; but to-day faith rests not only upon promises, but upon work actually performed by the Redeemer of Job when he stood upon the earth in the latter day or the Fourth Age.

Job's faith also indicates his belief in the begetting of the Son who, in the body prepared for him, came to do the will of God. What is a portion of this will?

It is (see Rom. viii. 28-30) the justification and glorification of those whom he predestinated and called; according to his purpose, that which was predestinated and called (see Gen. i. 26-28) was man, for man was made after the likeness and image of God; which clearly shows predestination and calling. Through the body thus prepared for the Son Job recognizes his Redeemer; for into this body Job will eventually be regenerated or born, and it, the body prepared for the Son, will become the flesh of Job; hence Job further says (xix. 26-27), " And *though* after my skin *worms* destroy this *body*, yet in my flesh shall I see God:

" Whom I shall see for myself, and mine eyes shall behold, and not another; *though* my veins be consumed within me." Hence the flesh of Job in which he shall see God will be of the pure, spotless, unblemished body that was prepared for the Son suitable for this purpose, and will not be the corrupt body of flesh and blood in which he knew evil and transgression: for (see text xix.) the corrupt body will be consumed within him. From these references indications are clear that the counsel of Job's wife was as foolishness to him: for why should he curse God and die when he knew that his Redeemer lived?

Job's reply to his wife, "Shall we receive good at the hand of God, and shall we not receive evil?" indicates the righteousness of the penalty of transgression that pertains to the First Covenant: for if there were no penalty for transgression the offence could not abound, judgment could not be rendered, and, hence, Evil could not be overthrown; whence it follows that the evil that came upon Job was a consequent of his transgression, and that he fell under the machinations of the Power of Evil in whose hand he, as a free agent, was, through the Law, left by the Almighty.

II. 11. "Now when Job's three friends heard of all this evil that was come upon him, they came every one from his own place; Eliphaz the Temanite, and Bildad the Shuhite, and Zophar the Naamathite: for they had made an appointment together to come to mourn with him, and to comfort him."

Thus three friends of Job came to mourn with him and to comfort him.

III. 1-10. "After this opened Job his mouth, and cursed his day.

"And Job spake, and said,

"Let the day perish wherein I was born, and the night *in which* it was said, There is a man child conceived.

"Let that day be darkness; let not God regard it from above, neither let the light shine upon it.

"Let darkness and the shadow of death stain it; let a cloud dwell upon it; let the blackness of the day terrify it.

"*As for* that night, let darkness seize upon it; let it not be joined unto the days of the year; let it not come into the number of the months.

"Lo, let that night be solitary; let no joyful voice come therein.

"Let them curse it that curse the day, who are ready to raise up their mourning.

"Let the stars of the twilight thereof be dark; let it look for light, but *have* none; neither let it see the dawning of the day:

"Because it shut not up the doors of my *mother's* womb, nor hid sorrow from mine eyes."

This lament of Job, couched in such powerful language, indicates his great grief at the failure of his mission, his calling. As the first-born of, and as the progenitor of, the Third Race of men, the command was given Job (see the mission of man, Gen. i. 28) to subjugate Evil; but instead of subjugating Evil the Evil element overcame him and brought him into bondage. Is it any wonder, therefore, that Job should curse the day of his bringing forth? Is it any wonder that, after his fall, he should lament his fate with bitter lamentation? Not at all; for the vale of death yawns to receive him, while sorrow (see Gen. iii. 17-19) shall be his portion all the days of his life; all of which is in addition to his grief of heart at the failure of the great mission to which he had been called. Job contiues his lament,—

III. 11-16. "Why died I not from the womb? *why* did I *not* give up the ghost when I came out of the belly?

"Why did the knees prevent me? or why the breasts that I should suck?

"For now should I have lain still and been quiet, I should have slept: then had I been at rest,

"With kings and counsellors of the earth, which built desolate places for themselves;

"Or with princes that had gold, who filled their houses with silver:

"Or as a hidden untimely birth I had not been; as infants *which* never saw the light."

Had Job died at the time of his bringing forth, or,

rather, at the time the Law entered for his government, he would still have been a transgressor; for without transgression (see Rom. vii. 8–11) he was alive, for death is not adjudged without transgression; but, in his case, with transgression came pain and tribulation, not as yet, however, the death-like sleep that pertains to the shadowy vale; for Job had mission to fulfil other than the subjugation of Evil; still, had he descended into the grave, he would have rested with the kings and counsellors of the earth that had been called into existence before his day.

The text further indicates that infants born alive, but which at the time of their birth give up the ghost, rest with kings and counsellors also; but (see verse 16) a hidden untimely birth is as though it had not been; hence, as a thing which hath not been cannot be recalled into existence, so, by the text, neither can the infant that never saw the light be recalled into existence or to the light; if otherwise, then the hidden untimely birth could not be classed in essential result with that which hath not been. Of the place of rest above indicated Job states,—

III. 17–19. "There the wicked cease *from* troubling; and there the weary be at rest.

"*There* the prisoners rest together; they hear not the voice of the oppressor.

"The small and great are there; and the servant *is* free from his master."

Such are the conditions that surround the dwellers in the valley of the shadow of death. They sleep an untroubled sleep, their rest is unbroken; neither the voice of the oppressor nor the hand of the wicked can evermore arouse them from slumber to pain. Blessed sleep for the weary; for, should no Redeemer arise, even then no pain or tribulation could, evermore, find in them a conscious habitation, although the text calls them prisoners; hence the indication is evident that the day will come when the length and breadth of this dark land will be visited by One who shall proclaim the Divine command (see Eph. v. 14), "Awake thou that sleepest, and arise from the dead, and Christ shall give thee light."

To Job, in his great affliction, this land of rest was a haven more desirable than all the treasures earth could cluster around him; for, from his day, not a few years only must pass away; but a myriad lay marked on the chart of time before the First fruit from the dead will call him to the light undimmed by shadow. Job continues,—

III. 20-22. "Wherefore is light given to him that is in misery, and life unto the bitter *in* soul;

"Which long for death, but it *cometh* not; and dig for it more than for hid treasures;

"Which rejoice exceedingly, *and* are glad, when they can find the grave?"

These questions of Job point to mission other than the subjugation of evil; what can it be? and why should not man descend into the valley of the shadow of death immediately after his transgression is manifested? Indications follow that life is given to the bitter in soul that they may fulfil their part in the great Plan that leads to the redemption and restoration of others than man. Job knew that his Redeemer lived, but the Redeemer of Job is the Redeemer of others besides Job; for (see Rev. xii. 3, 4) Satan cast a host into the earth which, clearly, did not pertain to man of Adam's race, neither was it (see Rev. xii. 7-9) Satan's immediate army. This host (see Eph. iii. 4-6) is the host of Gentiles that was created by the Almighty prior to the calling of man, and they fell into transgression prior to the calling of man; although at the time of their fall (see Rom. v. 13, 14) sin was not imputed. But what has this to do with the preservation of man as a transgressive creature that he should continue and not find the grave? The indications are that the welfare of the Gentile host is bound up with the welfare of man of Adam's race, and that the redemption of the Gentile host reaches fulfilment through man of Adam's race as a priesthood and a nation of priests; hence that subjugation of evil does not comprehend all the mission to which man was predestinated and called; therefore light is given to him that is in misery, and life unto the bitter in soul, that he may fulfil that mission of his individual calling; mission that is shrouded in mistery and hidden from sight. Job appears to indicate this where he asks,—

III. 23. "*Why is light given* to a man whose way is hid, and whom God hath hedged in?"

Thus the indication is strongly marked that the hidden mystery (see Col. i. 23-27) was open as a question to the mind of Job; wherefore Job continues:

III. 24-26. "For my sighing cometh before I eat, and my roarings are poured out like the waters.

"For the thing which I greatly feared is come

upon me, and that which I was afraid of is come unto me.

"I was not in safety, neither had I rest, neither was I quiet; yet trouble came."

The conditions indicated by the text would certainly follow with the calling of man as a priest; for persecution will fall upon the creature that seeks in any way to undo the works of Satan, the powerful King of Evil. Inasmuch, therefore, as the priests (see Ex. xxix. 32, 33) shall eat those things wherewith the atonement was made, so Job partook or ate of something that brought upon him dire tribulation; and even before he had eaten fear came upon him; hence what could Job have eaten that could or would thus bring down upon him Satan's wrath, if it were not something wherewith atonement had been, was, or would be made? Did not Aaron and his sons, the Levitical priesthood, eat of those things wherewith the atonement was made? They did certainly; hence, if atonement was made by the things that were eaten, then the indications come forth that the well-being of some host or hosts is bound up in the eating thereof; and if such be the case, so, also, the eating spoken of by Job may pertain to the well-being of some host or hosts, in consequence of which the devices of Satan were zealously devised against him.

Now, although Job was created perfect and upright, yet (see verse 26) he was not in safety; and although he was a worker, evidently for the good of others, yet trouble came upon him, which trouble, with little doubt, was due to the great strength of Satan, in that he caused Job to transgress.

IV. 1–6. "Then Eliphaz the Temanite answered and said,

"*If* we assay to commune with thee, wilt thou be grieved? but who can withhold himself from speaking?

"Behold, thou hast instructed many, and thou hast strengthened the weak hands.

"Thy words have upholden him that was falling, and thou hast strengthened the feeble knees.

"But now it is come upon thee, and thou faintest; it toucheth thee, and thou art troubled.

"*Is* not *this* thy fear, thy confidence, thy hope, and the uprightness of thy ways?"

Even as Eliphaz states, Job (see i. 5) upheld him that was falling, instructed many, and strengthened the weak hands; but, at the time, he himself (see ii. 1–6) had not been given into the hand of Satan. Later, however (see ii. 7), Satan did hold him in bondage, and smote him with sore boils from the sole of his foot to his crown.

Eliphaz further intimates that the righteousness of Job, as shown in his dealings with others, points to righteousness under the Law, righteousness by works, righteousness through free agency, and that this righteousness is induced through fear of the penalties carried with transgression; hence, when personal trouble overtook Job, Eliphaz asks, "*Is* not *this* thy fear, thy confidence, thy hope, and the uprightness of thy ways?" evidently referring to Job's righteousness by works as having been induced through fear of trouble. Eliphaz continues,—

IV. 7. "Remember, I pray thee, who *ever* perished, being innocent? or where were the righteous cut off?"

These questions of Eliphaz were propounded in the Third Age of man; hence, who, under the ruling of the First Covenant, ever perished or was cut off that was perfectly innocent and righteous? The First Covenant ordains to life through righteousness by works; therefore what power can cut off the perfectly innocent and righteous? The indication is clear that, inasmuch as the First Covenant or Law was established by the Almighty, no power exists that can make void the Law by cutting off the perfectly innocent and righteous. Jesus Christ the righteous (see 1 John ii. 1; St. John x. 14–18), at the end of his ministry, laid down his life for his people; of his own free will and accord he laid it down; no man took it from him: for he had power to lay it down and to take it up again; but when (see Isa. liii. 1–9) the Messiah was cut off out of the land of the living, his perfection was marred by the heavy burden of sinful flesh that pertained to others; wherefore he was numbered with the transgressors. This cutting off took place in the Fourth Age, while the stand-point of the text, as hidden history, is in the beginning of the Third Age, or before the Messiah made his advent in the flesh as the Redeemer of man; hence the words of Eliphaz are directed against Job as man of Adam's race, and do not of necessity include the Messiah as Jesus Christ the righteous. The context is confirmatory of these indications as follows:

IV. 8–11. "Even as I have seen, they that plough iniquity, and sow wickedness, reap the same.

"By the blast of God they perish, and by the breath of his nostrils they are consumed.

"The roaring of the lion, and the voice of the fierce lion, and the teeth of the young lions, are broken.

"The old lion perisheth for lack of prey, and the stout lion's whelps are scattered abroad."

By the Law the things which Eliphaz depicts will befall the transgressor, let him pertain to which host he may, for the Law is immutable; hence the afflictions that have come upon Job constitute evidence that he is not wholly righteous, and, hence, that he is a transgressor. Eliphaz continues,—

IV. 12-21. "Now a thing was secretly brought to me, and mine ear received a little thereof.

"In thoughts from the visions of the night, when deep sleep falleth on men,

"Fear came upon me, and trembling, which made all my bones to shake.

"Then a spirit passed before my face; the hair of my flesh stood up:

"It stood still, but I could not discern the form thereof: an image *was* before mine eyes, *there was* silence, and I heard a voice, *saying*,

"Shall mortal man be more just than God? shall a man be more pure than his Maker?

"Behold, he put no trust in his servants; and his angels he charged with folly:

"How much less *in* them that dwell in houses of clay, whose foundation *is* in the dust, *which* are crushed before the moth?

"They are destroyed from morning to evening: they perish forever without any regarding *it*.

"Doth not their excellency *which is* in them go away? They die, even without wisdom."

The reasoning of Eliphaz indicates that man cannot be more just than God, and be more pure than his Maker, or that he cannot equal the justness and purity of God. Why? Because by the Law immortality would clothe the creature that transgressed in nothing; but inasmuch (see 1 Tim. vi. 14–16) as none hath immortality but God, the creature must be counted as a transgressor, whether such creature be man or angel. By the Law, therefore, all are included under sin,—man and angel,—for none are perfect like God; and, hence, by the Law, all, whether man or angel, must die; which conditions Eliphaz makes manifest in his words to Job. If all die through the Law, then Eliphaz concludes that they perish forever; for the First Covenant or Law provides no way for the redemption of the transgressor. In support of his views Eliphaz says to Job,—

V. 1, 2. "Call now, if there be any that will answer thee; and to which of the saints wilt thou turn?

"For wrath killeth the foolish man, and envy slayeth the silly one."

Hence, where can Job turn for a witness in confutation of Eliphaz's words? The Law forbids the return of the dead from their graves, whether as the saint, the foolish, or the silly. Eliphaz continues,—

V. 3–5. "I have seen the foolish taking root: but suddenly I cursed his habitation.

"His children are far from safety, and they are crushed in the gate, neither *is there* any to deliver them.

"Whose harvest the hungry eateth up, and taketh it

even out of the thorns, and the robber swalloweth up their substance."

Thus prosperity may hover around the creature for a time, but sooner or later the transgressive element will manifest itself; the city wall, built through free agency for protection, will crumble and fall prostrate. Who or what can then deliver? The Law? No; hence Eliphaz says, "Neither *is* *there* any to deliver." Wherefore Eliphaz recognizes no ruling beyond the First Covenant that entered for the overthrow of evil; hence the position he assumes, while it is against Job, yet it also militates against the Kingdom of Evil, the source and fountain of pain and tribulation.

That the Kingdom of Evil is the source and fountain of pain and tribulation is indicated by Eliphaz in the context, as follows:

V. 6, 7. "Although affliction cometh not forth of the dust, neither doth trouble spring out of the ground;

"Yet man is born unto trouble, as the sparks fly upward."

The dust and the ground are God's creatures; hence, as (see Gen. i. 1) "in the beginning God created the heaven and the earth," so trouble and affliction cannot come forth from them, they having been pronounced to be very good; and, as man is born unto trouble, so God does not institute it; hence pain and tribulation must pertain to the Kingdom of Evil as the source and fountain thereof. Eliphaz further counsels Job,—

V. 8–16. "I would seek unto God, and unto God would I commit my cause:

"Which doeth great things and unsearchable; marvellous things without number:

"Who giveth rain upon the earth, and sendeth waters upon the fields:

"To set up on high those that be low; that those which mourn may be exalted to safety.

"He disappointeth the devices of the crafty, so that their hands cannot perform *their* enterprise.

"He taketh the wise in their own craftiness: and the counsel of the froward is carried headlong.

"They meet with darkness in the daytime, and grope in the noonday as in the night.

"But he saveth the poor from the sword, from their mouth, and from the hand of the mighty.

"So the poor hath hope, and iniquity stoppeth her mouth."

In these verses Eliphaz acknowledges and asserts the supremacy of God; but, at the same time, he indicates that evil flows through the creature, and as it is driven out so the creature rises into safety, yet not (see iv. 19, 20; v. 4) into eternal life. This plan, however, provides no way for the overthrow of Evil; for with the continued advent of the creature new fields arise in which the Adversary preserves the vigor and activity of his kingdom.

The deductions of Eliphaz (verse 16), "So the poor hath hope, and iniquity stoppeth her mouth," are not sound except in a very limited sense, for the elevation of a poor man does not stop the mouth of iniquity, else (see verse 7) man would not be born unto trouble; it being evident that as long as there is trouble there is iniquity also. But should the individual be raised or exalted above trouble and iniquity for his natural life that the mouth of iniquity may, in his case, be stopped, no guarantee is given of a renewed existence to that individual after his natural life shall have expired; neither is any guarantee given that the mouth of iniquity is not opened with greater effect in another direction, even as the changing wind of a cyclone does not, of necessity, indicate a less degree of force. Eliphaz continues,—

V. 17, 18. "Behold, happy *is* the man whom God correcteth: therefore despise not thou the chastening of the Almighty:

"For he maketh sore, and bindeth up: he woundeth, and his hands make whole."

From the stand-point of Eliphaz the chastening of the Almighty would result in the elevation of the chastened above his enemies during his natural life, so that he would not be cut off before the years thereof should have become fulfilled; in confirmation of which Eliphaz continues,—

V. 19-27. "He shall deliver thee in six troubles: yea, in seven there shall no evil touch thee.

"In famine he shall redeem thee from death: and in war from the power of the sword.

"Thou shalt be hid from the scourge of the tongue: neither shalt thou be afraid of destruction when it cometh.

"At destruction and famine thou shalt laugh: neither shalt thou be afraid of the beasts of the earth.

"For thou shalt be in league with the stones of the field: and the beasts of the field shall be at peace with thee.

"And thou shalt know that thy tabernacle *shall be* in peace; and thou shalt visit thy habitation, and shalt not sin.

"Thou shalt know also that thy seed *shall be* great, and thine offspring as the grass of the earth.

"Thou shalt come to *thy* grave in a full age, like as a shock of corn cometh in in his season.

"Lo this, we have searched it, so it *is;* hear it, and know thou *it* for thy good."

Thus Eliphaz confirms his position, that, as in the case of Job, the creature may rise in his natural life above iniquity and trouble, and, consequently, sin not; whereby he may live out the years of his natural life surrounded with great blessings; but, alas! just as the haven is reached death covers; then—a blank; for, by the philosophy of Eliphaz (see iv. 18–21; v. 1), even the saints perish forever.

VI. 1–3. "But Job answered and said,

"Oh that my grief were thoroughly weighed, and my calamity laid in the balances together!

"For now it would be heavier than the sand of the sea: therefore my words are swallowed up."

Should Job's grief and calamity be laid in the balances on the one hand, and the position accorded Job by the philosophy of Eliphaz in the other, the indication is given that the struggles of Job to preserve his uprightness, his failure, and his great afflictions cannot find adequate compensation in the few years, the ripe age, allotted him by the reasoning of Eliphaz. Truly, what intelligence would desire life, and the knowledge of life, the limits of which are so briefly set, and with them the certainty that tribulation will permeate the whole? Scarce one; for (see Gen. xlvii. 9) Jacob the patriarch said unto Pharaoh, "The days of the years of my pilgrimage *are* a hundred and thirty years: few and evil have the days of the years of my life been." Thus at or near the end of his earthly life (for he survived this episode only seventeen years), Jacob leaves a record of the undesirability of an earthly pilgrimage or of the natural life; hence if Jacob's griefs and calamities were weighed in the balances on the one hand, and his unmixed joy on the other, then the indication is clear that the scale bearing Jacob's griefs and calamities would far exceed in weight the one that bore the counter-freight of joy. What if there were no beyond to Jacob? Would not Jacob then have exclaimed with Job, "Oh that my grief were thoroughly weighed, and my calamity laid in the balances together!" Jacob's summary and Job's exclamation embody the same conclusion,—viz., that this life without a future existence is far more undesirable than though (see iii. 16) it had never been.

Job's calamities are evidence of his transgression; and because of his transgression and his calamities, his words, even as he says (verse 3), are swallowed up. How are they swallowed up? They are swallowed up in that, because of transgression, he failed in his mission as a subjugator of evil. As a free agent, and as untransgressive, Job's words were full of strength; but as a free agent and as a transgressor they are swallowed up, they are without force. How is it known that Job is a transgressor? Job's own words indicate the reply, as follows:

VI. 4. "For the arrows of the Almighty *are* within me, the poison whereof drinketh up my spirit: the terrors of God do set themselves in array against me."

How can such conditions possibly arise should Job still be perfect and upright? or, does God shoot poisoned arrows at the upright and righteous? The indications are that he does not; hence it follows that Job suffers afflictions consequent upon transgression through the ruling of the First Covenant or Law that was instituted by the Almighty for the government not only of man, but of all hosts, that judgments might come not only upon man but upon all hosts also. These conditions Job indicates as follows:

VI. 5. "Doth the wild ass bray when he hath grass? or loweth the ox over his fodder?"

Therefore the indication follows that as the wild ass does not bray when he hath plenty of grass, and as the ox loweth not over his fodder, which the Lord provided them, neither should Job have had cause to complain of the goodness of the Almighty before he fell under the devices of Satan; or evil would have been present in the garden of Eden independent of Satan, King of Evil; hence the words of Job are confirmative of his fallen state, a condition that befell him subsequent to the day when (see ii. 3–7) he was placed in the hand of Satan; wherefore Job says,—

VI. 6, 7. "Can that which is unsavoury be eaten without salt? or is there *any* taste in the white of an egg?

"The things *that* my soul refused to touch *are* as my sorrowful meat."

Hence, as the unsavory cannot be eaten without salt, neither can the life of Job in his fallen state be bearable without a Redeemer, and as the white of an egg is tasteless without something to redeem it, so Job's life to him, in his fallen condition, is valueless without a Redeemer, while the things which Job's soul refused to touch are become as his sorrowful meat, which condition Paul puts in plain words when he states (Rom. vii. 15), "For what I would, that do I not; but what I hate, that do I." Job continues,—

VI. 8-10. "Oh that I might have my request; and that God would grant *me* the thing that I long for!

"Even that it would please God to destroy me; that he would let loose his hand, and cut me off!

"Then should I yet have comfort; yea, I would harden myself in sorrow: let him not spare; for I have not concealed the words of the Holy One."

The request of Job, in that he longs for God to cut him off, carries with it this comfort,—viz., that as he should thus be cut off, so most assuredly the evil host that compassed his downfall, the source and fountain of pain and tribulation, would be cut off also, never more to afflict or make aggression upon any field however great or however small. Job's conscience is clear in his expressed desire; for he has not concealed the words of the Holy One; and, by the words of the Holy One (see Gen. ii. 16, 17), the transgressor shall surely die; hence Job could harden himself in his sorrow; hence Job could say "let him not spare;" for with the fulfilment of transgression the host of Evil will eventually be judged and destroyed forever. But the evils which have been heaped upon Job help to fill up the measure of iniquity that pertains to the Evil Kingdom; wherefore, even like Samson (see Jud. xvi. 30), Job desired to die with his enemies, he well knowing that evil once dead would never more be resuscitated or brought back to life. Job continues,—

VI. 11. "What *is* my strength, that I should hope? and what *is* mine end, that I should prolong my life?"

In this verse Job reverts to his free agency as a subjugator of Evil; but what is Job's strength that he should hope? Can he really hope to overthrow, to cast down Satan, the mighty Power of Evil? or can he hope to obtain life through a perfect fulfilment of Law, or through righteousness by works? The evidence is clear that he cannot, for he asks, "What *is* mine end, that I should prolong my life?" Job knows that, at this time, he is a transgressor; wherefore his end approaches by an immutable decree; hence a few days added to his life, be they sunshine or cloud, cannot change the result, and can never make Job, as a free agent, the subjugator of Evil. Job continues by asking,—

VI. 12, 13. "*Is* my strength the strength of stones? or *is* my flesh of brass?

"*Is* not my help in me? and is wisdom driven quite from me?"

Thus Job contrasts his strength with the strength of the Adversary, in whose hand he was placed by the Law. How, then, can he hope to overthrow the Adversary through his free agency? He cannot, for he asks, "*Is* not my help in me?" thus indicating his free agency under the Law; and he further asks, "Is wisdom driven quite from me?" thus indicating his weakness as a free agent. Job continues,—

VI. 14. "To him that is afflicted pity *should be shewed* from his friend; but he forsaketh the fear of the Almighty."

The afflictions of Job are consequent upon transgression; hence pity finds place, for if Job had not transgressed, and had not fallen under the devices of Satan, whence would he have had need of pity? or did pity have a habitation in the garden of Eden before the fall? The possibility is remote; but after the fall affliction seeks condolence such as one friend should show to another. Eliphaz, however, in condoling with Job, wrings all the comfort from his words by limiting Job's existence (see iv. 18-20; v. 26) to his natural life, thus confirming the lasting rule of the First Covenant as the ministration of death upon all the good as well as the bad. This position is not tenable, for after the fall it is stated (Gen. iii. 14, 15), "And the Lord God said unto the serpent, Because thou hast done this, thou *art* cursed above all cattle, and above every beast of the field; upon thy belly shalt thou go, and dust shalt thou eat all the days of thy life:

"And I will put enmity between thee and the woman, and between thy seed and her seed; it shall bruise thy head, and thou shalt bruise his heel." Had Eliphaz heeded these words of the Lord God he would not have forsaken the fear of the Almighty, for by them the promise is carried that the serpent shall be overthrown by one greater than Adam and stronger than Satan.

The overthrow of Satan, however, does not by any means fill out the labors of the Subjugator, for (see 1 John iii. 8) "the Son of God was manifested, that he might destroy the works of the devil." The destruction of the works of the devil involves the redemption of the Fallen; the redemption of the Fallen involves the separation of the good from the evil; wherefore, after the good shall have been separated from the evil, then the eternal life which was promised the creature (see 1 John ii. 26) can be conferred upon it notwithstanding the ministration of death that pertains to the First Covenant.

This beyond does not appear in the reasoning of Eliphaz; but the reasoning of Eliphaz endorses and proclaims the overthrow and blotting out of evil through the ruling of the Law. Job continues,—

VI. 15–18. "My brethren have dealt deceitfully as a brook, *and* as the stream of brooks they pass away;

"Which are blackish by reason of the ice, *and* wherein the snow is hid:

"What time they wax warm, they vanish: when it is hot, they are consumed out of their place.

"The paths of their way are turned aside; they go to nothing, and perish."

As the ice-bound brook seems to afford footholds strong as the earth itself, so the reasoning of Eliphaz (see v. 1–27) seems to be full of strength, vitality, and comfort; but when the sun takes a higher range in the heavens and pours his heated rays upon the icy mass till it melts and passes away, so the reasoning of Eliphaz weakens and disappears under the steady light that comes from above, and, hence, no longer points to a pathway that can safely be trodden. Job continues,—

VI. 19–21. "The troops of Tema looked, the companies of Sheba waited for them.

"They were confounded because they had hoped; they came thither and were ashamed.

"For now ye are nothing; ye see *my* casting down, and are afraid."

As the reasoning of Eliphaz loses its strength, so those treading the same pathways become confounded; and as Job is cast down because of his transgression, so they, by seeing it, are afraid, for the Law that cast down Job will surely cast them down also. Eliphaz accorded Job a full natural life, and an easy descent into oblivion, under the ruling of the First Covenant; for Job was both good and evil; but such compensation will not outweigh his grief and calamity that he should have been called into existence; hence a myriad of Jobs would not cast down evil, or lessen the power of the Evil Kingdom. Such being the situation, why call the creature into existence? The call of the creature resulted, eventually, in the entering of the Law by which the host of evil is brought under its rulings in a thoroughly righteous manner, so that if offence abound judgment may be rendered against the offender, be the offender whence he may.

The casting down of Job, by the text, makes others afraid; hence they begin to realize the immutability of the Law that makes the offence abound. Evil, therefore, will not be crushed until after there shall have been a thorough comprehension of the Law that entered with man. Job continues,—

VI. 22, 23. "Did I say, Bring unto me? or, Give a reward for me of your substance?

"Or, Deliver me from the enemy's hand? or, Redeem me from the hand of the mighty?"

These words indicate that Job did not seek for evil things; that he did not, of his own free will, seek to join hands with evil, either for protection or reward.

The evidence is clear (see ii. 3-5) that before the fall, yet after the Law had entered, Satan could make aggression upon Job in the way of temptation, or of inspiring terror at his presence, for he is (see Psalm lii. 1-4) a mighty man, while the Law becomes a potency in his hand for entering a doubt. Job continues,—

VI. 24. "Teach me, and I will hold my tongue: and cause me to understand wherein I have erred."

Truly wherein did Job err? That he did err is palpable, but if Job did not say to the Evil Host, "Bring unto me, or, Give a reward for me of your substance, or, Deliver me from the enemy's hand, or, Redeem me from the hand of the mighty," how could the Evil Host, the companions of Sheba, or even Eliphaz, make Job understand wherein he had transgressed without condemning themselves? For if Job did not go to them, then they must have come to him. Job does not claim to be perfect and upright, but the indications are that the aim of his remarks is to place evil upon its own base, that sin (see Rom. vii. 13), "that it might appear sin, working death in me," or by the text, in Job, "by that which is good; that sin by the commandment might become exceeding sinful." Job continues,—

VI. 25. "How forcible are right words! but what doth your arguing reprove?"

Does the argument of Eliphaz reprove evil or does it not? If the creature (see iv. 19-21) becomes dead forever through the influence of evil, and evil still exists as an aggressive power, then the argument of Eliphaz does not reprove evil. If it does not reprove evil, then, as the text asks, what does it reprove? The answer becomes limited: it reproves the creature, and lets evil go free. How false, therefore, the resultant, and how forcible are right words! hence the indication is manifest that the creature, the victim, the spoiled, shall not bear all the reproof and the penalty, while the Source of the evil fountain that overwhelms it continues freely on its evil rejoicing way. The creature cannot be condemned without the condemnation of evil follow; but the redemption of the creature does not bring with it the redemption of evil; for (see 1 John iii. 9), " Whosoever is born of God doth not commit sin; for his seed remaineth in him: and he cannot sin, because he is born of God." Hence, whosoever is born of God is regenerated, or born into the body that was prepared for the Son suitable for this purpose; and this Seed or body (see Heb. x. 5–10; Gal. iii. 16) is Christ; wherefore, as he that is born of God will be raised up in this body, he cannot sin, because he is regenerated or born into its perfection. Evil, however, cannot be regenerated or born into the body that was prepared for the Son; therefore, while the redemption of the creature can be brought about, the redemption of evil will never be realized. Job continues,—

VI. 26, 27. " Do ye imagine to reprove words, and the speeches of one that is desperate, *which are* as wind?

" Yea, ye overwhelm the fatherless, and ye dig *a pit* for your friend."

Here, again, Job confronts Eliphaz with the condemnation of the creature under bondage to sin, and the consequent tribulations that follow through his arguments and positions. By the argument of Eliphaz the words and speeches of one that is rendered desperate through mental and physical suffering are reproved, the fatherless are overwhelmed, and a pit is dug for the creature; but what hope does Eliphaz hold out to Job of any future existence beyond a ripe old age? Very little, if any; hence the reproof of Eliphaz is directed against the creature, rather than against the Source of evil, based upon the ruling of the Law or First Covenant. Job continues,—

VI. 28. "Now therefore be content, look upon me; for *it is* evident unto you if I lie."

Thus Job, covered with boils and overwhelmed with sorrow, presents, in himself, a proof of his own words; for were he without sin these afflictions would not have befallen him; but inasmuch as they have befallen him, then, through them, the pit is dug into which the argument of Eliphaz would fling Job forever. Job continues,—

VI. 29. "Return, I pray you, let it not be iniquity; yea, return again, my righteousness *is* in it."

Which, therefore, shall it be, iniquity or righteousness? It is evident that through the philosophy of Eliphaz iniquity will sweep the creature out of existence; hence Job prays Eliphaz to recede from his position, further saying, "Let it not be iniquity;" for why should iniquity reign to the eternal destruction of the creature? Job further said, "My righteousness *is* in it." In what? Evidently in the non-imputation of iniquity. Should such a condition arise, then the duality of man is brought forward,—that is, the conditions of good and evil that envelop or environ him. Hence, through the evil element pervading man, Eliphaz digs a pit for the creature, and into which he consigns him forever; but Job, through the good that pervades the creature, looks forward to the separation of the good from the evil, and consequently to the establishment of righteousness, that the creature through the good may escape from the pit and find a life beyond it. Job intimates these two positions as follows:

VI. 30. "Is there iniquity in my tongue? cannot my taste discern perverse things?"

By which Job perceives things which are both good and evil, and which pertain to a state higher than the physical. Job continues,—

VII. 1-3. "*Is there* not an appointed time to man upon earth? *are not* his days also like the days of a hireling?

"As a servant earnestly desireth the shadow, and as a hireling looketh for *the reward of* his work;

"So am I made to possess months of vanity, and wearisome nights are appointed to me."

The fall of man having been foreseen, the time of man upon the earth (see Acts xvii. 26) was before appointed, and also the bounds of their habitation. Job asks, evidently of man, are not his days also like the days of a hireling? thus indicating mission.

The mission of man is given (Gen. i. 28), and it involved the subjugation of the earth, and of every living thing that moved upon it. Man, however, failed in this part of his mission, and, hence, the result of his labors is manifested by his reward. What is this reward? Vanity and wearisome nights,—Job continuing,—

VII. 4–6. "When I lie down, I say, When shall I arise, and the night be gone? and I am full of tossings to and fro unto the dawning of the day.

"My flesh is clothed with worms and clods of dust; my skin is broken, and become loathsome.

"My days are swifter than a weaver's shuttle, and are spent without hope."

Such is the reward that falls to the lot of sinful flesh; and to and in himself—that is, through his own free agency—Job's days are spent without hope, for the penalty of the First Covenant rests irrevocably upon him. Job continues,—

VII. 7–10. "Oh remember that my life *is* wind: mine eye shall no more see good.

"The eye of him that hath seen me shall see me no *more:* thine eyes *are* upon me, and I *am* not.

"*As* the cloud is consumed and vanisheth away; so he that goeth down to the grave shall come up no *more.*

"He shall return no more to his house, neither shall his place know him any more."

If such be the case, wherein does Job's reasoning differ in result from that of Eliphaz? For Job condemned the philosophy of Eliphaz. The indications come forth that Job and Eliphaz accord as far as the destruction of the natural body is concerned; but, while Eliphaz buries both soul and sinful flesh deeply within the pit never more to reappear, Job consigns the body of sinful flesh—the natural body—only to such destruction.

If man be regenerated or born into a new body, what need is there for the old one? more especially as the old one is irrevocably overwhelmed by the ministration of death pertaining to the First Covenant? Can the immutable Law that was given in the garden of Eden stand fulfilled while the natural body, or the body of sinful flesh, is in existence? The probability is exceedingly doubtful; hence, that the body of sinful flesh might be cast off forever, man was and is regenerated into the body that was prepared for the Son suitable for this purpose; wherefore the body of sinful flesh dies, sinks into the pit, and (see text) neither shall its place know it any more.

The spirit of man that is regenerated or born into the body of the Son that was prepared for him died with the Son when he laid down his life a propitiation for sin. If, therefore, the body of sinful flesh be dead upon its own base, and if the spirit of man be regenerated or born into a new body that is without "spot, wrinkle, or blemish," what call is there for a resurrection of the old or natural body? Is not the resurrection of the spirit of man clothed with the perfect body of the Son sufficient for all things? It undoubtedly is sufficient; and, hence, if sufficient, then the body of the sinful flesh, the natural body, will never more rise into existence; but the image of the earthy (see 1 Cor. xv. 49; St. Luke xxiv. 36–43) will supersede the earthy; and in which body individual identity will be established and reproduced as perfectly as the individual identity of the Saviour was perceptible to his disciples after his resurrection.

Job's lament takes cognizance of his calling, his

mission, the strength of the Adversary, his weakness, his fall, and his consequent tribulation; wherefore he says,—

VII. 11–16. "Therefore I will not refrain my mouth; I will speak in the anguish of my spirit; I will complain in the bitterness of my soul.

"*Am* I a sea, or a whale, that thou settest a watch over me?

"When I say, My bed shall comfort me, my couch shall ease my complaint;

"Then thou scarest me with dreams, and terrifiest me through visions:

"So that my soul chooseth strangling, *and* death rather than my life.

"I loathe *it;* I would not live alway: let me alone; for my days *are* vanity."

Truly, what is the life of the creature that he should continue forever? or what is the life of a creature that, as a class, order, or genus, he should live forever? Can he, through his free agency, hope (see Isa. xiv. 14) to rise above the heights of the clouds, and be like the Most High? No. If not, where can tribulation cease? There is no limit, for exquisite happiness on the one hand will be met with exquisite torture on the other, however high the degree of perfection, no system existing whereby, through free agency, the power and progress of Evil may be stayed; hence it follows that free agency must give place to a ruling power that is perfect in all its attributes, not a power that will be, or may be, or can be, for that is not perfection. A perfect power must have been perfect as a power throughout the infinite past, which is a condition that does not pertain to progress or development; hence the perfect power is not a creature. The indication is clear that the creature cannot create the perfect power, but the perfect power may, can, or does create the creature.

The inanimate creature is more obedient to order than the animate, as witnessed in the movements of the sun, moon, and stars; whence it follows that the former is governed by a perfect creative power, while the latter is not so governed (the Law being the governing principle). If, however, there is no perfect creative governing power, how is it that the inanimate is more obedient to order than the animate? The fact that the inanimate is more obedient to order than the animate is proof of the existence of a perfect creative governing power; while the dereliction of the animate is proof that the perfect .creative governing power permits such dereliction in accordance with some plan or purpose which he has established.

Inasmuch, therefore, as the perfect creative governing power permits dereliction from perfect order, then the existence of a power contrary to, and adverse to, the perfect power is indicated. This adverse power is the one which mars the perfection of the creature, whether such creature be great or small; hence it becomes rival to and stands up against the perfect creative governing power. If therefore the perfect power established a great purpose, the indications are that this purpose involves the complete downfall and overthrow of the adverse power that makes aggression upon and mars every creature; hence it now follows that of these two powers one is the Lord of hosts and the other is Satan, King of Evil; wherefore (see Isa. xiv. 24–27) "the

Lord of hosts hath sworn, saying, Surely as I have thought, so shall it come to pass; and as I have purposed, *so* shall it stand :

"That I will break the Assyrian in my land, and upon my mountains tread him under foot: then shall his yoke depart from off them, and his burden depart from off their shoulders.

"This *is* the purpose that is purposed upon the whole earth: and this *is* the hand that is stretched out upon all the nations.

"For the Lord of hosts hath purposed, and who shall disannul *it?* and his hand *is* stretched out, and who shall turn it back?"

If the perfect Power permits dereliction of order in the animate, intelligent creature, then the indication comes forth that such intelligent creature is a free agent; but, that the perfect Power might retain his perfection, the Law entered (see Gen. ii. 16, 17) for the government of all hosts, heavenly and earthly.

Under the rule of the perfect Power (see Rom. vii. 9) man was safe, but under the Law (see iii. 25–26; Rom. vii. 9) man was not in safety. Why? Because of his free agency. Why because of his free agency? As a free agent man was not in safety because of the great strength of Satan, King of Evil. If, therefore, man as a free agent is not in safety because of the great strength of Satan, truly what is the life of the creature that he as a class, order, or genus should live forever compassed with pain and sorrow? Live forever! would not the creature rather choose death, and with Job say of life, "I loathe *it*, I would not live alway?" Job continues,—

VII. 17–19. "What *is* man, that thou shouldest magnify him? and that thou shouldest set thine heart upon him?

"And *that* thou shouldest visit him every morning, *and* try him every moment?

"How long wilt thou not depart from me, nor let me alone till I swallow down my spittle?"

Man was predestinated and called as a great and peculiar instrumentality in the overthrow of the Power of Evil, and in the redemption of the Fallen. With man the Law entered by which the offence abounded; by the abounding of the offence evil could be judged, and judgment could be rendered against it. Should man, however, be perfect under the Law, then righteousness by works on the part of the creature would be established, but the creature would undergo trial every moment that, perchance, the offence might abound; Job, however, longs for a respite from the grievous trial that has befallen him. Job continues,—

VII. 20–21. "I have sinned; what shall I do unto thee, O thou preserver of men? why hast thou set me as a mark against thee, so that I am a burden to myself?

"And why dost thou not pardon my transgression, and take away mine iniquity? for now shall I sleep in the dust; and thou shalt seek me in the morning, but I *shall* not *be*."

Thus Job admits transgression and sin on his part; but why is it that his life is spared, and that tribulation still compasses him? If the life of Job is spared after his fall into sin, and if his transgression and iniquity are not forgiven, then the indications are that Job has some special mission to fulfil outside of his own immediate welfare; for he said (verse 20), " What shall I do unto thee, O thou preserver of men?" thus recognizing God as the preserver of men; which recognition is not comprehended in the arguments of Eliphaz. If God is the Preserver of men, then he must be the Redeemer of men also, for all men are included under sin; hence the permitted tribulation that continues in the House of Man indicates mission on the part of fallen man.

Under the Law, with his iniquity and transgression upon him, Job would indeed sleep in the dust, and would be no more, so that even the Preserver of men would seek for him and find him not. Why? Because the Law entered for the destruction of Evil, and when the destruction of Evil shall have been accomplished, then the Preserver of men will find it no more, or the Law would have entered in vain; hence Job's transgression must be pardoned and his iniquity taken away through the labors of his Redeemer.

Job as the progenitor of the Third Race may be considered as representative of the Third Race; wherefore the transgression of Job becomes a different quantity from his iniquity. Job's transgression, as the representative of the Third Age, may indicate the transgressions of the people of the Third Age; while Job's iniquity indicates the iniquity of both the First and Second races of men that has fallen upon him as representative of the Third Race.

The descent of iniquity from father to son, or from

one generation to another, is governed by a law, which law is specially proclaimed as follows (Ex. xxxiv. 7): "Visiting the iniquity of the fathers upon the children, and upon the children's children, unto the third and to the fourth *generation*,"—in which the four generations point to the Four Ages of Man, and of which Job is representative of the Third. Hence Job's questions embody a prayer for the forgiveness of his transgression and for the taking away of the iniquity that has fallen upon him through the operation of the great Law of Iniquity.

VIII. 1-3. "Then answered Bildad the Shuhite, and said,

"How long wilt thou speak these *things?* and *how long shall* the words of thy mouth *be like* a strong wind?

"Doth God pervert judgment? or doth the Almighty pervert justice?"

The words of Job (see vii. 20, 21) still indicated his faith in the redemption of men by the Preserver of men; not only those of his own Age, but those of the two Ages preceding him. Bildad, however, evidently siding with the philosophy of Eliphaz, considers Job's words as wind; as vain, visionary, baseless. Why? Because through the ruling of the Law, or First Covenant, the transgressor shall surely die. Therefore, standing upon the immutability of this decree, Bildad asks, "Doth God pervert judgment?" In the face of this immutable decree, even as Bildad implies, how is it possible for man's transgression to be forgiven and his iniquity pardoned without perverting the judgment of God? for the host of Evil is under the ruling of the Law also; or how is it possible that man's iniquity be pardoned, and the iniquity of the Evil Host rest upon its own base, without perverting the justice of the Almighty?

These great questions find a solution in the manner of the redemption as set forth in the records of both the Old Testament and the New. What is the manner of the redemption as thus set forth? It is this,—viz., that a body (see Heb. x. 4–10; Ps. xl. 6–8) was prepared for the Son that in it he might do the will of God. This body is not the flesh of man, but was and is (see Col. i. 13–15) the first-born of every creature; and the beginning (see Rev. iii. 14) of the creation of God; and which (see Rev. xii.) was invested by the Son before the calling of man.

As, therefore, the Word of God invested this body, so the Word became the only begotten Son of God; and, by the investment, this body became his flesh. The Son of God in this body (see St. John x. 17, 18) possesses the power of laying down his life and of taking it up again; should, therefore, any one be regenerated, or born into this body, then such a one would die with the Son when he made his great atonement for sin, and would rise again with him from the dead.

The regeneration of man is accomplished (see Ex. xxix. 33) through the eating of those things wherewith the atonement was made; therefore, as the atonement for the sins of man was made by the Son in the body that was prepared for him, so this body must be eaten by man; and by the eating thereof the spirit of man becomes regenerated, or born into it, thus becoming clothed with it.

If the spirit of man dies with Christ in this body, and if it rises with Christ in this body, wherein is the judgment of God perverted? or wherein is the justice of the Almighty perverted? Is not the Law fulfilled to the very letter as far as man is concerned? and does not the body of sinful flesh lie dead forever? Moreover, does not the spirit of man die an absolute death in Christ, the Messiah? The judgment and justice of the Almighty are clear, the Law is fulfilled to the very letter, the spirit of man, clothed with its unblemished body, lives in the regeneration and redemption thus provided, while the body of sinful flesh, unsightly, undesired, moulders to its kindred dust never to be recalled; yet the image of the earthy, even from youth to old age, may ever be assumed to reveal the loved ones to their friends. Bildad, however, like Eliphaz, seems to see no beyond for the transgressor; the yawning abyss becomes his finality; for he states,—

VIII. 4–7. "If thy children have sinned against him, and he have cast them away for their transgression;

"If thou wouldest seek unto God betimes, and make thy supplication to the Almighty;

"If thou *wert* pure and upright; surely now he would awake for thee, and make the habitation of thy righteousness prosperous.

"Though thy beginning was small, yet thy latter end should greatly increase."

Wherefore Bildad considers the destruction of Job's children (see i. 18, 19), because of their transgression, as a final casting away, but that Job may, if he make supplication to the Almighty, and if he were pure and upright, increase and multiply and become greatly increased again at the latter end; which end, doubtless, is that of his natural life; hence Bildad's deductions coincide with the views of Eliphaz as expressed (v. 25–27). Bildad continues,—

VIII. 8–10. "For inquire, I pray thee, of the former age, and prepare thyself to the search of their fathers:

"(For we *are but of* yesterday, and know nothing, because our days upon earth *are* a shadow:)

"Shall not they teach thee, *and* tell thee, and utter words out of their heart?"

In the light that Job is the progenitor or Adam of the Third Race, then the former age referred to by Bildad would indicate the Second Race, while their fathers would indicate the First Race; hence, by research into the history of these two Ages (for Job, as the Adam of the Third Race, was created before the destruction of the Second), the increase and multiplication of the races pertaining thereto would be brought to Job's notice as indicating the probable increase and multiplication of the Third Race.

Inasmuch, however, as both the First and Second races of men were swept away because of their transgressions, it is not improbable but that Job's personal trial took place about the time of the great Heddekelic Famine that destroyed the Second; hence the words of both Eliphaz and Bildad, in which they pointed to the probable increase and multiplication of Job, could have been based upon their knowledge of the longevity and fate of the first two races, and as considering Job to be the escaping remnant or the Noah of the Third race, as well as the Adam or progenitor thereof, for with the destruction of the Second race many of the Third must have perished also; the parallel being witnessed later (see Gen. vi., vii.), in the history of the Deluge that overwhelmed the Third race and nearly all of the Fourth that lived contemporary with it.

The Adam of the Fourth race did not survive until the Deluge; wherefore Noah was chosen as the escaping remnant; but the overlap of the Second and Third Ages or Races was about three hundred years less than the overlap of the Third and Fourth, whereby the actual years of Job's life are brought within the scope of probability.

The words of Bildad, "For we *are but of* yesterday, and know nothing, because our days upon earth are a shadow," also point to the earlier years of the Third Age, or to the overlap of the Second and Third races, while the history of the preceding ages will indicate a scale for approximating the years of the Third. Bildad continues,—

VIII. 11–19. "Can the rush grow up without mire? can the flag grow without water?

"Whilst it *is* yet in his greenness, *and* not cut down, it withereth before any *other* herb.

"So *are* the paths of all that forget God; and the hypocrite's hope shall perish:

"Whose hope shall be cut off, and whose trust *shall be* a spider's web.

"He shall lean upon his house, but it shall not stand: he shall hold it fast, but it shall not endure.

"He *is* green before the sun, and his branch shooteth forth in his garden.

"His roots are wrapped about the heap, *and* seeth the place of stones.

"If he destroy him from his place, then *it* shall deny him, *saying*, I have not seen thee.

"Behold this *is* the joy of his way, and out of the earth shall others grow."

Thus Bildad adheres to the philosophy of Eliphaz that the transgressor is cast out of his place forever, and also, that his place shall deny him, saying, "I have not seen thee," while out of the earth others shall grow; hence, according to Bildad, as one generation or race is swept away, or passes from the scene, others rise up to take its place; but not one word significant of redemption or of restoration is let fall. Bildad continues,—

VIII. 20–22. "Behold, God will not cast away a perfect *man*, neither will he help the evil doers:

"Till he fill thy mouth with laughing, and thy lips with rejoicing.

"They that hate thee shall be clothed with shame; and the dwelling place of the wicked shall come to nought."

Here Bildad accords life to a perfect man; but who is perfect? None. Hence Bildad intimates that help must come to evil-doers that they be not cast away before their days have run out (for by comparison with previous ages he accredited Job with length of days,—that is, with a full natural life); but, he continues, "the dwelling place of the wicked shall come to nought," by which the destruction of the transgressor, whether or no his days have run, only is indicated.

IX. 1, 2. "Then Job answered and said,

"I know *it is* so of a truth: but how should man be just with God?"

Job, of a truth, knows that God will not cast away a perfect man; but how can a man be just with God? or how can a man be perfect with God? That he cannot, under the Law, Job indicates as follows:

IX. 3. "If he will contend with him, he cannot answer him one of a thousand."

If, under the Law, man cannot answer God one of a thousand, be they thoughts, words, or actions, then the situation becomes evident that man cannot be perfect or just with God; for his answers would be full of error; whence, inasmuch as (see Heb. ii. 4; Gal. iii. 11) the just shall live by faith, it follows that the Law must be set aside that all thought and action be justified through the Word or assenting Power of the Infinite Majesty which alone is all-wise and capable to order, answer, and govern all things. Job continues,—

IX. 4. "*He is* wise in heart, and mighty in strength: who hath hardened *himself* against him, and hath prospered?"

Is it possible for one under the Law to contend with the Almighty and prosper? Even an upright man contending for righteousness may fall into error, how much less, then, can one that is a transgressor contend against God and prosper,—that is, fulfil the

Law; wherefore the indication follows still further that justification of thought and action can only be found through the assenting Power of the Infinite Majesty,

IX. 5-12. "Which removeth the mountains, and they know not; which overturneth them in his anger;

"Which shaketh the earth out of her place, and the pillars thereof tremble;

"Which commandeth the sun, and it riseth not; and sealeth up the stars;

"Which alone spreadeth out the heavens, and treadeth upon the waves of the sea;

"Which maketh Arcturus, Orion, and Pleiades, and the chambers of the south;

"Which doeth great things past finding out; yea, and wonders without number.

"Lo, he goeth by me, and I see *him* not: he passeth on also, but I perceive him not.

"Behold, he taketh away, who can hinder him? who will say unto him, What doest thou?"

Such is the Word or Assenting Power of the Infinite Majesty in whom (see Col. ii. 9) all the fulness of the Godhead dwells bodily. Can ought but perfection follow the assent of such a Power? No; hence the text continues,—

IX. 13. "*If* God will not withdraw his anger, the proud helpers do stoop under him."

Thus the proudest stoop under the anger of the Supreme Unity. Job continues,—

IX. 14, 15. "How much less shall I answer him, *and* choose out my words *to reason* with him?

"Whom, though I were righteous, *yet* would I not answer, *but* I would make supplication to my judge."

Thus Job, even though he were righteous, throws himself altogether into the hands of the Almighty, that the Almighty may justify him in all his thought and action, word and deed. Job continues,—

IX. 16–18. "If I had called, and he had answered me; *yet* would I not believe that he had hearkened unto my voice.

"For he breaketh me with a tempest, and multiplieth my wounds without cause.

"He will not suffer me to take my breath, but filleth me with bitterness."

Inasmuch as all of this happens to Job under the ruling of the Law, how can Job discriminate between the penalties due to his own transgression, and how much is due to the aggression of the Adversary? for the latter by his aggression fills the measure of his iniquity. Let the Almighty take his protection from the creature, and let the creature stand upon his free agency, what follows? Transgression : the penalty of which is death. Should the protection of the Almighty be taken from the transgressor, be the transgression ever so slight, then the Evil Kingdom will overwhelm and plunge him into deep tribulation far beyond all commeasurable or equitable call.

Should the Almighty permit this tribulation, then Job's words gain their strength in that the Almighty did not prevent it; but the Law entered that the offence should abound and judgment be rendered; hence it follows that the protecting arm of the Almighty is continually stretched forth over the creature lest an excess of grief and woe should fall upon it, or that an excess of tribulation, calamity greater than it could bear, should fall upon any one generation. Many calls, therefore, to the Almighty are answered, but the answer is unknown, unrecognized, because tribulation is not entirely taken away, and the Law completely set aside. Job continues,—

IX. 19, 20. "*If I speak* of strength, lo, *he is* strong: and if of judgment, who shall set me a time *to plead?*

"If I justify myself, mine own mouth shall condemn me: *if I say,* I *am* perfect, it shall also prove me perverse."

These words are evidently the words of a creature that is under transgression, and under the Law; wherefore, high as the standard of Job's excellence may be, he is far too weak to fulfil all the Law. Job continues,—

IX. 21, 22. "*Though* I *were* perfect, *yet* would I not know my soul: I would despise my life.

"This *is* one *thing,* therefore I said *it,* He destroyeth the perfect and the wicked."

Why should Job despise his life were he perfect? The indications are that, were Job perfect, he would live in the Law; and were he to live in the Law, then the temptation to do evil would ever be before him. Should evil ever be before him, then the Law would become established as a ruling principle by which the shadowy vale would be filled with countless victims that never more would awaken into renewed life. Job as a perfect man might live in the Law, but myriads would perish, while Evil would become enthroned forever; hence all must die, perfect and imperfect, that Evil die the same death: Christ the perfect, to separate the good from the evil; and the Evil, for its transgression. When this shall have become fulfilled, then it is evident that the Law has reached its vanishing point, and that justification of all thought and action by and through the Word or Assenting Power of the Infinite Majesty will forever be the ruling principle in the government of all hosts; well, therefore, may Job despise a perfect life under the Law. Job continues,—

IX. 23. "If the scourge slay suddenly, he will laugh at the trial of the innocent."

Thus the perfect or the innocent may be slain or changed (see 1 Cor. xv. 51, 52) "in a moment, in the twinkling of an eye;" but, again, the innocent may be given over to great trial that the aggressive spirit of the Evil Kingdom be proved beyond all question or doubt; hence Job continues,—

IX. 24. "The earth is given into the hand of the wicked: he covereth the faces of the judges thereof; if not, where, *and* who *is* he?"

The truth of this saying is palpable, for evil is met with and seen on every side. Who is the author of all the misery thus witnessed? Job, himself, evidently asks the same question. Shall it be laid to the charge of the Kingdom of Righteousness? or shall it be laid to the charge of the Kingdom of Evil? Undoubtedly to the Kingdom of Evil; for, should the excess of misery that befalls the creature emanate from the Kingdom of Righteousness, what guarantee can possibly exist, or can be given, that misery will ever be abolished? Clearly none; hence the supreme perfection of the Infinite Power forbids the conclusion that misery emanates from the Kingdom of Righteousness. Wherefore, as the condition of good and the condition of evil are manifest to and in each individual intelligence, why, as Job intimates, should there not be judges or heads thereto?

The indications are that there is a head to the Kingdom of Righteousness that is purely righteous, that there is a head to the Kingdom of Evil that is the source and fountain of all essential evil, and that the earth is given into the hand of the latter,—as witnessed in the history of Job and his family,—that he may prove himself to be the source and fountain of evil. Job continues,—

IX. 25, 26. "Now my days are swifter than a post: they flee away, they see no good.

"They are passed away as the swift ships: as the eagle *that* hasteth to the prey."

These verses contain a summary of Job's labors under the Law. What is this summary? Failure, failure, failure: his days pass; they see no good: his days pass; they are as the wake of a swift ship that is soon lost forever in the troubled surge of the ocean: his days pass; they are like the path of the eagle whose swift flight leaves no mark upon the air. Under the Law man cannot throw down the mighty power of Satan; as a free agent man cannot repulse evil in all its varied forms; hence, as one broken link severs the chain, some misstep throws down the subjugator, breaks his calling, and leaves him bondman to evil. Job continues,—

IX. 27, 28. "If I say, I will forget my complaint, I will leave off my heaviness, and comfort *myself;*

"I am afraid of all my sorrows, I know that thou wilt not hold me innocent."

If Job is a transgressor,—of which there is little doubt,—any disregard of his transgression would be counted against him; and should he comfort himself by compromising with evil, then he could not be counted innocent. Job continues,—

IX. 29. "*If* I be wicked, why then labour I in vain?"

If Job is a transgressor, why then, even as he asks, does he labor in vain? or why does he continue to labor? or why is he not cut off for his transgression? for continued labor on his part cannot restore his pristine purity, neither can future labors on his part cast down evil and fulfil his mission as a subjugator; which conditions Job indicates as follows:

IX. 30, 31. "If I wash myself with snow water, and make my hands never so clean;

"Yet shalt thou plunge me in the ditch, and mine own clothes shall abhor me."

Hence no future righteousness on the part of Job can ever take away his transgression and restore him to his original purity; moreover, the Law (see Gen. ii. 16, 17) positively declares that the transgressor shall die. Should, therefore, any righteous action on the part of Job take away his sin, then the Law would be made void, and with it the Word of the Power giving it forth. Job's words, however, clearly point to the impossibility of free agency or righteousness by works following transgression to nullify such transgression;

wherefore Job accepts the certainty of the fulfilment of the Law that was established by the Most High for the overthrow of the transgressor irrespective of host. Furthermore, of the Most High Job states,—

IX. 32, 33. "For *he is* not a man, as I *am, that* I should answer him, *and* we should come together in judgment.

"Neither is there any daysman betwixt us, *that* might lay his hand upon us both."

In these verses Job recognizes and acknowledges the supremacy of the Most High, and hence the immutability of the Law that he set forth for the government of all hosts. No power exists, therefore, or can arise in the future, that can come together in judgment with the Most High, the Supreme Unity, that it should disannul and bring to naught any of his decrees, that it should restore the transgressor, or that it should endow the transgressor with life. Job continues,—

IX. 34, 35. "Let him take his rod away from me, and let not his fear terrify me:

"*Then* would I speak, and not fear him; but *it is* not so with me."

The rod of the Most High spoken of by Job appears to be the Law or First Covenant. Should the Law be taken away from Job, then he could speak and not fear, for without the Law (see Rom. v. 13) sin is not imputed, although transgression may exist; hence under such conditions Job could utter many sinful things with impunity; but it is not so with him; wherefore the fear of the Most High through the Law terrifies him; hence he continues,—

X. 1–3. "My soul is weary of my life; I will leave my complaint upon myself; I will speak in the bitterness of my soul.

"I will say unto God, Do not condemn me; shew me wherefore thou contendest with me.

"*Is it* good unto thee that thou shouldest oppress, that thou shouldest despise the work of thine hands, and shine upon the counsel of the wicked?"

Under the Law with its penalties Job is weary of his life; but death comes not to his relief; hence he seeks to know why the Almighty contends with him, but first uttering the prayer, "Do not condemn me," evidently because of his inquiry. The continued tribulation of Job instead of his cutting off seems to indicate that the Lord despised the work of his hands, and that he upheld the counsel of the wicked; for Job is the Lord's creature, while Satan is not. Of this mysterious indication Job seeks solution; hence his inquiry of the Almighty. Job continues,—

X. 4–6. "Hast thou eyes of flesh? or seest thou as man seeth?

"*Are* thy days as the days of man? *are* thy years as man's days,

"That thou inquirest after mine iniquity, and searchest after my sin?"

These verses indicate that the search after sin and iniquity by the Almighty is far beyond that which the eyes of man can see or the days of man can comprehend; hence the creature sins and knows it not; but if sin must be blotted out of existence, and evil be overthrown, then such sin and iniquity must be imputed that the offence abound whether the creature (see Lev. iv.) recognize or have knowledge of such transgression or not. Job continues,—

X. 7. "Thou knowest that I am not wicked; and *there is* none that can deliver out of thine hand."

This verse indicates that Job's transgression is unknown to him, that he has sinned through ignorance, but that the offence is known to the Almighty. The indication is clear, however, that an unknown, unrecognized sin produces a corresponding blight somewhere, and it points to vitality on the part of the Evil Kingdom; hence the eyes of man cannot discern evil in all its ramifications that he should successfully meet it at every step. Moreover, man is not the only sin-tinctured host that is under the Law; but the Law that judges man judges all hosts; wherefore it follows that man, from the strength and magnitude of these hosts, does not comprehend evil in all its reaches. Job continues,—

X. 8–12. "Thine hands have made me and fashioned me together round about; yet thou dost destroy me.

"Remember, I beseech thee, that thou hast made me as the clay; and wilt thou bring me into dust again?

"Hast thou not poured me out as milk, and curdled me like cheese?

"Thou hast clothed me with skin and flesh, and hast fenced me with bones and sinews.

"Thou hast granted me life and favour, and thy visitation hath preserved my spirit."

By these verses Job is clothed with skin and flesh, bones and sinews, and is made as the clay; hence the indications are strongly marked that he is man of Adam's race. When, therefore, such a one under tribulation says (see verse 7), "Thou knowest that I am not wicked," the indications are that he is a transgressor suffering under unknown, unrecognized sin; yet notwithstanding this transgression, life and favor is granted him, and the visitation of God has preserved his spirit; wherefore he continues,—

X. 13. "And these *things* hast thou hid in thine heart: I know that this *is* with thee."

Thus by his belief in the knowledge of God concerning these things Job's faith in a life beyond the natural existence of man is indicated. Both Eliphaz and Bildad, however, consider the grave as sealing the sum of existence. Job continues,—

X. 14–17. "If I sin, then thou markest me, and thou wilt not acquit me from mine iniquity.

"If I be wicked, woe unto me; and *if* I be righteous, *yet* will I not lift up my head. *I am* full of confusion; therefore see thou mine affliction;

"For it increaseth. Thou huntest me as a fierce lion: and again thou shewest thyself marvellous upon me.

"Thou renewest thy witnesses against me, and increasest thine indignation upon me; changes and war *are* against me."

Hence if Job sin he will not be acquitted from his iniquity, for no future righteousness on his part (see ix. 30, 31) can make void the Law that entered for the overthrow of Evil. If Job sin then he will bear the mark of his transgression; therefore, are the afflictions that compass him marks of transgression, or are they not? The indications are that the sorrowful condition of Job is due to his clothing of sinful flesh;

that he is suffering because of transgression; for why, under the Law, should a perfectly righteous creature suffer? That he will not suffer is plainly set forth as follows (Ex. xv. 26): "If thou wilt diligently hearken to the voice of the Lord thy God, and wilt do that which is right in his sight, and wilt give ear to his commandments, and keep all his statutes, I will put none of these diseases upon thee, which I have brought upon the Egyptians: for I *am* the Lord that healeth thee." Hence, as God is no respecter of persons, the same ruling is over all his creatures; wherefore it follows that Job suffers tribulation because of transgression; and that woe is unto him because of transgression.

If, however, Job should be righteous, yet would he not lift up his head. Why? Because Job's righteousness would be established through the Law; and if through the Law, then it would be established through free agency; and if through free agency, then all sin-tinctured creatures would be cut off by the Law never more to reappear; while nothing would or could insure righteousness to the forthcoming creature; for it is certain that while the Law shall stand supreme as the ruling principle, Evil will exist as an aggressive energy; hence Job is full of confusion; wherefore it follows that if Job alone were perfectly righteous he alone would live in his righteousness.

Of the two conditions Job calls the Lord's attention to the transgressive. Why? Because there is a possibility of the redemption of the creature under transgression that may be general. How can a general redemption of the creature be accomplished? It can be accomplished by the separation of the good from the evil, "the precious" (see Jer. xv. 19) "from the vile." When, therefore, the good shall have been separated from the evil, and each shall rest upon its own base, to which will the creature pertain? The indications are that the unresurrected body of sinful flesh points to the empty triumph of evil, to the habitation of the creature's iniquity, while the spirit of man, risen with Christ from the dead and clothed with Christ's body, the body that was prepared for him suitable for this purpose, stands witness of the marvellous glory that followed Christ's labors in separating the good from the evil, and in setting the good upon its own base.

In order to separate the good from the evil it is manifest that the great Separator must be cognizant of both the good and evil that permeates the creature; wherefore Job says, "Thou huntest me as a fierce lion: and again thou shewest thyself marvellous upon me." Job continues,—

X. 18, 19. "Wherefore then hast thou brought me forth out of the womb? Oh that I had given up the ghost, and no eye had seen me!

"I should have been as though I had not been; I should have been carried from the womb to the grave."

Why should Job thus lament anew his bringing forth into the world? Is it simply because of the physical suffering that has come upon him? The indications are that his lamentation is not due simply because of physical suffering, but that his great grief springs from the knowledge of the failure of his mission as the subjugator of evil. Had Job never been brought forth as an intelligent creature,—he being the progenitor or first man of a newly-created race of men, —the thought finds place in the heart of Job that perhaps another would have arisen, through the labors of the Creative Power, stronger and better adapted for the work of man's calling than he. Inasmuch, however, as he failed, he states,—

X. 20-22. "*Are* not my days few? cease *then, and* let me alone, that I may take comfort a little,

"Before I go *whence* I shall not return, *even* to the land of darkness and the shadow of death;

"A land of darkness, as darkness *itself; and* of the shadow of death, without any order, and *where* the light *is* as darkness."

As, therefore, Job's days are few, and as he is overwhelmed with affliction, the indication becomes strongly marked that he does not suffer as a perfectly righteous man, but as a transgressor. The penalty of transgression (see Gen. iii. 17) is death; but the land of darkness to which Job refers as a dwelling-place for himself is not actual death; wherefore, as the shadow is not the substance, so neither is the shadow of death actual death. Job may lay aside his natural life and take his place with others in the shadowy vale, but inasmuch as rest in this vale is not actual death, so the spirit of Job would not be dead, but would sleep a sleep entirely free from all knowledge of life and light; the darkness would be complete.

How can this land be the shadow of death simply, and not actual death, if Job shall not return from thence?

It is the land of the shadow of death in that all descend into it because of transgression. If all descend into it because of transgression, then, clearly, it cannot be actual death, or the creature would surely pay the penalty of his transgression in his own person as called for by the Law. If the creature pay the penalty of his own transgression in his own person, then no redeemer can arise; he would have nothing to redeem; a restorer might recall the creature to life again, but such recall would bring back the unregenerated body of sinful flesh; hence the land of the shadow of death cannot be actual death; but as the land of the shadow of death, wherein the departed lie sleeping, the possibility that a Redeemer arose becomes a probability.

The retention of Job in the land of the shadow of death indicates that, as a free agent and a transgressor, he cannot throw aside the ruling of the Law and return from thence at his will; and that he is held there a prisoner until a redeemer shall arise and set him free from his bondage. The fact that Job shall go to the land of the shadow of death carries with it the certainty that a redeemer shall arise; otherwise such dwelling would, essentially, be absolute death.

Such being the case, the indication becomes clear that from the reign of death among men in the First Age until the resurrection of the Messiah in the Fourth the departed slept unconscious of any existence. That they were not absolutely dead is indicated (St. Luke xx. 37, 38); for, in the day of Moses, the God of Abraham, the God of Isaac, and the God of Jacob was the God of the living; hence, although Abraham, Isaac, and Jacob dwelt in the land of the shadow of death, and their natural bodies were mouldered into dust, yet spiritually they were living and were not absolutely dead. After the resurrection of the Messiah, however, the situation of the departed was and is very different; for now the indications are that the grave cannot hold its victim beyond three days and three nights as fulfilled by the Messiah.

XI. 1-4. "Then answered Zophar the Naamathite, and said,

"Should not the multitude of words be answered? and should a man full of talk be justified?

"Should thy lies make men hold their peace? and when thou mockest, shall no man make thee ashamed?

"For thou hast said, My doctrine *is* pure, and I am clean in thine eyes."

What is Job's doctrine? Job's doctrine is the resurrection of the creature into a new and pure life after he shall have laid away the body of sinful flesh that pertains to the natural life; that is, Job believes in the redemption of the creature from the bonds and penalties that accrue to him through transgression under the Law. Zophar, however, considers Job's doctrine a lie; wherefore the indication follows that Zophar endorses the arguments and reasonings of both Eliphaz and Bildad, that there is no life to the creature beyond the grave.

The cleanness of Job's hands consists in the positive declaration of his doctrine even though he himself be a transgressor. Moreover, by Job's transgressive condition the force of his doctrine becomes more strongly marked and comprehended. Zophar continues,—

XI. 5, 6. "But oh that God would speak, and open his lips against thee;

"And that he would shew thee the secrets of wisdom, that *they are* double to that which is! Know therefore that God exacteth of thee *less* than thine iniquity *deserveth*."

If Job's doctrine embodies the redemption of the creature under transgression, then Zophar's words (verse 5) make God condemn redemption through the utterances of Job. This position Zophar further confirms where he states in substance that God exacts of Job less than his iniquity deserves; hence, considering Job's affliction, what else remains but to cut him off entirely? Zophar continues,—

XI. 7–9. "Canst thou by searching find out God? canst thou find out the Almighty unto perfection?

"*It is* as high as heaven; what canst thou do? deeper than hell; what canst thou know?

"The measure thereof *is* longer than the earth, and broader than the sea."

Truly, as Zophar asks, who can comprehend the Almighty in his perfection? None. Wherein, then, does Job derive his doctrine of redemption, seeing that the Law condemns the transgressor and in no way provides for the redemption of the transgressor? Job's doctrine is based upon the charge given to the Third Race, as follows (Rev. iii. 1–6): "And unto the angel of the church in Sardis write; These things saith he that hath the seven Spirits of God, and the seven stars; I know thy works, that thou hast a name that thou livest, and art dead.

"Be watchful, and strengthen the things which remain, that are ready to die: for I have not found thy works perfect before God.

"Remember therefore how thou hast received and heard, and hold fast, and repent. If therefore thou shall not watch, I will come on thee as a thief, and thou shall not know what hour I will come upon thee.

"Thou hast a few names even in Sardis which have not defiled their garments; and they shall walk with me in white: for they are worthy.

"He that overcometh, the same shall be clothed in white raiment; and I will not blot out his name out of the book of life, but I will confess his name before my Father, and before his angels.

"He that hath an ear, let him hear what the Spirit saith unto the churches."

Through this charge, therefore, Job as the progenitor and Adam of the Third Race based his doctrine of the redemption of the creature under transgression. The Law, however, which irretrievably condemns the transgressor to death forms the basis of the philosophy of Eliphaz, Bildad, and Zophar.

In the charge to the people of the Third Age the promise is given by the Spirit,—which is the Fulfilling Power of the Infinite Majesty,—that he that overcometh, the same shall be clothed in white raiment; and his name shall not be blotted out of the book of life. This promise would be empty and vain unless one arise that shall overcome all things; hence belief in the promise indicates faith in the existence of or in the arising of such a one; and that he, through his excellence and strength, shall fulfil the mission of man as set forth (Gen. i. 28) for the subjugation and government of all things. The only one that overcame all things was Jesus Christ the righteous; hence by the promise Jesus Christ will be endowed with eternal life. Who is Jesus Christ? He is (see Col. i. 13-15) the Son of God, and the first-born of every creature. How is it possible for the Son of God to be the first-born of every creature? It is possible (see Psalm xi. 6-8; Heb. x. 4-7) through the investment, by the Word of God, of the body that was prepared for the Son in and as the very beginning of the creation of God, that he might do the will of God. If this body was prepared for the Son, then it, the body, was a creature; wherefore this body, as the first-born of all creatures, was (see Rev. iii. 14, 20, 21) the beginning of the creation of God.

When the Word or Assenting Power of the Infinite Majesty invested this body that he might come and do the will of God, then the Word became the Son of God, or otherwise the Living Bread; hence those regenerated or born into this body through the eating thereof will (see Heb. ii. 11) become brethren, and (see St. John vi. 48-58; Gal. iv. 4-7) sons of God also.

Job's doctrine concerning redemption, therefore, is based upon promises and grounds that entered far beyond the working of the Law; and, by his wonderful faith in the promise and charge to the people of the Third Age, he felt assured that his Redeemer lived; and also that the promise and charge were not given as empty and meaningless issues. Zophar continues,—

XI. 10-12. "If he cut off, and shut up, or gather together, then who can hinder him?

"For he knoweth vain men: he seeth wickedness also; will he not then consider *it*?

"For vain man would be wise, though man be born *like* a wild ass's colt."

Thus Zophar fails to see beyond the Law. Truly the Law is irrevocable, and Job is a transgressor; wherefore, from Zophar's stand-point, wickedness must be considered, and also from the immutability of the Law wickedness must be considered. If wickedness must be considered, and if the Law is unchangeable, then of a surety the transgressor must die whether such transgressor be man or spirit; hence in condemning Job Zophar condemns himself, and also condemns the transgressor irrespective of host. Zophar continues,—

XI. 13–20. "If thou prepare thine heart, and stretch out thine hands toward him;

"If iniquity *be* in thine hand, put it far away, and let not wickedness dwell in thy tabernacles.

"For then shalt thou lift up thy face without spot; yea, thou shalt be steadfast, and shalt not fear:

"Because thou shalt forget *thy* misery, *and* remember *it* as waters *that* pass away:

"And *thine* age shall be clearer than the noonday; thou shalt shine forth, thou shalt be as the morning.

"And thou shalt be secure, because there is hope; yea, thou shalt dig *about thee, and* thou shalt take thy rest in safety.

"Also thou shalt lie down, and none shall make *thee* afraid; yea, many shall make suit unto thee.

"But the eyes of the wicked shall fail, and they shall not escape, and their hope *shall be as* the giving up of the ghost."

In this summary Zophar indicates possibility of life through righteousness by works; that is, the transgressor may by his own free will and effort leave behind him transgression and consequential misery, and live in safety. In this case, however, the Law governing transgression would not be immutable, for the creature would redeem himself through reformation; but should not the creature reform and put away his iniquity, then Zophar consigns him to hopeless death.

Thus, while Zophar stands upon the Law, he ignores and makes of none effect the ruling of the Law in the earlier stages of transgression. The overthrow of the Evil Kingdom clearly demands the consideration of every transgression, first or last, great or small, that no loop-hole be found or left for the escape of Evil, and that the absolute justice and equity of the Almighty be preserved free from all blemish.

XII. 1-3. "And Job answered and said,

"No doubt but ye *are* the people, and wisdom shall die with you.

"But I have understanding as well as you; I *am* not inferior to you: yea, who knoweth not such things as these?"

Job's words indicate that the exposition of the Law as set forth by his friends is well known, and even commonplace; but to Job there is a beyond that finds no lodgement in their philosophy. Job continues,—

XII. 4. "I am *as* one mocked of his neighbour, who calleth upon God, and he answereth him: the just upright *man is* laughed to scorn."

The afflictions that compass Job and the exemption therefrom of his friends make it seem as though Job was forsaken of God, and that his friends, his neighbors, with all their fallacious reasoning and incomplete deduction, were heeded, answered, and specially cared for by the Almighty. Job knows that his doctrine is based upon sure promises,—promises that go far beyond the Law; and, although a transgressor, yet he declares the truth thereof in the face of all his tribulation; by which the grandeur of his faith is manifested. Job continues,—

XII. 5. "He that is ready to slip with *his* feet *is as* a lamp despised in the thought of him that is at ease."

Hence the tribulation that besets a creature is no indication of the true worth of the sufferer. Job continues,—

XII. 6. "The tabernacles of robbers prosper, and they that provoke God are secure; into whose hand God bringeth *abundantly*."

Hence, on the other hand, so may prosperity cover the greater transgressor. Job continues,—

XII. 7-10. "But ask now the beasts, and they shall teach thee; and the fowls of the air, and they shall tell thee:

"Or speak to the earth, and it shall teach thee; and the fishes of the sea shall declare unto thee.

"Who knoweth not in all these that the hand of the Lord hath wrought this?

"In whose hand *is* the soul of every living thing, and the breath of all mankind."

By these words tribulation is permitted among all flesh for some wise purpose; the pursuer may, however, be a greater transgressor than the pursued; but, as stated (verse 5), "He that is ready to slip with *his* feet *is as* a lamp despised in the thought of him that is at ease." Job continues,—

XII. 11. "Doth not the ear try words? and the mouth taste his meat?"

Weigh, then, Job's words (verses 7-10), and sift them, when it will be found that the universal tribulation that besets the creature will, at some time, confront the Evil Kingdom as evidence that the Evil Kingdom is the source and fountain of such tribulation. Job continues,—

XII. 12-14. "With the ancient *is* wisdom; and in length of days understanding.

"With him *is* wisdom and strength, he hath counsel and understanding.

"Behold, he breaketh down, and it cannot be built again: he shutteth up a man, and there can be no opening."

Such are the attributes and power of the Infinite Majesty, the Sublime Unity, that governs all things: there is nothing that He cannot understand and control, from the wisdom that lies concealed in the ultimate atom to the comprehension and binding of the Strong Man that sends his evil emissaries throughout the habitation of the creature. Job continues,—

XII. 15, 16. "Behold, he withholdeth the waters, and they dry up: also he sendeth them out, and they overturn the earth.

"With him *is* strength and wisdom: the deceived and the deceiver *are* his."

These verses point to the power of the Infinite Majesty over the waters: by withholding them the deadly famine is brought about, and by sending them out the destructive deluge finds place; but because Satan (see 1 Kings xix. 11-13) is permitted to sway these elements, and thus bring tribulation upon the creature because of transgression, supremacy as a ruler must not be accorded him, neither must the resulting tribulation be considered proof of unrestrainable power; for, even as the text declares, "the deceived and the deceiver *are* his;" that is, Satan and all his host of evil, his followers, and adherents are in the power of the Infinite Majesty and under his control, even to imprisonment and death. Job continues,—

XII. 17–21. "He leadeth counsellors away spoiled, and maketh the judges fools.

"He looseth the bond of kings, and girdeth their loins with a girdle.

"He leadeth princes away spoiled, and overthroweth the mighty.

"He removeth away the speech of the trusty, and taketh away the understanding of the aged.

"He poureth contempt upon princes, and weakeneth the strength of the mighty."

By these verses no other power can approach unto the Sublime Unity in strength and wisdom; they are as nothing before him, and, under his glance, they sink into nothingness; their vacant places neither miss them nor know them any more. Job continues,—

XII. 22. "He discovereth deep things out of darkness, and bringeth out to light the shadow of death."

Thus the Infinite Majesty is Creator, Redeemer, Restorer. Job continues,—

XII. 23–25. "He increaseth the nations, and destroyeth them: he enlargeth the nations, and straiteneth them *again*.

"He taketh away the heart of the chief of the

people of the earth, and causeth them to wander in a wilderness *where there is* no way.

"They grope in the dark without light, and he maketh them to stagger like a drunken man."

These verses indicate the bringing forth and enlarging of the nations, the great Races of Men, their destruction, and their dwelling in the darksome vale where there is no way. They are not dead, however,—that is, not spiritually dead,—for life without aim is indicated by the text. This vale or wilderness evidently is that described by Job (x. 21, 22) as the land of darkness and the shadow of death,—

"A land of darkness, as darkness *itself;* and of the shadow of death, without any order, and *where* the light *is* as darkness." Job continues,—

XIII. 1, 2. "Lo, mine eye hath seen all *this,* mine ear hath heard and understood it.

"What ye know, *the same* do I know also: I *am* not inferior unto you."

Thus Job fully comprehends the philosophy of his three friends, not, however, because they first advanced it, but from his own knowledge and investigation of the Law that elevates or casts down those under the ruling thereof. Job continues,—

XIII. 3–5. "Surely I would speak to the Almighty, and I desire to reason with God.

"But ye *are* forgers of lies, ye *are* all physicians of no value.

"Oh that ye would altogether hold your peace! and it should be your wisdom."

In the eye of Job the wisdom of his three friends

becomes foolishness; nay, worse: for by misconstruction of the Law and of the charges given man (see Rev. ii., iii. 16) their statements turn to falsity. Why? Because they ignore the promises thus given man of a life hereafter. These promises are not given to man as a perfect creature, but as a transgressor,—see also the promise given man after the fall (Gen. iii. 1-16); hence the wisdom of Eliphaz, Bildad, and Zophar becomes foolishness in the eye of Job; wherefore silence on their part indicates more wisdom than uttered foolishness, or as indicated by the text, silence in the foolish passes for wisdom. Moreover, even as Job declares, his friends are physicians of no value. Why? Because they cannot recover the transgressor: for they consigned him (see iv. 17-21) to eternal forgetfulness. Of what value to the sick man is the physician who tells his patient that he will die? Of what value to the sick man is the physician who masses the symptoms of disease and overwhelms his patient with their deadly properties, with the hopelessness of escape, and with the certainty of decease? None; hence the wisdom of such a physician would be in his silence: for the patient might recover notwithstanding the deadly properties shadowed by the symptoms of his disease. Job continues,—

XIII. 6-8. "Hear now my reasoning, and hearken to the pleading of my lips.

"Will ye speak wickedly for God? and talk deceitfully for him?

"Will ye accept his person? will ye contend for God?"

By ignoring the promises of life to the transgressor

the reasoning of Eliphaz, Bildad, and Zophar becomes wickedness in the eyes of Job. Why? Because God knew that the creature would transgress, and (see 2 Tim. ii. 26) would become captive to Satan at his will. With this foreknowledge (see Rom. viii. 28-30) man was predestinated and called according to the purpose of God; and whom he predestinated and called, them he also justified: and whom he justified, them he also glorified. If, therefore, man was predestinated and called to justification and glory, who and what are Eliphaz and Bildad and Zophar, that they should deny the probability or possibility of the accomplishment thereof? It is true that Paul summed up in a few words the greatness of the reward that should rest upon man long after the day of Job and his friends, yet the substance thereof is given to the churches in Rev. ii., iii., and in many other portions of the Scriptures where the history of the first three ages of man is taken up.

The charges to the churches, the summing up of Paul, the deductions of Job, all indicate that the Law or First Covenant must be superseded that the promises given man may become fulfilled and the word of God established. Job's friends, however, rest entirely upon the Law as the ultimatum; they see no beyond. Job continues,—

XIII. 9. "Is it good that he should search you out? or as one man mocketh another, do ye *so* mock him?"

Will the philosophy of Job's friends bear searching out, or not? The indications are that it will not. Why? Because it is based on partial grounds only; hence it is incomplete. Job continues,—

XIII. 10-12. "He will surely reprove you, if ye do secretly accept persons.

"Shall not his excellency make you afraid? and his dread fall upon you?

"Your remembrances *are* like unto ashes, your bodies to bodies of clay."

These verses indicate the partial grounds upon which the reasoning of Eliphaz, Bildad, and Zophar is based, for they secretly accept persons or things; that is, they accept and ignore as may be convenient; wherefore their remembrance is like unto ashes, or as the uncared-for *débris* of greater things. Job continues,—

XIII. 13-16. "Hold your peace, let me alone, that I may speak, and let come on me what *will*.

"Wherefore do I take my flesh in my teeth, and put my life in mine hand?

"Though he slay me, yet will I trust in him: but I will maintain mine own ways before him.

"He also *shall be* my salvation: for a hypocrite shall not come before him."

Thus Job, as a transgressor, positively declares his belief in his redemption,—not, however, through his own free agency or his righteousness by works, but that through God his Redeemer his salvation shall be accomplished; and that even though he should be slain yet will he trust in his God for the fulfilment of the promises that man should be justified and glorified.

Why will not Job give up his own way before God? It is because Job's actions are righteous in that he strives to fulfil the Law; and also that Job's way comprehends life, while the way of his friends terminates in absolute death; Job's righteous works also give proof of his faith in his Redeemer.

Moreover, Job's way points to the separation of the good from the evil, whereby evil can be set upon its own base, be judged, and be blotted out of existence forever, by the ruling of the Law that forms the basis of Eliphaz's argument. Job, however, by his own position, will, as a transgressor, surely die; which fact he appears clearly to recognize, for he states, " Wherefore do I take my flesh in my teeth, and put my life in mine hand?" The reason why Job puts his life in his hand is manifest; for by his death the evil pertaining to him will be separated from the good; and although Job in himself possesses not the power of returning back to life, yet he feels assured that the God of his salvation will provide a way for such return. Job continues,—

XIII. 18. " Behold now, I have ordered *my* cause; I know that I shall be justified."

Thus Job, although a transgressor, expresses his faith in his justification; and if justified, then (see Rom. viii. 30) he will be glorified. If justified and glorified after transgression, then the indication is clear that he must have been redeemed from his transgression. Job continues,—

XIII. 19. "Who *is* he *that* will plead with me? for now, if I hold my tongue, I shall give up the ghost."

This verse indicates that it is incumbent upon Job to define his position, wherefore he states,—

XIII. 20–22. " Only do not two *things* unto me; then will I not hide myself from thee.

"Withdraw thine hand far from me: and let not thy dread make me afraid.

"Then call thou, and I will answer: or let me speak, and answer thou me."

Thus, at the outset, Job seeks for freedom of speech in the declaration of his position, but as a free agent and as an instrumentality in the purpose of God. Owing to the sacredness of the situation, reverential freedom (see Isa. vi. 5-8) must be accorded the creature that silence seal not his lips forever. Job continues,—

XIII. 23. "How many *are* mine iniquities and sins? make me to know my transgression and my sin."

In the light that Job as the progenitor and Adam of the Third Race of men represents the Third Race, then the iniquity and sin resting upon him comprehends and includes that of both the First and Second races; their iniquity and sin having been transmitted from father to son through the operation of the great Law of Iniquity that is set forth (Ex. xx. 5, 6; xxxiv. 5-7). The indication is clear, however, that to the transgression thus transmitted to the Third Race their own immediate iniquity must be added. The indication is also manifest that the trangression of Job simply as a man is unknown to him, and, hence, that he has transgressed through ignorance. Job continues,—

XIII. 24. "Wherefore hidest thou thy face, and holdest me for thine enemy?"

This verse points to the children under transgression that (see Ex. xx. 5) hate the Lord; their transgression being counted as enmity to the Lord. In his own eyes, Job, as a man simply, has lived an upright life, and knows not wherein he has transgressed that he should be held as an enemy of the Lord by the Lord; but Job, as representative of the Third Age or Race, comprehends not the iniquity that has been transmitted to him from the preceding Ages that he in any way should be held responsible for it. Job continues,—

XIII. 25, 26. "Wilt thou break a leaf driven to and fro? and wilt thou pursue the dry stubble?

"For thou writest bitter things against me, and makest me to possess the iniquities of my youth."

These verses further indicate the transmission of iniquity from father to son. The fathers (see xii. 23–25) wandering in the wilderness, groping in the land of darkness, are as leaves driven to and fro, and are as the dry stubble; shall, therefore, they be pursued?

By the descent of iniquity from father to son the age of Job, as representative of the Third Race of men, is made to possess the iniquity of his youth; wherefore it follows that although the fathers dwell (see x. 21, 22) in the land of darkness and of the shadow of death, and are as leaves driven to and fro, that they still will be pursued; which pursuit is made manifest in the bitter things that are written against Job as representative of the Third Age, to whom the iniquity of the fathers was transmitted. This iniquity must not become lost to sight, for every scrap carries with it the penalty of the Law; which penalty pertains to the original transgressor or to the transgressor from whom it first was transmitted, even though such transmission cover a myriad of years. Job continues,—

XIII. 27, 28. "Thou puttest my feet also in the stocks, and lookest narrowly unto all my paths; thou settest a print upon the heels of my feet.

"And he, as a rotten thing, consumeth, as a garment that is moth-eaten."

These verses indicate the search after the iniquity that pertains to Job as representative of the Third Race, for cognizance must be taken of his own transgression as well as that which has been transmitted through the Law of Iniquity. Moreover, the Third Race was also called as a subjugatory and governing element; hence failure in governmental duty would involve failure in mission, by which transgression would be imputed. Thus the Lord God watches for and seeks out all iniquity and remission, that the evidence may be overwhelming as to who alone can be the Subjugator and Ruler of all things that none suffer through neglect or ignorance. When, therefore, such proof shall have become full, then, through the Edenic Law, through the First Covenant with its ministration of death, the iniquitous as a rotten thing will be consumed, and be as a garment that is moth-eaten. Job continues,—

XIV. 1, 2. "Man *that is* born of a woman *is* of few days, and full of trouble.

"He cometh forth like a flower, and is cut down: he fleeth also as a shadow, and continueth not."

Why should man that is born of woman be of few days and full of trouble? It is because of transgression. Created man was physically constituted to continue indefinitely; for as a perfect creature, endowed with perfect recuperative faculties, no change could occur in the perfect organism already established; hence youth would continually be renewed, and length of years would bring forth no wrinkle to mark the aged man. With transgression, however, the Divine law is broken; wherefore things of pain creep in, overwhelm the creature, and sap the vitals of his longevity; hence his days become few and are full of trouble; hence, as the text states, "He cometh forth like a flower, and is cut down: . . . and continueth not," but fleeth as a shadow (see x. 21, 22) to the land already dark as darkness itself. Such is man in the hand of the mighty Power of Evil. Job continues,—

XIV. 3. "And dost thou open thine eyes upon such a one, and bringest me into judgment with thee?"

Therefore, considering the weakness of man as compared with the strength of the Adversary, how can the perfection and strength of such a one be brought into judgment with the perfection and strength of the Almighty? The indication is clearly marked that they cannot; hence, though man was created perfect and upright, and though under the Law he, as a free agent, could not retain his perfection and uprightness,—although specially commanded (see Gen. i. 28) to subdue the earth,—the position does not follow that the Almighty's power for such subjugation is exhausted, the fall of man of Adam's race being no proof or evidence of weakness on the part of the Creator. Job continues,—

XIV. 4. "Who can bring a clean *thing* out of an unclean? not one."

Although man was commanded to subdue the earth with its host of Evil, how could he reform Evil even should he subjugate it? or how could he bring a clean thing out of an unclean? Job himself briefly answers these questions by replying, "Not one." Hence, if Evil cannot be reformed or made clean, or if no clean thing can be brought forth from Evil, then it is a total depravity or a totally unclean thing; and as such will, by the Law, be blotted out of existence; for of the holy city Jerusalem it is said (see Rev. xxi. 27), "there shall in no wise enter into it anything that defileth, neither *whatsoever* worketh abomination, or *maketh* a lie: but they which are written in the Lamb's book of life." Job continues of man,—

XIV. 5, 6. "Seeing his days *are* determined, the number of his months *are* with thee, thou hast appointed his bounds that he cannot pass;

"Turn from him, that he may rest, till he shall accomplish, as a hireling, his day."

These verses indicate that the bounds of the habitation of man are fixed, and that the number of months thereof are with the Lord (see also Deut. xxxii. 7, 8; Acts xvii. 26). Such being the case, the indication is clear that the fall of man was foreseen; and if foreseen, then provided for that an empty triumph grace the banners of the Adversary.

With the fall came rest in the land of shadow and darkness, but not absolute death, which rest Job likens to the cutting down of a tree, as follows:

XIV. 7–9. "For there is hope of a tree, if it be cut down, that it will sprout again, and that the tender branch thereof will not cease.

"Though the root thereof wax old in the earth, and the stock thereof die in the ground;

"*Yet* through the scent of water it will bud, and bring forth boughs like a plant."

Thus by the figure the semblance of a death is indicated, and also the semblance of a resurrection through which the tree survives until a later day; wherefore, by the figure, man rests in the valley of the shadow of death; but through great laws his iniquity, blood, and characteristics are transmitted to and live in a later generation; hence there is hope that in a later generation the Water of Life will not fail that shall awaken the dwellers of the dark valley from their sleep, and raise their names up again in the land of the living,— for the root still lives, the sap still flows, but the stock thereof, the body of sinful flesh, lies dead in the ground; which indications Job further confirms as follows:

XIV. 10-12. "But man dieth, and wasteth away: yea, man giveth up the ghost, and where *is* he?

"*As* the waters fail from the sea, and the flood decayeth and drieth up;

"So man lieth down, and riseth not: till the heavens *be* no more, they shall not awake, nor be raised out of their sleep."

Thus man, natural man, the body of sinful flesh, the stock of the tree, will die, waste away, and be no more; Job further stating, "till the heavens *be* no more, they shall not awake, nor be raised out of their sleep." Can the heavens be no more? The heavens (see Ps. lxxxix. 34-37) will endure forever; hence the body of sinful flesh was cast off that hope of a renewed life might enter in. As the tree is not cut down to renew life to the stock, so neither is man's body of sinful flesh cut off that renewed life may be given it. How, then, can life be renewed in man? The indication is clear that the spirit of man will have been regenerated or born into a new body before absolute death shall overtake him; hence, as both the body of sinful flesh and the new body die an absolute death, so the resurrection of the spirit of man clothed with the new body that is without spot or blemish is altogether possible under the Law, in which case, even as the text indicates, the revival of the body of sinful flesh would be uncalled for. Job continues,—

XIV. 13. "Oh that thou wouldest hide me in the grave, that thou wouldest keep me secret, until thy wrath be past, that thou wouldest appoint me a set time, and remember me!"

Job longs for rest from the great trials that are upon him; not so much, probably, on account of the physical suffering as for the terrible struggle between the good and evil that compasses him. He also craves an appointed time for rest and forgetfulness, and an appointed time for awakening. Why should Job crave any awakening? It is because of his faith (see xiii. 15, 16) in his salvation by the Lord. Job continues,—

XIV. 14. "If a man die, shall he live *again?* all the days of my appointed time will I wait, till my change come."

Job's faith answers this question in the affirmative; wherefore all the days of his natural life will he wait, till the change come or till he shall die. What then? Job states,—

XIV. 15. "Thou shalt call, and I will answer thee: thou wilt have a desire to the work of thine hands."

Thus after death the Lord shall call, and shall have a desire to the work of his hands. Such call and such desire surely can never bring back into existence aught that is tinctured with evil? Therefore, inasmuch as essential evil is not the work of the hands of the Lord, and does not spring from the Kingdom of Righteousness, the indication is clear that the good will have been separated from the evil, the good body from the sinful body, before the creature shall enter upon his new life. Job continues,—

XIV. 16, 17. "For now thou numberest my steps: dost thou not watch over my sin?

"My transgression *is* sealed up in a bag, and thou sewest up mine iniquity."

These verses indicate the transmission and accumulation of iniquity that it may be separated from the good. Job continues,—

XIV. 18. "And surely the mountain falling cometh to nought, and the rock is removed out of his place."

This mountain indicates the accumulated mass of man's iniquity; it will surely fall and come to naught, while the rock, the instigator of this iniquity, will be removed out of his place. Job continues,—

XIV. 19–22. "The waters wear the stones: thou washest away the things which grow *out* of the dust of the earth; and thou destroyest the hope of man.

"Thou prevailest for ever against him, and he passeth: thou changest his countenance, and sendest him away.

"His sons come to honour, and he knoweth *it* not; and they are brought low, but he perceiveth *it* not of them.

"But his flesh upon him shall have pain, and his soul within him shall mourn."

As the waters wear away the stones, so the Lord takes away the things that grow out of the dust of the earth; the chief of which is man. Man, as a free agent under the Law, and as a subjugatory element, passes away, the grave closes over him, and the land of shadow and darkness receives him. In the day of Job countless numbers dwelt in this dark land, oblivious to all existence; their sons arose to honor, but no voice could make them glad with the cheerful news; their sons were brought low, but still they slept unconscious of all. If such be the condition of him that dwells in the land of the shadow of death, how is it that his flesh upon him shall have pain, and his soul within him shall mourn? The indications are that these conditions can only be filled by the transmission of blood through the Law of Generation. If the iniquity of the fathers shall be transmitted to the children, then the flesh and blood must be transmitted also to a greater or less extent; wherefore, even as the text indicates, the flesh of the fathers shall have pain through the children, the conditions of the Edenic Promise (see Gen. iii. 14–16), the Law of Iniquity, and the Law of Generation requiring it.

XV. 1–3. "Then answered Eliphaz the Temanite, and said,

"Should a wise man utter vain knowledge, and fill his belly with the east wind?

"Should he reason with unprofitable talk? or with speeches wherewith he can do no good?"

Thus Eliphaz indirectly denies the position expressed by Job, that iniquity, blood, and characteristics are transmitted from father to son, that through such transmission the highway to redemption may be opened, and whereby life beyond the grave may become an established fact. Eliphaz stands upon the sure fulfilment of the Law that sweeps the transgressor from existence; with him an upright life after transgression may give length of days, and even a ripe old age to the transgressor, but it cannot redeem him nor confer upon him eternal life; hence any system of redemption becomes unprofitable talk in the eyes of Eliphaz, vain knowledge, and speeches wherewith no good can be done. But is it so? Can no system exist or be brought about for the redemption of the creature under transgression that shall not interfere with or make void the Law? The indications are strongly marked that such a system can exist whereby the creature may be redeemed and the Law fulfilled to the very letter.

This system finds substance in the transmission of the iniquity and blood of the creature from father to son— for the blood (see Deut. xii. 23) is the life—until it shall fall upon the One that shall lay down his life in full payment for such iniquity. The Law is fulfilled to the letter, whether the creature die an absolute death in his own individual person, or whether he die in the person of the Redeemer; but the exceeding great difference in the manner of the two possible absolute deaths lies in the facts that, should the creature or transgressor, irrespective of host, die in his own individual person, then the grave would close over him for evermore; while, on the other hand, should the transgressor die in the person of the Redeemer, into whose body he had been regenerated, then, in the regenerated body, he could and would return to life from absolute death clothed with this unblemished body, the body that was prepared for the Son suitable for this purpose. Eliphaz continues,—

XV. 4. "Yea, thou castest off fear, and restrainest prayer before God."

Even as Eliphaz states, the reasoning of Job casts off fear and restrains prayer before God. Why? Because Job's faith in the promises of God engenders love, and love casts off fear, while by it prayer and supplication give place to "joy, thanksgiving, and melody." Eliphaz, however, discards the faith of Job, he being governed by the Law; wherefore, by his philosophy, fear and prayer before God must continue that, perhaps, a full life, a good old age, may be accorded the creature under the Law. Eliphaz continues,—

XV. 5, 6. "For thy mouth uttereth thine iniquity, and thou choosest the tongue of the crafty.

"Thine own mouth condemneth thee, and not I: yea, thine own lips testify against thee."

Thus Eliphaz considers Job's uttered hope of a future life as iniquitous, and that, as iniquitous uttering, his mouth condemns him. Why? As already indicated, it is because Job looks beyond the Law, or First Covenant, with its ministration of death, to the charges and promises (see Rev. ii., iii.) that embody a newer and better covenant.

These charges and promises Eliphaz ignores or misapprehends because of the failure of the preceding races to which the charges were given. To his senses their transgression resulted in their disappearance from the face of the earth, and that the destruction implied by the charges had overwhelmed them forever; wherefore Eliphaz continues,—

XV. 7–10. "*Art* thou the first man *that* was born? or wast thou made before the hills?

"Hast thou heard the secret of God? and dost thou restrain wisdom to thyself?

"What knowest thou, that we know not? *what* understandest thou, which *is* not in us?

"With us *are* both the grayheaded and very aged men, much elder than thy father."

The question of Eliphaz, "*Art* thou the first man *that* was born?" implies that Job was not the first man that was born; hence in the light that Job is the progenitor or Adam of the Third Race of men, then other men were born (see Rev. vi., xii.) or brought forth before his day. These men, as races, peopled the First and Second Ages of Man; wherefore Eliphaz likens them to the grayheaded man, and the very aged man, both of which are much older than the father of Job, or the Third Age from the beginning thereof to the particular day of Job's affliction. Eliphaz claims to be familiar with the history of these two races of men; and, therefore, inasmuch as death reigned among them from the calling of the first man thereof, and as instead of a resurrection there was brought forth a new creature, Eliphaz, by their fate, felt convinced that the Law ruled as absolute monarch; and, hence, as it was with them, so it would be with Job,—he would live out his years, pass away, and be no more, while a new creature would be brought forth to fill his place.

Job's dissent, however, brings forth Eliphaz's question, "Hast thou heard the secret of God?" It is not because Job has heard the secret of God, or that he understands the fulness of what God comprehends in his purpose, but it is because Job's mind grasps, to a certain degree, the revelations made by the charges to the churches that Evil should be overthrown and the works thereof undone. With unlimited space as a field, progression or development does not call for the destruction of the creature. Why, therefore, should not a system exist whereby man of to-day could be redeemed? If there is a Creator, then no good reason appears why man, with his intellectual faculties just bursting into bloom and setting with fruit, should be cut off, annihilated, that another, simply as man, might occupy his place and take up his labors.

If no good reason appears why he should be cut off, then the promises of the Creator that he should be restored may well be considered. To cut off the creature because of the evil dwelling within him would be a sacrifice of the good, but the separation of the good from the evil would be a foundation upon which the creature, through the good, might stand in the hope of restoration and life. Job evidently bases his faith of future life upon the separation of the good from the evil, "the precious from the vile;" but Eliphaz considers such faith as without foundation, vain. Eliphaz continues,—

XV. 11. "*Are* the consolations of God small with thee? is there any secret thing with thee?"

Hence, as Eliphaz intimates from Job's faith and hope, does Job really need small consolation of God? Job's faith and hope carry him beyond the need of consolation, for in the future life consolation will be unknown; wherefore the entering into this hope lessens the consolations of God. Consolation betokens a suffering state or condition; hence, as the Kingdom of Righteousness draws nearer to the creature, so consolation gives place to joy and thanksgiving, and, consequently, consolation must lessen. This is the secret thing that is with Job, but which secret Job abundantly declares. Eliphaz continues,—

XV. 12, 13. "Why doth thine heart carry thee away? and what do thy eyes wink at,

"That thou turnest thy spirit against God, and lettest *such* words go out of thy mouth?"

The Law entered for the government of all hosts, and by it the transgressor shall die, for such is the decree of the Most High; but Job, being a transgressor, hopes to live, and expresses his hope in plain words. Eliphaz considers that such a hope is contrary to the Law, and hence against the Power that instituted it; he also considering that Job's wishes rather than the Law laid the foundation of his hope. Further, Eliphaz asks,—

XV. 14–16. "What *is* man, that he should be clean? and *he which is* born of a woman, that he should be righteous?

"Behold, he putteth no trust in his saints; yea, the heavens are not clean in his sight.

"How much more abominable and filthy *is* man, which drinketh iniquity like water?"

These verses point to the various sin-tinctured hosts that people the earth, and, also, even to impurity in the heavens. Why should the heavens be counted impure? It is because of the wickedness of the Evil Host (see

Rev. xii. 7–9) that once found place there; wickedness that was manifest to and perceived of the angels of heaven; hence the judgment of the Lord God as set forth in Deut. xii. 2—"Ye shall utterly destroy all the places, wherein the nations which ye shall possess served their gods"—will apply to the heavens, that they may be purified from all knowledge and remembrance of sin by the fulfilment of the Law. From these indications it follows that the angels of heaven are not perfect, that man born of woman is not righteous, and that sin-tinctured man, let him pertain to which host he may, according to the philosophy of Eliphaz, drinks iniquity like water; yet, outside of the philosophy of Eliphaz, the indication becomes evident that the creature, be he man or angel, cannot govern all things so perfectly that he should not transgress through ignorance or through error of judgment.

If the angels of heaven in their superiority and grandeur are not perfect, how can man of Adam's race hope to rise above the Law and be perfect, and thus obtain eternal life? If man stands upon the ruling of the Law, simply like Eliphaz, then he never can rise above the Law, and his argument and reasoning will never go beyond the ruling of the Law, and hence, as a transgressor far below the angels, he will by the Law be swept out of existence.

The reasoning of Eliphaz, therefore, while it condemns man to eternal annihilation, also condemns the Evil Host to the same fate; for the ruling of the Law is over them also; but Job, while realizing these conditions, as well as Eliphaz, also knows that no condemnation rests over the good. If, therefore, condemnation rests over the evil, and the good is uncondemned, then it follows that the ministration of death pertaining to the Law or First Covenant has no hold upon the good that it should die; wherefore the good must be separated from the evil, or the Law itself would become unrighteous, which cannot be. Job's faith and hope rest upon the certainty of such a separation; but Eliphaz discards the position as untenable; he evidently considering man with his various qualities as a spontaneous growth, or atomic development, and not as a creature that could independently be engrafted with good and with evil. Eliphaz continues,—

XV. 17–19. "I will shew thee, hear me; and that *which* I have seen I will declare;

"Which wise men have told from their fathers, and have not hid *it:*

"Unto whom alone the earth was given, and no stranger passed among them."

Through the philosophy of Eliphaz these verses become indicative of spontaneous growth or at least progression from some created atomic or molecular system of life, unto which the earth was given as a field of progress, and hence, none other passed among them; wherefore, from the atomic life thus created, man was developed, and, from the excellence of his development, continued and existed as the possessor of the earth. Eliphaz continues his saying,—

XV. 20–24. "The wicked man travaileth with pain all *his* days, and the number of years is hidden to the oppressor.

"A dreadful sound *is* in his ears: in prosperity the destroyer shall come upon him.

"He believeth not that he shall return out of darkness, and he is waited for of the sword.

"He wandereth abroad for bread, *saying,* Where *is it?* he knoweth that the day of darkness is ready at his hand.

"Trouble and anguish shall make him afraid; they shall prevail against him, as a king ready to the battle."

Eliphaz has already declared (see iv. 17–21; xv. 14–16) that man without exception is wicked, and that he shall perish forever; yet here again he pictures the fall of man, for he concludes that all men are wicked. In this picture man is hopeless of a return from the land of darkness: when, therefore, the grave shall close over him a final adieu will have been made to all that sparkles with light and life; and, as the age rolls on, others arise, but there is no awakening for him; time progresses, and even ages unfold, but the darkness deepens; no glimmer steals a momentary glance or shoots a single ray to light the self-digged pit that clasps him. Hopeless, helpless, dead; barren, uncalled for, uncared for; broken forever he lies, a rusting link in the remorseless chain that finds its bitter end in the dark chamber of death. Who would not seek escape from such a fate? Even the wicked man (see verse 23) "wandereth abroad for bread, *saying,* Where *is it?*" for he knows that his hour is at hand. Eliphaz, however, does not believe in this bread or in any redeemer, that escape may be had; for, with him, trouble and anguish shall prevail against the transgressor as a king ready to the battle. Of the wicked man Eliphaz continues,—

XV. 25-28. "For he stretcheth out his hand against God, and strengtheneth himself against the Almighty.

"He runneth upon him, *even* on *his* neck, upon the thick bosses of his bucklers:

"Because he covereth his face with his fatness, and maketh collops of fat on *his* flanks.

"And he dwelleth in desolate cities, *and* in houses which no man inhabiteth, which are ready to become heaps."

According to the philosophy of Eliphaz, the wicked man stretches out his hand against God in that he does not keep to the ruling of the Law that ordains to life; and, hence, that he transgresses. Transgression, however, is not all; but Eliphaz intimates that in his transgression man brings forth his own wisdom to offset the ministration of death that pertains to the Law, as in the case of Job, whose hopes, notwithstanding transgression, lead him to look for life in the future. The philosophy of Eliphaz points to the utter futility of such hopes under the Law, where he consigns the wicked man to a ruinous dwelling in a desolate city, which no man inhabiteth. Eliphaz further points to the futility of hopes such as those held by Job where he states,—

XV. 29, 30. "He shall not be rich, neither shall his substance continue, neither shall he prolong the perfection thereof upon the earth.

"He shall not depart out of darkness; the flame shall dry up his branches, and by the breath of his mouth shall he go away."

Thus by the breath of his mouth man shall go away, or, when man ceases to breathe, then, by the position of Eliphaz, he ceases to exist forever,—nothing can recall him out of the deep darkness into which he has descended, and no perfection pertaining to him shall be prolonged upon the earth. If this is not annihilation, what is it? for Eliphaz recognizes no Redeemer. Eliphaz continues,—

XV. 31. "Let not him that is deceived trust in vanity: for vanity shall be his recompense."

These words evidently are directed against all holding such hopes as those expressed by Job; for Eliphaz considers such hopes as vain, vanity; and, hence, that a vain, empty recompense will be the reward of him that so trusts. Eliphaz continues,—

XV. 32, 33. "It shall be accomplished before his time, and his branch shall not be green.

"He shall shake off his unripe grape as the vine, and shall cast off his flower as the olive."

In this statement Eliphaz brings forward the loss of Job's children as a proof of the truth of his position; but, from Job's stand-point, such evidence cannot be accepted as proof that they shall not return again. Eliphaz consigns Job's children to the land of absolute darkness, to absolute death; but Job considers that they descended into the land of the shadow of death, not absolute death, but into the shadow or semblance of death; in which case there is hope of a return: but from absolute death no return is possible, except it be through the resurrecting power of the Infinite Majesty; which power (see St. John x. 18) was conferred upon the Son that he might fulfil the will of the Father in the redemption of the world. Eliphaz further continues his reasoning,—

XV. 34, 35. "For the congregation of hypocrites

shall be desolate, and fire shall consume the tabernacles of bribery.

"They conceive mischief, and bring forth vanity, and their belly prepareth deceit."

By which continued transgression only confirms the final sentence of the wicked, among whom Eliphaz classes Job.

XVI. 1, 2. "Then Job answered and said,

"I have heard many such things: miserable comforters *are* ye all."

If the words of Job's three friends really contained any substantial indications of a future life, why should they be called miserable comforters? Can the promise of future life be considered miserable comfort? By no means; but if there were no future life, how much better would it have been for the creature had the creature never seen the light! Job's afflictions make it manifest to him that something beyond the natural life of man is called for, even though (see v. 26) the last days of man should be lightened with sunshine. The sunshine of life, however, carries with it stronger proof of future existence than affliction; for should this sunshine die a great blot would take its place never more to be removed. The setting sun brings many an unsolved pang into the heart of the beholder, but hope clings to the last lingering ray not as to a departing friend, but as to one soon to come again. How great the misery should the thought arise, and find fulfilment, that a final adieu was given to the source of light! Who could banish the sun, the glorious sun, and give its place forever to the blackness of night? Miserable comforters, did Job say? Aye, worse than miserable are those who would consign Job's sunshine to eternal darkness, and who would open a pit no future could ever fill; for the grave would grow as fast as eternity should unroll its limitless scroll, and would bury within its precincts the most precious treasures of earth. Job continues,—

XVI. 3, 4. "Shall vain words have an end? or what emboldeneth thee that thou answerest?

"I also could speak as ye *do:* if your soul were in my soul's stead, I could heap up words against you, and shake mine head at you."

To Job the words of his friends are vain; they embody vanity,—vanity of calling, vanity of being, vanity of mission. Vain calling, vain mission! The grave restores the primordial condition of darkness to the creature that existed as though he had never been. What, then, emboldens Eliphaz that he should answer Job's hope of life with his belief in the certainty of absolute, eternal death? The boldness of Eliphaz evidently comes from his knowledge of the Law that embodies the ordination to life to the righteous, and the ministration of death to the unrighteous, coupled with the apparent fulfilment of the latter condition in the destruction that has befallen man of Adam's race from the calling thereof (see viii. 7–10; xv. 9, 10) in the First Age to the day of Job.

Job recognizes the fact that it is easy to heap up words against the transgressor; but from his standpoint there is something besides death on which the transgressor may lean, for the ordination to life that pertains to the Law was not made in vain. In fact, the ordination to life embodies the very essence involved in the calling of the creature, for what would the Law be without the ordination to life? It is clear that Jesus Christ, the righteous, lived in the Law, in that he fulfilled it; and, hence, through his life others may live also, even though they be transgressors; for the life of Christ invested the body into which the transgressor was and is born or regenerated; but if, as the argument of Eliphaz implies, the ordination to life that pertains to the Law is made dead through transgression, and only the ministration of death remain, then no redeemer can arise, and the transgressor will, in his own person, at the end of his natural life, lay down his life forever. Thus the reasoning of Eliphaz is a continual condemnation of Job, and heightens rather than softens his grief, wherefore Job continues,—

XVI. 5. "*But* I would strengthen you with my mouth, and the moving of my lips should assuage *your grief*."

Hence through his faith and knowledge Job could and would speak words of comfort to the transgressor that was overwhelmed through the ruling of the Law. Job continues,—

XVI. 6. "Though I speak, my grief is not assuaged: and *though* I forbear, what am I eased?"

This verse indicates that the tribulation of Job comes from a source beyond his control. What, therefore, is this source? Some spontaneous growth more powerful than man that it should mock his will and cast his physique to the ground? If so, whence comes order that the fire freeze not, or that the water boil not in an ice-bound habitation? The sufferings of Job prove that the source of his tribulation is an active, intelligent, powerful being; one whose strength is far beyond that of Job or any man of Adam's race; one that understands the properties of pain, the methods of producing it, and who is not slow in bringing it about.

The mission of man (see Gen. i. 28) is the subjugation of this power; wherefore, can man rise above and subdue it, the great Power of Evil? Can man say to the fire burn not, and it burn not? If man fails in the possession of this power, then he cannot subdue the Evil Power that tortures the creature with heat and cold; for by its created properties fire will burn the creature whether applied directly by the Power of Evil or by his emissaries.

If the Power of Evil be subdued, then he cannot control fire or any pain-giving element; whence it becomes evident that as long as tribulation shall beset the creature, whether great or small, that a power stronger than the creature rules over him for harm; hence this power (see ii. 1–7) is Satan, king of Evil.

Man may hope by his own efforts to rise above and rule over Satan, but, should such be the case, how conflict among great excellencies could be avoided does not very plainly appear, unless one mind, one sentiment, should actuate them all; in which case a universal sameness of thought and action would find place, which, in itself, is distasteful. The Laws of Order (see Gen. i.) point to a far better state of things, for by them one Head is given to all things; for by them One that is a God, a Creator, a Subjugator, a Redeemer, and a Restorer is made manifest that is infinite, supreme, and perfect in all his attributes. Such a One can subdue the Power of Evil, and can say to the fire, burn not, and it shall not burn; neither shall any tribulation beset the creature, be it great or small, under his rule; but all excellencies, however great they may be, will live in harmony, each free to enjoy the gifts with which they are endowed, whereby beauty and variety will be manifest on every side, and every one will find pleasure in his own work and in the work of his neighbor. Job continues,—

XVI. 7–10. "But now he hath made me weary: thou hast made desolate all my company.

"And thou hast filled me with wrinkles, *which* is a witness *against me:* and my leanness rising up in me beareth witness to my face.

"He teareth *me* in his wrath, who hateth me: he gnasheth upon me with his teeth; mine enemy sharpeneth his eyes upon me.

"They have gaped upon me with their mouth; they have smitten me upon the cheek reproachfully; they have gathered themselves together against me."

The wrinkles and leanness of Job stand witness of his transgressive state; but transgression is one thing and wrinkles and leanness another. Why? Because transgression indicates sin without reward or punishment. With the entering in of the Law transgression or sin was made punishable by death; the Law (see Gen. ii. 16, 17) does not say that transgression shall be punished by wrinkles and leanness, but by death; hence wrinkles and leanness follow with transgression through the rule of some power other than God, and which is greater than man. This power (see i., ii.) is Satan; hence he it is that tears Job and makes his natural life a burden to him. Job himself indicates this as follows:

XVI. 11-14. "God hath delivered me to the ungodly, and turned me over into the hands of the wicked.

"I was at ease, but he hath broken me asunder: he hath also taken *me* by my neck, and shaken me to pieces, and set me up for his mark.

"His archers compass me round about, he cleaveth my reins asunder, and doth not spare; he poureth out my gall upon the ground.

"He breaketh me with breach upon breach; he runneth upon me like a giant."

If the ungodly and wicked are not Satan and his host, who are they? Was not Job (see ii. 3-7) placed in the hand of Satan, who smote him with great affliction? Undoubtedly; but because God took away his special protection from Job, and left him standing upon his free agency to battle under the Law with Satan, and also in fulfilment of the command (Gen. i. 28) for the government of all things, the indication does not follow that, because of Job's weakness, the Almighty brought the ills and afflictions upon Job, but, rather, that he permitted Satan to inflict them; for Job after transgression became subject to the Kingdom of Evil, and, hence, as a subject, was open to such tribulation as the Evil Kingdom might see fit to inflict.

Job, however, is a transgressor, but he is not wholly evil,—that is, transgression does not make the creature a total depravity; hence the Kingdom of Righteousness must take cognizance of the good that dwells within him. Job continues,—

XVI. 15-17. "I have sewed sackcloth upon my skin, and defiled my horn in the dust.

"My face is foul with weeping, and on my eyelids *is* the shadow of death;

"Not for *any* injustice in mine hands: also my prayer *is* pure."

From these verses it is evident that Job's tribulation is due to unrecognized transgression, yet the penalty of transgression is over him just as certainly as over manifest transgression; hence the afflictions that befall a righteous man transgressing through ignorance indicate the certainty of the fulfilment of the Law upon the transgressor, irrespective of host, that no loop-hole exists for the escape of Evil, be it either small or great, known or unknown.

The afflictions that befall righteous men become, therefore, real signs to all hosts of the immutability of the Law, and that the establishment of the Kingdom of Righteousness requires the absolute blotting out of Evil as an energy or power.

Thus Job's hands, from man's stand-point, may be free from injustice, and his prayer may be pure, but still his affliction marks transgression in some intricate, unknown path that brings him under the ruling of the Law; hence (see 1 Kings viii. 46) "*there is* no man that sinneth not." Job continues,—

XVI. 18, 19. "O earth, cover not thou my blood, and let my cry have no place.

"Also now, behold, my witness *is* in heaven, and my record *is* on high."

Thus, should Job's blood be shed through transgression, the call for investigation as to why it was shed would bring the oppressor to the judgment-seat. Job does not wish that his cry be shut up or silenced, for (see text) his witness is in heaven, and his record is on high. The good works of Job do not insure redemption for him, or deliverance from the hand of the oppressor, but they are proofs of his faith in the promises of redemption, and hence it follows that his faith, as a good thing, or essence, shall, like that of Abraham, be counted to him for righteousness. Job continues,—

XVI. 20-22. "My friends scorn me: *but* mine eye poureth out *tears* unto God.

"Oh that one might plead for a man with God, as a man *pleadeth* for his neighbour!

"When a few years are come, then I shall go the way *whence* I shall not return."

Job's friends scorn his faith in a future life, but he turns unto God; and, although turning unto God, he knows that the word of God concerning the transgressor is immutable and cannot be changed; hence he states, "When a few years are come, then I shall go the way *whence* I shall not return." This saying evidently relates to Job's body as transgressive man, for the body of sinful flesh must be left behind forever. Job unregenerated represents this body; Job regenerated represents the body that shall be; hence it follows that the unregenerated must give place to the regenerated, which condition does not pertain to and follow with the philosophy of Eliphaz. Job continues,—

XVII. 1. "My breath is corrupt, my days are extinct, the graves *are ready* for me."

By this verse graves—not the grave or a grave, but graves—are ready for Job. Why graves? Because the body of sinful flesh, the unregenerated body, shall sleep in one grave, while the regenerated body, or the body into which man is and shall be born, sleeps or shall sleep in another. These conditions involve the separation of the good from the evil, "the precious from the vile;" hence one grave will hold the natural body of man, and one grave will hold the body that was prepared for the Son, suitable for the regeneration and restoration of man, and into which man was and is born or regenerated. Job continues,—

XVII. 2. "*Are there* not mockers with me? and doth not mine eye continue in their provocation?"

Who, therefore, is it that mocks Job in his sublime faith? Is it not his three friends with their fallacious reasoning and arguments? Yet, notwithstanding the indicated difference in the final result of their respective reasonings, Job will continue in the faith which, to his friends, is as great a provocation as their argument is a provocation in the eye of Job. Job continues,—

XVII. 3. "Lay down now, put me in a surety with thee; who *is* he *that* will strike hands with me?"

Thus who will agree with Job's philosophy, that they should strike hands with him? His friends? No; for of them Job says,—

XVII. 4. "For thou hast hid their heart from understanding: therefore shalt thou not exalt *them*."

Job continues,—

XVII. 5. "He that speaketh flattery to *his* friends, even the eyes of his children shall fail."

Flattery leads to false deductions; but the term in the mouth of Job evidently points to a species of deceit that will cause or tend to cause others to fall into grave error; hence the more powerful the flatterer the greater the downfall. Job continues,—

XVII. 6–8. "He hath made me also a byword of the people; and aforetime I was as a tabret.

"Mine eye also is dim by reason of sorrow, and all my members *are* as a shadow.

"Upright *men* shall be astonished at this, and the innocent shall stir up himself against the hypocrite."

In his affliction Job has become a byword of the people where once, as the Adam and progenitor of the Third Race, he was looked upon (see i. 1–3) as the head and front of human greatness.

The tribulation of Job is brought about (see i., ii.) through the devices of Satan, who, by his great power, caused transgression on the part of Job; not great, glaring transgression, but imperceptible transgression, or (see Lev. iv. 13, 14) transgression through ignorance. If transgression through ignorance should not be imputed how could the offence abound that Evil be judged? The indications are that every jot of transgression pertaining to man must and will be imputed that the minor offences of the Evil Host be imputed also.

If by such rigid construction every jot of transgression shall be imputed, then the transgressor will come under the rule of the Evil Kingdom, and, if under the rule of the Evil Kingdom, then the resources of the Evil Kingdom will be over him for evil, be the transgression great or small. The indications are clear that the tribulations besetting Job are far in excess of all commensurate call; wherefore the text states, "Upright *men* shall be astonished at this, and the innocent shall stir up himself against the hypocrite." Under the circumstances developed by the text of Job, who is the righteous and innocent that shall be astonished, and shall stir up himself? It evidently is the one that shall counteract, throw down, and make void the works of evil that threaten to sink the creature forever in the pit of oblivion. Job further speaks of this one as follows:

XVII. 9. "The righteous also shall hold on his way, and he that hath clean hands shall be stronger and stronger."

The essence of this saying cannot apply to the transgressor, for by the Law he shall not be stronger and stronger; for the transgressor cannot make void the Law by reformation any more (see Heb. xii. 16, 17) than Esau could recover his birthright, with its accompanying blessings, after his transgression; wherefore it follows that the righteous that shall be stronger and stronger is one that is without transgression, one (see Deut. xxxii. 4) without iniquity, one that is just and right; hence the righteous that shall be stronger and stronger is the God of truth. Such a One, therefore, by the words of Job, shall stir up himself against the flatterer whose Evil Kingdom bears such bitter fruit. Job continues,—

XVII. 10. "But as for you all, do ye return, and come now: for I cannot find *one* wise *man* among you."

Inasmuch, therefore, as the reasoning of Job's friends does not provide any way for the abolishment of tribulation,—except it be through righteousness by works, the failure of which is proved by the universal fall of man and his subsequent tribulation,—Job cannot find one wise man among them. True wisdom will find a means or way for casting down pain and tribulation forever; for what kind of perfection would that be which, when beyond suffering itself, could calmly look down upon the misery of countless thousands as they are brought into existence, live a short, unhappy life, and die overwhelmed with physical and mental distresses? Should such perfection become the standard of excellence of the creature, then the heart of that creature would be harder than "the nether millstone," and the excellence thereof but a byword in the mouth of evil-doers. Job continues,—

XVII. 11-13. "My days are past, my purposes are broken off, *even* the thoughts of my heart.

"They change the night into day: the light *is* short because of darkness.

"If I wait, the grave *is* mine house: I have made my bed in the darkness."

The broken purposes of Job indicate his failure as a subjugator; wherefore the night is as the day, and the day is as the night; hence, even if Job wait or continue, the grave, under the Law, would be his house, and darkness, through his failure, would be his bed; no reformation being sufficiently strong in itself to insure righteousness, or to redeem the transgressor. Job continues,—

XVII. 14. "I have said to corruption, Thou *art* my father: to the worm, *Thou art* my mother, and my sister."

Thus Job's intimate relation to corruption points to him as being a transgressor; for it is written (Ps. xvi. 10), "Neither wilt thou suffer thine Holy One to see corruption;" wherefore, being a transgressor, Job continues,—

XVII. 15, 16. "And where *is* now my hope? as for my hope, who shall see it?

"They shall go down to the bars of the pit, when *our* rest together *is* in the dust."

Job's hope of filling out his mission as subjugator is gone; when, therefore, he shall rest in the dust, with corruption and the worm for companions, then those who shall go down to the bars of the pit wherein Job lies will see Job's hope blasted by failure and death; hence he makes no claim to redemption or life through his own righteousness; but he does claim (see verses 8, 9) that "the innocent shall stir up himself against the hypocrite," and that "The righteous also shall hold on his way, and he that hath clean hands shall be stronger and stronger;" the innocent and righteous evidently pointing to the Redeemer.

XVIII. 1, 2. "Then answered Bildad the Shuhite, and said,

"How long *will it be ere* ye make an end of words? mark, and afterwards we will speak."

Thus Bildad considers Job's reasoning but empty logic, or words which reach the ear but leave no mark upon the brain deep enough to force conviction or whereupon to base a firm conclusion. Bildad continues,—

XVIII. 3. "Wherefore are we counted as beasts, *and* reputed vile in your sight?"

If the philosophy of Eliphaz, Bildad, and Zophar consigns the creature to absolute eternal death because of transgression, without any attempt to separate the good from the evil, then such philosophy decorates the banners of Satan with great tokens of victory. If there be a kingdom of good and a kingdom of evil, the one separate and distinct from the other, then the indication is clear that that which pertains to and forms part of the kingdom of good cannot be held prisoner forever by the kingdom of evil without the latter be at least equal to if not stronger than the former; in which case Evil could not be subjugated, neither could the precious (see Jer. xv. 19) be separated from the vile.

Is it at all probable that an infinite, all-wise, all-powerful God would leave any part of his kingdom in the hands of the Power of Evil forever? No; for the perfection of his Divine character and his foreknowledge completely shuts off any such conclusion. If the good is good, why predestinate the creature, call him forth, endow him with good, and then consign him into the hand of his Enemy forever? The philosophy of Job will not consign the creature to any such fate, neither will it accredit the Almighty Power with any such attributes, that he should bring forth the good to destroy it.

If the separation of the good from the evil be an utter impossibility, then, by the Law, the creature that is subject to the ruling of the two powerful kingdoms, both of which are far stronger than himself, would perish forever, even as indicated by the reasoning of Job's friends. Is it any wonder, therefore, that their philosophy should be rejected by Job, and be considered vile in his eyes? Not at all. Bildad continues,—

XVIII. 4. "He teareth himself in his anger: shall

the earth be forsaken for thee? and shall the rock be removed out of his place?"

The rock is the Law: shall it, therefore, be removed out of its place that Job be redeemed from its rulings, and live a renewed life beyond the valley of darkness? Bildad, standing upon the immutability of the Law, gives a negative reply as follows:

XVIII. 5–21. "Yea, the light of the wicked shall be put out, and the spark of his fire shall not shine.

"The light shall be dark in his tabernacle, and his candle shall be put out with him.

"The steps of his strength shall be straitened, and his own counsel shall cast him down.

"For he is cast into a net by his own feet, and he walketh upon a snare.

"The gin shall take *him* by the heel, *and* the robber shall prevail against him.

"The snare *is* laid for him in the ground, and a trap for him in the way.

"Terrors shall make him afraid on every side, and shall drive him to his feet.

"His strength shall be hungerbitten, and destruction *shall be* ready at his side.

"It shall devour the strength of his skin: *even* the firstborn of death shall devour his strength.

"His confidence shall be rooted out of his tabernacle, and it shall bring him to the king of terrors.

"It shall dwell in his tabernacle, because *it is* none of his: brimstone shall be scattered upon his habitation.

"His roots shall be dried up beneath, and above shall his branch be cut off.

"His remembrance shall perish from the earth, and he shall have no name in the street.

"He shall be driven from light into darkness, and chased out of the world.

"He shall neither have son nor nephew among his people, nor any remaining in his dwellings.

"They that come after *him* shall be astonished at his day, as they that went before were affrighted.

"Surely such *are* the dwellings of the wicked, and this *is* the place *of him that* knoweth not God." (Verse 21 in the text is rendered 12.)

Thus Bildad unequivocally declares his belief in the absolute eternal death of the wicked; there is no separation of the good from the evil; but the wicked, as individual embodiments, are chased out of the world, their names forgotten in the streets, their remembrance perished from the earth, while no remainder pertaining to him as an individual embodiment shall find place in his dwelling. The reasonings and conclusions of Bildad make no distinction between the sin-tinctured creature and the Host of Evil, which should be done, for the Law does take cognizance of the good dwelling within the creature that it lack not in equity.

XIX. 1–4. "Then Job answered and said,

"How long will ye vex my soul, and break me in pieces with words?

"These ten times have ye reproached me: ye are not ashamed *that* ye make yourselves strange to me.

"And be it indeed *that* I have erred, mine error remaineth with myself."

In these verses Job still condemns the arguments of

Bildad, and also shows that Bildad's words are directed against him personally. If Bildad's philosophy condemns Job to eternal darkness so that "his remembrance shall perish from the earth," what man of Adam's race could or can hope for any future life through such philosophy? Not one. If not one man of the thousands predestinated and called could or can hope for future life through the philosophy of Bildad, then, by the Scriptures, such philosophy must contain points that are radically wrong; for (see Rom. viii. 28-30) those whom he predestinated and called, them he justified and also glorified; which justification and glorification the philosophy of Bildad completely shuts out from the creature, as Job, who (see verse 4) in all probability is under error, and, hence, under transgression. Job continues,—

XIX. 5, 6. "If indeed ye will magnify *yourselves* against me, and plead against me my reproach;

"Know now that God hath overthrown me, and hath compassed me with his net."

Job's reproach is his transgression, and through this transgression Bildad applies the strength of his reasoning against Job. Job, however, proclaims and declares that God hath overthrown him and compassed him with his net; that is, the Law that was instituted by the Almighty holds him as a transgressor; by which holding the same ruling of the Law is over each and every transgressor. If, therefore, Job is overthrown by and compassed by the Law of God in its pertaining to transgression, so also each and every transgressor will be compassed by and overthrown by this pertaining irrespective of host; hence the Law reaches to the very heart of the Evil Kingdom, that it—the Evil Kingdom, not Job or the creature simply—may be compassed and overthrown by it. Job continues,—

XIX. 7. "Behold, I cry out of wrong, but I am not heard: I cry aloud, but *there is* no judgment."

This verse points to the free agency of Job, and not to that of Job only, but to the free agency of all hosts under the Law. Were there no free agency under the Law there would be no wrong, and were there no wrong there would be no cry, for the Almighty Ruler would govern all things; but with free agency under the Law the offence can abound, sin can be imputed, and judgment can be rendered against the transgressor irrespective of host. Moreover, by continued transgression under the Law, as witnessed in the excessive afflictions of Job, the measure of iniquity of the Evil Host (see Gen. xv. 16; Dan. ix. 24) will eventually become full, and then judgment will be rendered against it. Job continues,—

XIX. 8–10. "He hath fenced up my way that I cannot pass, and he hath set darkness in my paths.

"He hath stripped me of my glory, and taken the crown *from* my head.

"He hath destroyed me on every side, and I am gone: and mine hope hath he removed like a tree."

Job's crowning glory was his mission as the subjugator of Evil, but because of his failure this great glory is stripped from him; now afflictions beset him, all hope of accomplishing his mission is removed from him; wherefore the darkness that fills the land of the shadow of death lies in his path. Job continues,—

XIX. 11. "He hath also kindled his wrath against me, and he counteth me unto him as *one of* his enemies."

Thus the ruling of the Law over Job as a transgressor is the same as the ruling over any other transgressor, the transgressor being counted as an enemy of the Kingdom of Righteousness. Job continues,—

XIX. 12–20. "His troops come together, and raise up their way against me, and encamp round about my tabernacle.

"He hath put my brethren far from me, and mine acquaintance are verily estranged from me.

"My kinsfolk have failed, and my familiar friends have forgotten me.

"They that dwell in mine house, and my maids, count me for a stranger: I am an alien in their sight.

"I called my servant, and he gave *me* no answer; I entreated him with my mouth.

"My breath is strange to my wife, though I entreated for the children's *sake* of mine own body.

"Yea, young children despised me; I arose, and they spake against me.

"All my inward friends abhorred me: and they whom I loved are turned against me.

"My bone cleaveth to my skin and to my flesh, and I am escaped with the skin of my teeth."

Such is the situation and condition of Job, who, through unintentional transgression or transgression through ignorance, fell under bondage to the Evil Kingdom, and thus became prey to their evil devices. The afflictions of Job, even as already stated, are beyond all commensurate call, but by the fulness thereof the Evil Kingdom is filling up the measure of its iniquity and proving beyond all question the bitter qualities of its fruit. Job continues,—

XIX. 21. "Have pity upon me, have pity upon me, O ye my friends; for the hand of God hath touched me."

Here in his distress Job looks to his friends for pity and sympathy; but instead of pity or sympathy they heap up words against him, condemning him in this life, and consigning him to eternal darkness in the interminable hereafter, wherefore he asks,—

XIX. 22. "Why do ye persecute me as God, and are not satisfied with my flesh?"

Thus Job's friends are not satisfied with their condemnation of the body of sinful flesh, but (see xviii. 16–18) they would chase him out of the world so that neither root, branch, nor remembrance pertaining to him should evermore remain or be. With such merciless deductions forced upon him, Job exclaims,—

XIX. 23–27. "Oh that my words were now written! oh that they were printed in a book!

"That they were graven with an iron pen and lead in the rock for ever!

"For I know *that* my Redeemer liveth, and *that* he shall stand at the latter *day* upon the earth:

"And *though* after my skin *worms* destroy this *body*, yet in my flesh shall I see God:

"Whom I shall see for myself, and mine eyes shall behold, and not another; *though* my reins be consumed within me."

In these verses Job positively declares his knowledge and belief in the existence of his Redeemer in bold contradistinction from the reasoning of his friends that no future life shall be given the transgressor. This Redeemer, although in existence, has not, up to the day of Job, stood upon the earth as the Redeemer of man; for the text points to his advent as such in the latter day, or in the Fourth Age, Job being the Adam and progenitor of the Third Race, and hence he pertains to the Third Age.

Job implies (see verse 22) that the body of sinful flesh or the natural body will pass away forever, even as indicated by the reasoning of his friends; wherefore, then, the statement, "*Though* after my skin *worms* destroy this *body*, yet in my flesh shall I see God"? If the body of sinful flesh shall surely die never more to return, and if Job in his flesh shall see God, then the indication is strongly marked that Job must be regenerated or born into a new, unblemished body of flesh before absolute death shall overtake him; hence it follows that this new body is the one in which he shall see God; for by the regeneration the new body of flesh would really become his flesh, so that his eye, and not another, should behold his God; but the body of sinful flesh would eventually, or after regeneration, be consumed within him.

If man is regenerated, or born into a new body, then the spirit of man would be clothed with two bodies; but when Job shall see his God the indication is clear that the body of sinful flesh will have been consumed within him, so that (see Eph. ii. 15) of the twain one new man will have been made.

By the text, Job knew that his Redeemer lived; by Eph. i. 1–12, the Redeemer is Jesus Christ; by St. Mark xiv. 22, Jesus Christ gave his body to be eaten;

by St. John vi. 56, Jesus said, "He that eateth my flesh, and drinketh my blood, dwelleth in me, and I in him ;" hence man, by eating the Lord's body or the flesh of the Redeemer,—which body (see Heb. x. 4) was prepared for the Son,—is regenerated or born into the body or flesh of the Redeemer. If man is not regenerated or born into this body after eating thereof, how is it possible for him to dwell in the Redeemer and for the Redeemer to dwell in him?

The indications are almost wholly if not altogether probable that man is regenerated through the Communion of the Lord's body; that is, under the ministration of a priesthood of and after the order of Melchizedek. If man is born into the body of the Redeemer, what need is there for a return of the body of sinful flesh or the natural body? There seems to be none; for as an unclean, discarded thing it cannot (see Rev. xxi. 9-27) enter into the holy city, Jerusalem; but regenerated man—man born into and clothed with the body that was prepared for the Son, suitable for this purpose—can enter into the beloved city, bearing the image of the earthy in which he had walked from youth to old age as perfectly manifest as an individuality (see St. Luke xxiv. 32-43) as the Messiah was manifest to his disciples after his resurrection; hence Job says to his friends, who deny the future life,—

XIX. 28, 29. "But ye should say, Why persecute we him, seeing the root of the matter is found in me?

"Be ye afraid of the sword: for wrath *bringeth* the punishments of the sword, that ye may know *there is* a judgment."

Thus, although Job suffers affliction, because, through

transgression, he is in the hand of Satan, King of Evil, the indication is given by Job that his friends are bondmen to the same power, the root of Job's affliction being in them also; hence he cautions them to be afraid of the sword; for transgression bringeth wrath, and wrath bringeth the punishment of the sword, that, as a great sign, not only Eliphaz, Bildad, and Zophar may know there is a judgment, but that all hosts may know it also.

XX. 1-3. "Then answered Zophar the Naamathite, and said,

"Therefore do my thoughts cause me to answer, and for *this* I make haste.

"I have heard the check of my reproach, and the spirit of my understanding causeth me to answer."

According to these verses, Zophar comprehends the words of Job, that his Redeemer lived, and would stand upon the earth at the latter day, and that he, Job, would be raised up from the grave by his Redeemer after the complete destruction of his body of sinful flesh. What answer does Zophar give to Job's declarations? Zophar replies,—

XX. 4-7. "Knowest thou *not* this of old, since man was placed upon the earth,

"That the triumphing of the wicked *is* short, and the joy of the hypocrite *but* for a moment?

"Though his excellency mount up to the heavens, and his head reach unto the clouds;

"*Yet* he shall perish for ever like his own dung: they which have seen him shall say, Where *is* he?"

Thus Zophar condemns the wicked to eternal punishment; not to eternal torture, but to eternal punishment;

for once dead they never, by the Law, can return to life; wherefore the punishment of evil or of the wicked will be eternal.

Thus far the reasoning of Zophar regarding the eternal punishment of the wicked is based upon the immutability of the Law that condemns the transgressor to death; but inasmuch (see 1 Kings viii. 46) as there is no man that sinneth not, so the Law condemns all to death, and among them Job also.

The good dwelling within man possesses no weight with Zophar; no, even "though his excellency mount up to the heavens, and his head reach unto the clouds;" hence no separation of the good from the evil that dwells within man is comprehended in Zophar's reasoning, but the good shares the same fate as the evil, which, as a matter of equity, should not be. Moreover, the Law did not enter for the destruction of the good, but (see Rom. v. 20) it entered that the offence might abound. If the Law did not enter for the destruction of the good, then it follows that the good must be separated from the evil, lest the Law condemn other than the offence.

Should the good be separated from the evil, to which would the spirit of man pertain? To both, clearly. Such being the case, the indication is manifest that by the separation of the good from the evil an opportunity exists for the redemption of man notwithstanding the immutability of the Law. The reasoning of Zophar, however, rejects the separation of the good from the evil as a possible means for giving life to the transgressor, wherefore he continues,—

XX. 8, 9. "He shall fly away as a dream, and shall

not be found : yea, he shall be chased away as a vision of the night.

"The eye also *which* saw him shall *see him* no more; neither shall his place any more behold him."

Thus, by Zophar's reasoning, the transgressor, even "though his excellency mount up to the heavens," shall be seen no more, neither shall his place know him any more. If the statements of Zophar do not point to the utter annihilation of the transgressor, to what do they point? Some system of redemption whereby the transgressor may be known to his place, and whereby those who once beheld him shall behold him again? No; for the words of Zophar (verse 7), "he shall perish forever," are positive, and are given in answer to and as an offset to Job's hope of redemption as set forth (xix. 23–27). Zophar continues,—

XX. 10. "His children shall seek to please the poor, and his hands shall restore their goods."

Hence others shall arise to take the place of the departed, even as, in the past, the children stood up in the stead of their fathers; no recall is suggested, but—

XX. 11. "His bones are full *of the sin* of his youth, which shall lie down with him in the dust."

Such is the fate to which the philosophy of Zophar consigns the transgressor through the immutability of the Law. Job, however, looked beyond the Law, and beyond the Law he saw his Redeemer, through whom his place will know him again, and through whom those who once beheld him will behold him again. Job's philosophy recognizes the existence of an all-powerful, all-wise, all-seeing God that will not permit the overwhelming destruction of his creatures by a rival Power;

but Zophar's reasoning, while recognizing the supremacy and uprightness of the Most High, gives no head to evil that it, as a Power, should be swept out of existence forever. Of the transgressor Zophar continues,—

XX. 12-14. "Though wickedness be sweet in his mouth, *though* he hide it under his tongue;

"*Though* he spare it, and forsake it not, but keep it still within his mouth;

"*Yet* his meat in his bowels is turned, *it is* the gall of asps within him."

From Zophar's position of the inseparability of the union between good and evil in the one individuality, even though evil be hidden yet not forsaken by such individual, the Law will surely make itself manifest in tribulation; which tribulation, coming as it does because of transgression, Zophar likens to the gall of asps; hence, from Zophar's position, in order that the Law be fulfilled, and evil die, the good, not being separable from the evil, must die with the individual possessing it; but once dead there is no recall, while others rise up to take his place. From this position evil, as an energy, is not overthrown; but, however great the excellency of the creature may be, it, evil, still exists, bitter as the gall of asps. What is the summary of this philosophy? Darkness for the past, dim light for the present, and an improbable possibility of brilliancy for the future,—and that only as regards the natural life of the individual. Zophar continues of the transgressor,—

XX. 15. "He hath swallowed down riches, and he shall vomit them up again: God shall cast them out of his belly."

Thus, from Zophar's stand-point, the continuation is given that, however great the excellency that pertains to the transgressor, he must give it up, and—

XX. 16. "He shall suck the poison of asps: the viper's tongue shall slay him."

Wherefore it follows that because of his transgression he shall be slain, that his excellency (verses 6–9) shall know him no more, and that—

XX. 17. "He shall not see the rivers, the floods, the brooks of honey and butter."

Which rivers, from Zophar's stand-point (see Ezek. xlvii. 7–9; Deut. xi. 8, 9), point to a future life filled with happiness only for the creature that transgresses not. Of the transgressor Zophar continues,—

XX. 18. "That which he laboured for shall he restore, and shall not swallow *it* down: according to *his* substance *shall* the restitution *be*, and he shall not rejoice *therein.*"

This verse indicates that the increase or worldly wealth of the transgressor must be given up, left behind for others to dispense; and that according to his substance or wealth so shall the restitution be; hence he shall restore or leave all; none shall cling to him. Zophar continues,—

XX. 19–21. "Because he hath oppressed *and* hath forsaken the poor; *because* he hath violently taken away a house which he builded not;

"Surely he shall not feel quietness in his belly, he shall not save of that which he desired.

"There shall none of his meat be left; therefore shall no man look for his goods."

These verses plainly indicate that the transgressor

shall not retain any of his possessions; there shall none be left, and, therefore, that no man shall look for his goods. When such shall be the situation of the transgressor, then, of a surety, he will have passed away forever, and his place will know him no more. This situation and this result obtain through the Law; hence the reasoning of Zophar is based upon the Law, through which evil will be irretrievably overthrown; the Law having entered for the overthrow of evil in all its ramifications. From these indications it follows that the reasoning of Zophar contains great weight, and must not be cast aside as altogether fallacious, but, on the contrary, it points to the sure overthrow of the transgressor irrespective of host, even though it provides no system of redemption for the creature under transgression. Zophar continues,—

XX. 22-29. "In the fulness of his sufficiency he shall be in straits: every hand of the wicked shall come upon him.

"*When* he is about to fill his belly, *God* shall cast the fury of his wrath upon him, and shall rain *it* upon him while he is eating.

"He shall flee from the iron weapon, *and* the bow of steel shall strike him through.

"It is drawn, and cometh out of the body; yea, the glittering sword cometh out of his gall: terrors *are* upon him.

"All darkness *shall be* hid in his secret places: a fire not blown shall consume him; it shall go ill with him that is left in his tabernacle.

"The heaven shall record his iniquity; and the earth shall rise up against him.

"The increase of his house shall depart, *and his goods* shall flow away in the day of his wrath.

"This *is* the portion of a wicked man from God, and the heritage appointed unto him by God."

In all this there is no indication given of any redemption for the creature, or of any separation of the good from the evil that redemption may follow; hence by it annihilation shall overwhelm the transgressor from the day of his death, whether such transgressor be a total depravity or whether he be a creature simply in which dwells both good and evil.

XXI. 1–3. "But Job answered and said,

"Hear diligently my speech, and let this be your consolations.

"Suffer me that I may speak; and after that I have spoken, mock on."

These verses indicate that Job does not agree with the result indicated by the philosophy of his friends, that death seals the sum of existence pertaining to the creature. Job continues,—

XXI. 4–6. "As for me, *is* my complaint to man? and if *it were so*, why should not my spirit be troubled?

"Mark me, and be astonished, and lay *your* hand upon *your* mouth.

"Even when I remember I am afraid, and trembling taketh hold on my flesh."

Job's questions imply that his complaint is not to man, but to God; and that, even though it were so, sufficient cause was given whereby his spirit might well be troubled, for great affliction has come upon him in his natural life because of transgression through ignorance.

The tribulation thus indicated impairs his strength and saps his vitals, but why should his spirit be troubled? It is because of the magnitudes involved in the bringing about of this tribulation, and the apparent disregard of equity on the part of the ruling Power in the compensation for transgression; hence Job continues,—

XXI. 7–15. "Wherefore do the wicked live, become old, yea, are mighty in power?

"Their seed is established in their sight with them, and their offspring before their eyes.

"Their houses *are* safe from fear, neither *is* the rod of God upon them.

"Their bull gendereth, and faileth not; their cow calveth, and casteth not her calf.

"They send forth their little ones like a flock, and their children dance.

"They take the timbrel and harp, and rejoice at the sound of the organ.

"They spend their days in wealth, and in a moment go down to the grave.

"Therefore they say unto God, Depart from us; for we desire not the knowledge of thy ways.

"What *is* the Almighty, that we should serve him? and what profit should we have, if we pray unto him?"

Thus prosperity frequently surrounds the habitation of the wicked, while the comparatively righteous are overwhelmed with sorrows. Why should these things be? or why should they be permitted to exist? These things exist, or are permitted, under the ruling of the Law establishing responsible free agency among all hosts, that every such free agent may develop and give proof of the quality of the attributes dwelling within him or of which he is a unity. The Law will judge all free agents, from the highest to the lowest, for their actions under the Law with unquestionable equity, that the offence of the transgressor may cling to him and judgment be rendered against him; hence the tribulation that befalls an upright man is no sure evidence of the degree of transgression pertaining to that man, but it may be evidence of a persecution (see xix. 28, 29) due to another source; which source, by its persecution, is giving proof of the quality of the attributes that dwell within it, and of which it is a unity.

Hence a prosperous wicked man may not suffer physical pain, but, on the contrary (see text), may increase and multiply on every side, and finally depart in a moment, thus going down to his grave without a pang. If the grave were the end of all, as Zophar's reasoning implies, well might such a one say of God (see text), "Depart from me; for I desire not the knowledge of thy ways, and what profit shall I have if I pray unto him?" Could the prosperous wicked man, by the philosophy of Zophar, expect more, should he pray to the Almighty, than that accorded him by the text? Not very well. Then, such prosperity leads to the denial of any need of an Almighty God; for the wicked man can live a life of prosperity, increase and multiply, and go down to the grave in peace, while the upright man is overwhelmed by distress.

The prosperous wicked man doubtless is a persecutor; and if a persecutor, then an innocent man may suffer from his persecutions; hence he also gives proof of the quality of the attributes dwelling within him, and of which he is a unity. Thus it is with every transgressor; for the Law establishes responsible free agency; while by their free agency the attributes of individual unities are brought to light; hence it follows that, under the Law, the Almighty permits tribulation to befall the creature under transgression; but the perfectly upright and righteous man, not being a transgressor, can no power, under the Law, touch for harm. The latter condition preserves the character of the Almighty free from all blemish should affliction befall the transgressor; for the Law, not the Almighty, is, for the time being, judge.

Should the natural life be the end of all, then the affliction of the upright man and the prosperity of the wicked man clearly indicate a lack of equity in the government of the higher intellectualities, while, at the same time, laws of order are manifest which regulate the inanimate so that not one second is displaced or lost to sight in a solar cycle. How, then, can such incongruity exist? The indications follow that the natural life of the higher order of intelligencies is not the end of their existence; for the laws of order regulating the inanimate point to other laws and rulings that bear upon the intellectual after natural life shall have expired, or the worm that feeds upon the grave-clad flesh would be more hopeful than the flickering light that marks dissolution. Job, however, does not believe in the annihilation of the creature at the end of his natural life, wherefore he states of the wicked man,—

XXI. 16. "Lo, their good *is* not in their hand: the counsel of the wicked is far from me."

The good, therefore, that pertains to the creature is not in his hand; it certainly will be separated from the evil; hence the counsel of the wicked that no God, no Redeemer, is needed is far from Job. Job continues,—

XXI. 17. "How oft is the candle of the wicked put out! and *how oft* cometh their destruction upon them! *God* distributeth sorrows in his anger."

Hence a man is not prosperous simply because he is wicked, but tribulation oft comes upon him because of his transgression. God permits and God withholds suffering according to the greatness of his purpose; wherefore,—

XXI. 18. "They are as stubble before the wind, and as chaff that the storm carrieth away."

By which their deliverance into the hand of a power greater than themselves is indicated. Job continues of the transgressor,—

XXI. 19. "God layeth up his iniquity for his children: he rewardeth him, and he shall know *it*."

By the Law of iniquity (see **Ex. xxxiv. 7**) the iniquity of the fathers is visited upon the children. Should the iniquity of the fathers be visited upon the children, then the fathers, through the transmission of blood and characteristics, can be rewarded, both for good and for evil, and eventually, as the text implies, they will know it. Job continues,—

XXI. 20-22. "His eyes shall see his destruction, and he shall drink of the wrath of the Almighty.

"For what pleasure *hath* he in his house after him, when the number of his months is cut off in the midst?

"Shall *any* teach God knowledge? seeing he judgeth those that are high?"

These verses evidently apply to and include Satan,

King of Evil, the source and fountain of evil, the Power that takes the creature captive (see 2 Tim. ii. 26) at his will. Job looks to the overthrow of this Power; but the philosophy of Zophar simply casts down the creature that is tinctured with sin and gives his place to another that grows up an inseparable compound of good and evil. Job continues of the transgressor,—

XXI. 23-26. " One dieth in his full strength, being wholly at ease and quiet.

"His breasts are full of milk, and his bones are moistened with marrow.

"And another dieth in the bitterness of his soul, and never eateth with pleasure.

"They shall lie down alike in the dust, and the worms shall cover them."

Thus transgressors lie down alike in the dust, whether their natural lives were full of ease or full of pain. Why? Because by transgression, be it small or great, the same penalty thereof is over them. What is this penalty? It is (see Gen. ii. 16, 17) unquestionable death. If, then, the penalty of transgression—be the transgression small or great—is unquestionable death, and if the penalty is enforced (for the Law is immutable), then equity requires a judgment (see xix. 29) after the natural life of the creature shall have passed away that rewards and recompenses may be commeasurably set forth and established. Zophar's philosophy discards judgment after such death; for should the natural life of the creature seem total existence, then, of a surety, judgment could not follow; there would be nothing to judge. Job, however, looks beyond this position; for he states (xix. 23-27),—

"Oh that my words were now written! oh that they were printed in a book!

"That they were graven with an iron pen and lead in the rock for ever!

"For I know *that* my Redeemer liveth, and *that* he shall stand at the latter *day* upon the earth:

"And *though* after my skin *worms* destroy this *body*, yet in my flesh shall I see God:

"Whom I shall see for myself, and mine eyes shall behold, and not another; *though* my reins be consumed within me."

These sublime words indicate Job's positive belief in a new life after the natural life shall have expired,—a new life that is based upon the labors of a Redeemer, and not upon labors pertaining to himself. As the philosophy of Zophar discards judgment after death, so also the same philosophy discards the Redeemer, or any necessity that a Redeemer arise; for if after absolute death there would be nothing to judge, so neither would there be anything to redeem; hence Job continues,—

XXI. 27, 28. "Behold, I know your thoughts, and the devices *which* ye wrongfully imagine against me.

"For ye say, Where *is* the house of the prince? and where *are* the dwellingplaces of the wicked?"

Truly, where can Job point to the house of the prince, the Redeemer, in whose existence he has expressed such positive belief? Can he point it out to his friends in the order which marks the government of the universe? No; for universal order marks the Creator, not the Redeemer. Such being the case, Job must have received special light bearing upon redemption; which light, as the Adam and progenitor of the Third Race of Men, was accorded him (see Rev. iii. 1-6), even as special light was accorded (see Gen. i., ii., iii.; Rev. iii. 14-22) the Adam and progenitor of the Fourth Race.

By the charge given to the Adam of the Third Race (see Rev. iii. 5), the name of the one that overcometh shall not be blotted out of the book of life; by the charge to the Adam of the Fourth Race (see Rev. iii. 14-21), he that overcame was the beginning of the creation of God, and, hence, he must be the Son for whom a body (see Heb. x. 5) was prepared that he might do the will of God. The Son for whom a body was prepared (see Col. i.) is and was Jesus Christ the Redeemer; therefore Job's Redeemer is the beginning of the creation of God, and, hence, had an existence from the beginning of the creation of God.

By the charge to the Third Race (see Rev. iv. 4), the one that overcometh shall be clothed in white raiment. Jesus Christ was the only one that overcame all things, wherefore he will be clothed with the white raiment called for by the charge; but inasmuch as others also shall walk in white, it follows that their clothing is derived from the one that overcame, who, in consequence, is the Redeemer.

If the creature is regenerated, or born into the body that was prepared for the Son, and if the body that was prepared for the Son shall, because in it the Word overcame all things, be clothed in white, then the indication is clear that the redeemed shall have this white clothing also, even as called for by the charge. From these indications it follows that Job had great grounds for basing his faith in the existence of his Redeemer; but Zophar fails to comprehend them, pointing rather to the grave, which holds the transgressor a close unheard-from prisoner, and which has been his dwelling-place for ages. That Zophar is biased in his opinion by the silence of the grave is indicated by his inquiry (verse 28), "Where *are* the dwellingplaces of the wicked?" thus evidently pointing to their habitation in the grave; which indication Job further confirms, as follows:

XXI. 29. "Have ye not asked them that go by the way?"

By which the advent and destruction of the independent consecutive races of men, without any sign of a resurrection or return, are brought forward as great foundation-stones in the arguments of Eliphaz, Bildad, and Zophar, that the grave is the final resting-place of the creature. Job further continues,—

XXI. 29, 30. "And do ye not know their tokens,

"That the wicked is reserved to the day of destruction?"

Hence by Job's philosophy the silence of the grave is no indication of annihilation, but, rather, that the grave is a prison in which the wicked is reserved to the day of destruction; and, hence, that the grave, even as he states (see x. 21, 22), is a land of darkness and of the shadow of death; wherefore Job asserts,—

XXI. 30. "They shall be brought forth to the day of wrath."

Hence from Job's stand-point the natural life is not the sum total of existence. Job continues,—

XXI. 31–34. "Who shall declare his way to his face? and who shall repay him *what* he hath done?

"Yet shall he be brought to the grave, and shall remain in the tomb.

"The clods of the valley shall be sweet unto him, and every man shall draw after him, as *there are* innumerable before him.

"How then comfort ye me in vain, seeing in your answers there remaineth falsehood?"

Should the grave not give up its dead, who, indeed, would declare the way of the transgressor to his face? By the philosophy of Zophar, none. Who shall recompense the upright man for his pain and tribulation? By the philosophy of Zophar, none. Who shall reward the righteous man for his righteous acts? By the philosophy of Zophar, none. Hence by the philosophy of Zophar no day of wrath finds place, no judgment, no separation of "the precious from the vile," no redemption, no sign of redemption; nothing is visible but a yawning abyss filled with darkness, into which the waters of life plunge, disappear, never more to return to the light. Horrible comfort! Yea, horrible comforters are they that find not within themselves a confutation of the merciless, barren reasoning that would bind the girdle of calamity around every loved soul that once gladdened their eyes or brought sunshine within their doors. How can such answers cover only truth?

XXII. 1–4. "Then Eliphaz the Temanite answered and said,

"Can a man be profitable unto God, as he that is wise may be profitable unto himself?

"*Is it* any pleasure to the Almighty, that thou art

righteous? or *is it* gain *to him,* that thou makest thy ways perfect?

"Will he reprove thee for fear of thee? will he enter with thee into judgment?"

The indication is not possible that the creature was called as a source of profit to the Almighty, the Almighty being perfect within himself infinitely beyond all creatures and powers; he needs nothing to insure his pleasure or to increase his gain; as the Creator all things are his; as the Supreme Ruler all things are subject to him; hence he will enter into judgment with none that they should give him counsel. The creature, however, was called that it might enter into his pleasure, and, as an independent existence, enjoy the gifts with which it was endowed. Had there been no Power of Evil man would have continued a happy existence, free from every suspicion of tribulation or danger; but inasmuch as there was such a Power, man, being the weaker of the two, fell prey to its evil devices, and thereby came under its ruling; hence the possibility of profitableness such as that spoken of by Eliphaz is not at all probable in the calling of the creature; moreover, the Almighty foreknew the fall of the creature. Eliphaz continues,—

XXII. 5–11. "*Is* not thy wickedness great? and thine iniquities infinite?

"For thou hast taken a pledge from thy brother for nought, and stripped the naked of their clothing.

"Thou hast not given water to the weary to drink, and thou hast withholden bread from the hungry.

"But *as for* the mighty man, he had the earth; and the honourable man dwelt in it.

"Thou hast sent widows away empty, and the arms of the fatherless have been broken.

"Therefore snares *are* round about thee, and sudden fear troubleth thee;

"Or darkness, *that* thou canst not see; and abundance of waters cover thee."

The accusations of Eliphaz against Job doubtless are based upon the abundance of Job's afflictions, and not because he had been or was eye-witness of such transgression on the part of Job; for by the philosophy of Eliphaz the truly righteous man will be raised above tribulation in the day of his natural life, and the reward of his righteousness (see v. 17–27) will be reaped during the day of his natural life; Eliphaz not according man, be he upright or transgressive (see iv. 17–21), with any life hereafter or life after the semblance of death shall have closed the eyes of the natural body. Eliphaz continues,—

XXII. 12–14. "*Is* not God in the height of heaven? and behold the height of the stars, how high they are!

"And thou sayest, How doth God know? can he judge through the dark cloud?

"Thick clouds *are* a covering to him, that he seeth not; and he walketh in the circuit of heaven."

Thus, high as the stars may be, the God of heaven dwells far above them; there is no space or recess into which he does not penetrate; he is higher than the stars and more infinite than space; for space is too small to hold its own history, were it written in books or graven with the minutest lettering, but which history the Infinite God knows and comprehends in every detail.

Now, according to the reasoning of Eliphaz, should God judge the transgressor he would surely die, but Job hopes for redemption and life; to Eliphaz, therefore, Job's reasoning takes judgment from the Almighty that he judge not, for judgment must bring death.

Eliphaz accords the immutability of God's word concerning the transgressor, and, hence, the words which he puts in Job's mouth must convey the idea that, should Job as a transgressor live, God's eye does not pierce the clouds and settle upon the transgressor in his transgression; neither does he know anything of such transgression as he walks in the circuit that envelops the cloud-bound habitation of man. Eliphaz continues,—

XXII. 15–17. "Hast thou marked the old way which wicked men have trodden?

"Which were cut down out of time, whose foundation was overflown with a flood:

"Which said unto God, Depart from us: and what can the Almighty do for them?"

Here Eliphaz calls Job's attention to the race of men that has passed away, the First or Euphratic race that fell under the rule of the Adversary, who (see Rev. iii. 15–17) cast a flood of water after them. This Race (see Isa. iii. 14–26; Jer. iv. 11–31; Ezek. viii. 7–18) became very wicked, and were swept from the face of the earth because of their transgression. Under such circumstances, and such being their fate, Eliphaz asks Job, "What can the Almighty do for them?" for from his stand-point the grave never gives up its dead, owing to the immutability of the Law that was given forth and established by the Almighty for the sure destruction of Evil. Of this people Eliphaz continues,—

XXII. 18. "Yet he filled their houses with good *things:* but the counsel of the wicked is far from me."

Hence, although the Almighty filled the houses of these people with good things, yet they said unto God (verse 17), "Depart from us." Eliphaz, however, does not discard the protecting arm of the Almighty during his natural life, but considers that many blessings come upon the upright man because of his righteous acts. Eliphaz continues,—

XXII. 19. " The righteous see *it*, and are glad : and the innocent laugh them to scorn."

What do the righteous see that they are glad? It is, evidently, the destruction of the wicked that took place at the end of the First Age. Who are the righteous? They are, by the philosophy of Eliphaz (see also Isa. xiii. 9–12; Jer. iv. 27; Ezek. ix. 2–6), the escaping remnants of that great and dreadful day of the Lord.

According to the reasoning of Eliphaz, the escaping remnants, as righteous men, represented all those who were considered worthy of living out the days of their natural lives. Eliphaz continues,—

XXII. 20. " Whereas our substance is not cut down, but the remnant of them the fire consumeth."

By which the preservation of the righteous is indicated, even (see v. 26, 27) to the fulness of his days, while the wicked shall be cut off for their transgression ; which condition Eliphaz applies, the one to the escaping remnant, and the other to the overwhelmed. Eliphaz continues,—

XXII. 21, 22. " Acquaint now thyself with him, and be at peace : thereby good shall come unto thee.

"Receive, I pray thee, the law from his mouth, and lay up his words in thine heart."

Thus Eliphaz further indicates that his reasoning is based upon the fulfilment of the Law, either for good or for evil. Eliphaz continues,—

XXII. 23–30. "If thou return to the Almighty, thou shalt be built up, thou shalt put away iniquity far from thy tabernacles.

"Then shalt thou lay up gold as dust, and the *gold* of Ophir as the stones of the brooks.

"Yea, the Almighty shall be thy defence, and thou shalt have plenty of silver.

"For then shalt thou have thy delight in the Almighty, and shalt lift up thy face unto God.

"Thou shalt make thy prayer unto him, and he shall hear thee, and thou shalt pay thy vows.

"Thou shalt also decree a thing, and it shall be established unto thee: and the light shall shine upon thy ways.

"When *men* are cast down, then thou shalt say, *There is* lifting up; and he shall save the humble person.

"He shall deliver the island of the innocent: and it is delivered by the pureness of thine hands."

The sum of these verses is righteousness by works that the creature may rise above transgression, and thus live out his prescribed days entirely free from pain or evil experiences.

XXIII. 1–5. "Then Job answered and said,

"Even to day *is* my complaint bitter: my stroke is heavier than my groaning.

"Oh that I knew where I might find him! *that* I might come *even* to his seat!

"I would order *my* cause before him, and fill my mouth with arguments.

"I would know the words *which* he would answer me, and understand what he would say unto me."

Job groaning under the burden of the Law would seek unto the Almighty for relief. Truly, in the midst of his affliction he could fill his mouth with argument, and express his wonderment at the reign of tribulation; but with his great faith and his knowledge he could understand what the Lord would say unto him should he unfold the sheet whereon is written the mystery that permits terror to stalk forth even at noonday. Job continues,—

XXIII. 6. "Will he plead against me with *his* great power? No; but he would put *strength* in me."

In this verse Job does not accredit the Almighty with being the source of his troubles. No; but, on the contrary, the Almighty would put strength in him that he might cast them aside. Job continues,—

XXIII. 7. "There the righteous might dispute with him; so should I be delivered for ever from my judge."

Who or what is Job's judge? It is the Law, the irrevocable, the immutable Law that turns neither to the right hand nor to the left. Who is the righteous that he might come before the seat of the Lord (see verse 3), and there dispute with the Lord, so that Job should be delivered forever from the Law that judges him so severely? He is with little doubt (see xix. 23-27) Job's Redeemer; and hence, as the Redeemer, he must plead Job's cause before the Eternal Throne that Job may be freed forever from the Law. Job continues,—

XXIII. 8–10. " Behold, I go forward, but he *is* not *there;* and backward, but I cannot perceive him:

" On the left hand, where he doth work, but I cannot behold *him:* he hideth himself on the right hand, that I cannot see *him:*

" But he knoweth the way that I take : *when* he hath tried me, I shall come forth as gold."

Thus Job is left under the Law as a free agent; the Law, not the Almighty, being, for the time, both ruler and judge. That Job strives to be righteous under the Law is evident, but that he has transgressed is made manifest by his affliction. Now, although Job is a transgressor, yet his righteous works are a proof of his faith; wherefore his faith, not his works, will be counted for righteousness; through which belief he states " *when* he hath tried me, I shall come forth as gold." In all this Job looks forward to his deliverance from the Law, his judge; but the reasoning of Eliphaz indicates no such deliverance, for with him there is no life beyond the grave that grimly extends a welcome to every comer. Job continues,—

XXIII. 11, 12. " My foot hath held his steps, his way have I kept, and not declined.

" Neither have I gone back from the commandment of his lips; I have esteemed the words of his mouth more than my necessary *food.*"

In these verses Job indicates that he has kept the Law. If, therefore, Job has kept all the Law, and has not declined from it, then he will not taste death. By reference to xix. 25–27, however, Job indicates that death shall cover him, and also that his Redeemer lived. If Job is not a transgressor why does he need a Redeemer? if Job is not a transgressor why does he see death? The indications are that Job transgressed the Law (see Lev. iv. 22-24) through ignorance, which brought him into condemnation; wherefore his words doubtless would find place with those of Paul (Rom. vii. 16, 17), "If then I do that which I would not, I consent unto the law that *it is* good.

"Now then it is no more I that do it, but sin that dwelleth in me." Thus as with Paul (see also Phil. iii. 6) so with Job; hence, if Paul transgresses not, but sin that dwells within him is the transgressor, so neither does Job transgress, but sin makes him a transgressor. Such being the case, it follows that should the good be separated from the evil that are united in the individualities of Paul and Job, that both Paul and Job, notwithstanding the penalty of the Law, could stand up as righteous men free from sin.

How can such a wonderful result be brought about? or as Paul asks (Rom. vii. 24), "O wretched man that I am! who shall deliver me from the body of this death?" Paul gives the reply to his own question (Rom. vii. 25), "I thank God through Jesus Christ our Lord;" while Job states (xix. 25), "For I know *that* my Redeemer liveth."

Redemption, however, involves regeneration; hence, by being regenerated or born into the body that was prepared for the Son suitable for this purpose; hence, by being regenerated or born into the body that was prepared for the Redeemer (see St. John vi. 47-58), the possibility of the separation of the good from the evil is made manifest in a clear, strong, steady light. Job continues,—

XXIII. 13, 14. " But he *is* in one *mind,* and who can turn him? and *what* his soul desireth, even *that* he doeth.

" For he performeth *the thing that is* appointed for me: and many such *things are* with him."

These verses indicate purpose on the part of the Almighty and mission on the part of Job. What is the purpose of the Almighty? The great purpose of the Almighty is the establishment of a kingdom of righteousness in which all thought and action will be justified through the assenting power of the Infinite Majesty. The establishment of this Kingdom will necessitate the complete subjugation and overthrow of the Kingdom of Evil, the ruinous works of which are beheld on every side. What is the mission of man? The mission of man, in part (see Gen. i. 28), is the subjugation of the Evil Kingdom; but (see Ex. xix. 4–6) man is called also as a peculiar treasure above all people, as a kingdom of priests, and a holy nation. This part of the mission of man indicates instrumentality in the regeneration and redemption of such as shall be redeemed irrespective of host; hence Job states,—

XXIII. 15–17. "Therefore am I troubled at his presence: when I consider, I am afraid of him.

" For God maketh my heart soft, and the Almighty troubleth me:

" Because I was not cut off before the darkness, *neither* hath he covered the darkness from my face."

When man considers the magnitude of his calling, well may fear of the Almighty come upon him; and as the wonders of the overthrow of evil, the redemption of the fallen, and the restoration of the fallen are opened to his view, well may his heart become soft and troubled. Job's heart is made soft because through the mercy of the Almighty he was not cut off forever in his sins; that is, that he was not absolutely cut off before the special day of darkness that marked the absolute death of his Redeemer. Job continues,—

XXIV. 1. "Why, seeing times are not hidden from the Almighty, do they that know him not see his days?"

What are the times here spoken of? They evidently are the Four Ages of Man, of which a time, times, and the dividing of a time (see Dan. vii. 25; xii. 7; Rev. xii. 14) constitute three and one-half of the Four, or actual time from the calling of man in the First Age until the absolute death of the Messiah in the Fourth. These Times or Ages (see Acts xvii. 22–26) were before appointed, with the bounds thereof; and the bounds thereof (see Deut. xxxii. 8) were set according to the number of the children of Israel. Seeing then that these Times or Ages were known to the Almighty, even as Job asks, Why do they that know the Almighty not know his days? To be sure the veil is thrown over them to a great extent, yet sufficient light was accorded, even in the day of Job, for Eliphaz, Bildad, and Zophar (see viii. 7–10; xv. 7–10) to comprehend the first three Ages of Man.

Their knowledge of these Ages, however, did not develop a better result for the creature than a short existence followed by an eternal death. To them, as with the First Race of Men, so with the Second; as with the Second, so with the Third, of which Job was the Adam and progenitor; as with the Third, so with the indefinite succession of races that may follow. This system gives no bounds to time, neither does it limit or cripple the Power of Evil that it should cease to exist as an energy. Job, however, dissents from such a system, for he states substantially (see xix. 25) that his Redeemer shall stand at the latter day upon the earth, by which a limit is set to the power of Evil, and by which bounds to time are indicated.

Moreover, the words of the text indicate that bounds are set to time, Job asking, "Why, seeing times are not hidden from the Almighty, do they that know him not see his days?" thus referring to time as being limited by the Almighty.

Why is time limited? or why are bounds set to time? Bounds are set to time that all hosts may prove the qualities of their indwelling attributes through free agency; time is set apart that within its limits all that is evil shall be overthrown forever; time is set apart for the separation of the good from the evil; time is set apart that the mercy and justice of the Almighty may be preserved free from all blemish in the destruction of the wicked; but will the wicked turn from their evil way? but will the King of Evil cease from troubling those under bondage to him during the limits of time? Job indicates the reply as follows:

XXIV. 2-6. "*Some* remove the landmarks; they violently take away flocks, and feed *thereof*.

"They drive away the ass of the fatherless, they take the widow's ox for a pledge.

"They turn the needy out of the way: the poor of the earth hide themselves together.

"Behold, *as* wild asses in the desert, go they forth to their work; rising betimes for a prey: the wilderness *yieldeth* food for them *and* for *their* children.

"They reap *every one* his corn in the field: and they gather the vintage of the wicked."

Here, notwithstanding that limits are set to time and that the bounds of time limit the existence of the evil-doer, no attempt is made by many to turn from their evil ways; they remove the landmarks and say (see Ezek. xi. 3), "*It is* not near; let us build houses: this *city is* the caldron, and we *be* the flesh;" nevertheless (see Ezek. xi. 11) they shall be driven from the city and shall be judged in the border of Israel. Job continues,—

XXIV. 7–13. "They cause the naked to lodge without clothing, that *they have* no covering in the cold.

"They are wet with the showers of the mountains, and embrace the rock for want of a shelter.

"They pluck the fatherless from the breast, and take a pledge of the poor.

"They cause *him* to go naked without clothing, and they take away the sheaf *from* the hungry:

"*Which* make oil within their walls, *and* tread *their* winepresses, and suffer thirst.

"Men groan from out of the city, and the soul of the wounded crieth out: yet God layeth not folly *to them*.

"They are of those that rebel against the light; they know not the ways thereof, nor abide in the paths thereof."

Such are the wicked, the extremely wicked, that tempt the souls of men to error: they hate the light, and despise the ways thereof; they walk not in the paths thereof. Who can they be that even God layeth not folly to them? They must pertain to the Evil Host that shall be swept away with the expiring limit of time; for Paul said (see Rom. vii. 17), "It is no more I that do it, but sin that dwelleth in me," by which a power is indicated that is entirely independent from man. Job continues,—

XXIV. 14–18. "The murderer" [see i. 7; ii. 2] "rising with the light killeth the poor and needy, and in the night is as a thief.

"The eye also of the adulterer waiteth for the twilight, saying, No eye shall see me: and disguiseth *his* face.

"In the dark they dig through houses, *which* they had marked for themselves in the daytime: they know not the light.

"For the morning *is* to them even as the shadow of death: if *one* know *them, they are in* the terrors of the shadow of death.

"He *is* swift as the waters; their portion is cursed in the earth: he beholdeth not the way of the vineyards."

These verses seem to point to total depravities, or intelligencies in which no good thing exists. Should it be deemed an incredible thing that Satan's vast army contains within its numbers some that are total depravities? Not at all. If, then, total depravities exist they know not the light (see St. John i. 5) that shineth in darkness, even as the darkness comprehendeth not the light; neither do they know the way of the vineyards. What are the vineyards? They are (see the Song of Solomon;

Isa. v. 5) the Four Ages of Man. What is the way of the vineyards? It is the mission and calling developed in and by the setting apart of these Ages for the overthrow of Evil, and for the establishment of the Kingdom of Righteousness into which no evil thing can enter or find place; hence Job continues,—

XXIV. 19, 20. "Drought and heat consume the snow waters: *so doth* the grave *those which* have sinned.

"The womb shall forget him; the worm shall feed sweetly on him; he shall be no more remembered; and wickedness shall be broken as a tree."

Such is the fate of the evil-doer irrespective of host that wickedness may be broken completely; Paul also stating (2 Cor. v. 14), "For the love of Christ constraineth us; because we thus judge, that if one died for all, then were all dead," the indication being clear that, by the Law, every transgressor must die. After the universal death a resurrection must follow; for Christ the innocent also died an absolute death. If Christ the innocent died an absolute death, then the indication is clear that his death was connected with the resurrection or recalling of the good that went down to the grave with the sin-tinctured host of God's creatures. Absolute death, therefore, is the last link in the chain of labors that separates the good from the evil; the good shall come back, but the evil "shall be broken as a tree," and, as a power, be blotted out of existence forever. Job continues his speech,—

XXIV. 21–25. "He evil entreateth the barren *that* beareth not: and doeth not good to the widow.

"He draweth also the mighty with his power: he riseth up, and no *man* is sure of life.

"*Though* it be given him *to be* in safety, whereon he resteth ; yet his eyes *are* upon their ways.

"They are exalted for a little while, but are gone and brought low; they are taken out of the way as all *others*, and cut off as the tops of the ears of corn.

"And if *it be* not *so* now, who will make me a liar, and make my speech nothing worth ?"

These verses relate to the transgressor under the ruling of the Law. The Law ordained to life, but, because of the great power of Satan, no man was sure of it, even though the Law was given that he might be in safety ; hence they fell, and were taken out of the way as all others, and were cut off as the tops of the ears of corn ; hence, again, not only man will be cut off, taken out of the way, but all hosts will share the same fate. The reasoning of Job's friends points to the destruction of the evil that permeates the person of the transgressor as a creature, but provides no way for the overthrow of the source thereof. Job, however, looks to the complete overthrow of the source of evil through the fulness of the Law that entered for the condemnation of each and every transgressor. Should the Source of Evil be overthrown then the indication becomes clear that the creature can be influenced by it no more, and, hence, would live in safety. As a result, the overthrow of evil and the preservation of the creature is of far greater moment than the preservation of the source of evil and the overthrow of the creature ; if it be not so, who will make Job's speech " nothing worth ?"

XXV. 1–6. "Then answered Bildad the Shuhite, and said,

"Dominion and fear *are* with him; he maketh peace in his high places.

"Is there any number of his armies? and upon whom doth not his light arise?

"How then can man be justified with God? or how can he be clean *that is* born of a woman?

"Behold even to the moon, and it shineth not; yea, the stars are not pure in his sight.

"How much less man, *that is* a worm? and the son of man, *which is* a worm?"

Bildad's philosophy does not grasp any system whereby man can be justified with God, or whereby he can be made clean in the sight of God. With Bildad the Law with its ordination to life and its ministration of death bears with it all to which man can look forward or upon which to base hope.

Moreover, Bildad's philosophy indicates an innate or indwelling of evil or uncleanness in the creature that can, under the Law, only end in its eternal dissolution. His questions, therefore, do not answer Job's rigid construction of the Law, his faith in redemption, and his hope of a life after he shall have passed into the land of the shadow of death, and even after absolute death.

XXVI. 1, 2. "But Job answered and said,

"How hast thou helped *him that is* without power? *how* savest thou the arm *that hath* no strength?"

Truly wherein does the philosophy of Bildad help the creature that is taken captive (see 2 Tim. ii. 26), at the will of the Adversary? or wherein does the philosophy of Bildad save the creature that hath no strength? Bildad accords the Almighty (see **xxv.** 2) with dominion, yet God's creatures are tossed about at the will of a rival Power that hesitates not to plunge them into deepest pits of tribulation. Does Bildad's philosophy accredit the Almighty with any efforts tending to break the chains that bind the creature captive to the oppressor? No; the Law is the ruler. Does Bildad's philosophy accredit the Almighty with any efforts tending to save the creature from the ministration of death that pertains to the Law? No; but man, as a transgressor, must pass away with no hand to save him from his fall. What kind of a philosophy is it that accords dominion to a Power, and then makes that Power a listless spectator of the spoliation of his works by an acknowledged rival? Job continues,—

XXVI. 3. "How hast thou counselled *him that hath* no wisdom? and *how* hast thou plentifully declared the thing as it is?"

Who is the one that hath no wisdom? It is the foolish, the demented, the blind; yet such are transgressors. How has Bildad counselled the transgressor? Bildad's counsel is clearly set forth (xviii.); and by it the transgressor shall be driven from light into darkness, chased out of the world, his remembrance shall perish from the earth, and he shall have no name in the street. It is true that these things shall befall the transgressor, but had Bildad been more plentiful in declaring the thing as it really was, he would have considered the charge (see Rev. iii. 1–6) by which certain ones shall walk in white because of their worth; but Bildad's questions (xxv. 4), "How then can man be justified with God? or how can he be clean *that is* born of a woman?" clearly imply that, from his stand-point, none can be justified with God, or, otherwise, none can be worthy to walk in white; no, not even those who were afflicted from birth.

To walk in white, as thus recorded, redemption is necessary; for all, even as Bildad intimates, are under transgression; and to be redeemed a redeemer is necessary. Job has already expressed his knowledge and belief in his Redeemer; and if such a one be his Redeemer, then he is the Redeemer of others besides Job. Bildad, however, declares nothing of all this; for with him the works of the Almighty end rather with the bringing forth of the creature than future care for its preservation. Job continues,—

XXVI. 4. "To whom hast thou uttered words? and whose spirit came from thee?"

If a Redeemer is promised, then the words of Bildad would be uttered to those under transgression; as therefore his words possess no comfort for Job, so neither will they carry comfort to any host, except it be the immediate army of the Adversary that brought about transgression. If so, then the spirit that came from Bildad is a comfortless emanation from a tribulative source. Job continues,—

XXVI. 5, 6. "Dead *things* are formed from under the waters, and the inhabitants thereof.

"Hell *is* naked before him, and destruction hath no covering."

By these verses every grave contains a known occupant: not one individuality is lost to the eye of him that brought them forth; neither can the destruction that envelops them hide them from his view. The Almighty Power that possesses dominion will never permit an aggressive Enemy to throw down and annihilate that which he brought forth and pronounced good: no, the grave will give up its dead; and destruction will flee away and hide itself forever in the darkness that marks the blotted page of the Book of Life. Of the Almighty, Job continues,—

XXVI. 7-14. "He stretcheth out the north over the empty place, *and* hangeth the earth upon nothing.

"He bindeth up the waters in his thick clouds; and the cloud is not rent under them.

"He holdeth back the face of his throne, *and* spreadeth his cloud upon it.

"He hath compassed the waters with bounds, until the day and night come to an end.

"The pillars of heaven tremble, and are astonished at his reproof.

"He divideth the sea with his power, and by his understanding he smiteth through the proud.

"By his Spirit he hath garnished the heavens; his hand hath formed the crooked serpent.

"Lo, these *are* parts of his ways; but how little a portion is heard of him? but the thunder of his power who can understand?"

Many and great are the works which the Almighty has displayed to the wondering senses of man; physical combinations and marvellous properties meet him on every hand; as he walks abroad and scans the heavens each star in turn gives glance for glance in recognition of the universal Master that brought them forth and gave them place. These garnishments and bewildering actualities form part of the way of the Almighty, but, even as the text asks, "how little a portion is heard of him?" hence the physical, the manifest, the invisible, now point to instrumentalities rather than to the finished work of ultimate mission. But inasmuch as ultimate mission has an indefinite reach, so must it border infinity; wherefore the portion that is heard of the Almighty is small and ever will be small; for none can comprehend the fulness of purpose, and the power of him that "holdeth back the face of his throne, *and* spreadeth his cloud upon it."

XXVII. 1–6. "Moreover Job continued his parable, and said,

"*As* God liveth, *who* hath taken away my judgment; and the Almighty, *who* hath vexed my soul;

"All the while my breath *is* in me, and the spirit of God *is* in my nostrils;

"My lips shall not speak wickedness, nor my tongue utter deceit.

"God forbid that I should justify you: till I die I will not remove mine integrity from me.

"My righteousness I hold fast, and will not let it go: my heart shall not reproach *me* so long as I live."

Thus Job positively refuses to justify his friends in their reasoning that there is no redemption for the creature, no life hereafter, nothing but annihilation at the end of the natural life. The few days of enjoyment that fall to man cannot compensate for the miseries of life: Job himself saying, "I would not live alway." Job's integrity lies in his faith; he will not depart from it; he does not believe that the creature was brought forth simply to become the sport and prey of a power stronger than himself.

What more could Satan himself desire were he possessed of the creative power? Nothing so far as an aggressive field is concerned. Job's faith, therefore, is firm that the Almighty will not permit the aggression of the Adversary to be crowned with such triumphal ending; but, on the contrary, he believes that a path will be opened for the redemption and restoration of the creature, which faith and belief will be counted for and is his righteousness; hence he will hold it fast, and will not justify his friends in their clinging to the Law simply, and not to the higher attributes of the One that established the Law. Job continues,—

XXVII. 7. "Let mine enemy be as the wicked, and he that riseth up against me as the unrighteous."

Thus Job further condemns the philosophy of his friends that would hurl him into an eternal abyss of darkness never to return. It must be kept in mind (see ix. 30, 31) that Job does not expect to live again through his own works, but (see xix. 23–27) through his Redeemer, the latter condition not entering into the arguments of Eliphaz, Bildad, or Zophar. Job continues,—

XXVII. 8–10. "For what *is* the hope of the hypocrite, though he hath gained, when God taketh away his soul?

"Will God hear his cry when trouble cometh upon him?

"Will he delight himself in the Almighty? will he always call upon God?"

Who is the hypocrite thus spoken of by Job? some creature that is bound to the kingdom of evil through the power of Satan? or is he some one otherwise pertaining to the army of Satan? The latter doubtless, for Job looks forward to the separation of the good from the evil that the creature be redeemed. Evil, therefore, embodies the hypocrite of which Job speaks. Will God hear the cry of such a one when trouble comes upon him, and when God takes away his soul? How can it be possible? Or will such a one delight himself in the Almighty? will he always call upon God? How can it be possible? for evil is diametrically opposed to good. Job, however, gives the answer as follows :

XXVII. 11-17. "I will teach you by the hand of God: *that* which *is* with the Almighty will I not conceal.

"Behold, all ye yourselves have seen *it;* why then are ye thus altogether vain?

"This *is* the portion of a wicked man with God, and the heritage of oppressors, *which* they shall receive of the Almighty.

"If his children be multiplied, *it is* for the sword: and his offspring shall not be satisfied with bread.

"Those that remain of him shall be buried in death: and his widows shall not weep.

"Though he heap up silver as the dust, and prepare raiment as the clay;

"He may prepare *it*, but the just shall put *it* on, and the innocent shall divide the silver."

The portion of the wicked man is well known to the three friends of Job; and that which is with the Almighty, of which Job will teach and will not conceal, is seen also of his friends; but their deductions are very different, and the results thereof are very widely separated from those of Job. Job and his friends fully agree that the wicked are destroyed by the Law, but the Law simply is the starting-point of a new departure. By the philosophy of Eliphaz, Bildad, and Zophar all those who die by the Law are dead forever, whether they be total depravities, as the immediate army of Satan (see Rev. xvi. 13, 14), or whether they be sin-tinctured only, as man; but, by Job's reasoning, of those dying by or through the Law the sin-tinctured may live again through the separation of the good from the evil; hence the wicked man of the immediate text, from Job's stand-point, must be a total depravity or one that is wholly evil.

If through any system of redemption the good be separated from the evil, then the evil will be a total depravity; if not, what will it be? And if it be a total depravity, then it will be a wicked man; and if it be a wicked man, then it will surely be destroyed by the Law never more to rise into existence. But the good; what becomes of the good? Shall it die forever also? Will there be no return for it? Will no distinction be made between good and evil that both should share the same fate? Eliphaz, Bildad, and Zophar say no; but Job says yes. Why? Because the Law does not condemn the good, but evil only.

If evil shall be destroyed and the good shall not be destroyed, then it follows to a certainty that the good must be separated from the evil. How can it be done? or, as Bildad asks of Job (xxv. 4), "How then can man be justified with God?" Job indicates (xix. 25-27) that it is through a Redeemer. Can a Redeemer set aside the Law through power alone that it should be made void? No. How, then, can the Redeemer justify man and not make void the Law? He can justify man by satisfying the demands of the Law; for the Law demands nothing more than satisfaction. How can the Redeemer satisfy the demands of the Law that he be not a substitute instead of being an actual bearer of the transgressions that the Law holds in condemnation? He can satisfy the demands of the Law by taking upon himself the actual flesh of those under condemnation, and thus in himself pay the penalty that follows the transgressor. If he takes upon himself the actual flesh of the transgressor, then he is no more a substitute in the true sense of substitution, but becomes an actual bearer of man's transgression; hence the Law holds him and counts him (see Isa. iii. 12) as a transgressor.

If the Redeemer take upon himself the actual flesh of man, then it is evident, by the Law, that he must die; but if he die not, what would become of sinful flesh? Would the Redeemer take upon himself sinful flesh and remain clothed with it forever? Not at all; but when the fulness of time shall have come (see Gal. iv. 4, 5), then the Redeemer will lay down his life, and, at which time, the body of sinful flesh will be laid aside forever.

If, however, the Redeemer take not upon himself sinful flesh, how is it possible for him to be a Redeemer, for the Law is irrevocable? No way appears or seems to exist except through pure substitution; but pure substitution the Law will in nowise permit, for the Law condemns the transgressor, not the innocent. How is it possible for the Redeemer to take sinful flesh upon himself? Job negatively indicates the reply (see verses 14, 15), where the offspring of the wicked shall not be satisfied with bread that, evidently, they may live. If the wicked shall not be satisfied with bread that they may live, then the opposite condition is indicated that the good shall be satisfied with bread that they may live. What is this bread? It is (see Rev. ii. 17) the hidden manna of which Job had knowledge through the charge to the people of the Second Age; it is (see St. John vi. 48–50) the living bread that came down from heaven, that man may eat thereof and not die. What is the living bread that came down from heaven? It is (see St. John vi. 51) the flesh of Jesus Christ the Redeemer. What is the flesh of Jesus Christ the Redeemer? It is (see Heb. x. 5–7; Ps. xl. 6–8) the body that was prepared for the Son that he might do the will of God, and which body was entirely suitable for the purpose.

The flesh of the Redeemer (see St. John vi. 53–55) shall be eaten. Why? It is (see St. John vi. 56) that the Redeemer may dwell in the eater; hence by the eating of the flesh of the Redeemer; hence by the eating of the body that was prepared for the Son, suitable for this purpose, the Redeemer takes upon himself the actual flesh of the eater, and, therefore, dwells in him.

If the actual flesh of the Redeemer dwells in the actual flesh of the eater, then the Law will be fully satisfied should the Redeemer, thus clothed, die an absolute death; for pure substitution is left out entirely.

Now that the Law is fully satisfied, what follows? The statement is made (see St. John vi. 56), " He that eateth my flesh, and drinketh my blood, dwelleth in me, and I in him." Hence, when the eater partook of the flesh of the Redeemer, it was not that the Redeemer might take upon himself the flesh of the eater only, but that, at the same time, the eater might be regenerated or born into the flesh of the Redeemer, or that the eater might be transferred from the earthy body and be regenerated or born into the pure unblemished body that was prepared for the Son suitable for this purpose. When, therefore, the Redeemer died an absolute death, he bore with him to the grave the body of sinful flesh and the pure unblemished body into which the spirit of man had been regenerated.

Which body will the grave give up? Will it give up the body of sinful flesh? or will it give up the pure unblemished body into which the spirit of man had been regenerated? The latter beyond all question. Why? Paul states (2 Cor. v. 1), "For we know that, if our earthly house of *this* tabernacle were dissolved, we have a building of God, a house not made with hands, eternal in the heavens." This house, then, is of the body that was prepared for the Son in and at the very beginning of the creation of God (see Col. i. 15; Rev. iii. 14), suitable for the purpose; for the earthly tabernacle is dissolved and gives place to the house not made with hands; which indication Paul further confirms in the succeeding verse as follows: "For in this we groan, earnestly desiring to be clothed upon with our house which is from heaven."

Paul does not claim both tabernacles, but he expresses earnest desire to be clothed upon with the house not made with hands, although it might seem at first sight (see 2 Cor. v. 4) that he would not be unclothed; that is, that he would not lay aside the body of sinful flesh or the earthly tabernacle, but would be clothed over that. The indication is clear, however, that unclothing transgressive man would make him bare, and cast him into the pit, but by the spirit of man being clothed upon with the house not made with hands, or with the body that was prepared for the Son, mortality would be swallowed up of life.

Paul continues (2 Cor. v. 6–8), "Therefore *we are* always confident, knowing that, whilst we are at home in the body, we are absent from the Lord :

"(For we walk by faith, not by sight:)

"We are confident, *I say*, and willing rather to be absent from the body, and to be present with the Lord."

Here again the forsaking of the earthly tabernacle is indicated, and that while at home in the earthly tabernacle man is absent from the Lord; and, hence, from the house not made with hands and with which he would be clothed, even though, at the time, he be regenerated; for man believes in regeneration through faith, and not by sight.

By the text of Paul the two tabernacles are indicated: one of which is sinful flesh, and the other is of the body that was prepared for the Son who was (see Rev. iii. 14; Col. i. 15) the beginning of the creation of God, and the first-born of every creature; who took upon himself the sinful flesh of man; wherefore Paul further states (2 Cor. v. 16), "Henceforth know we no man after the flesh: yea, though we have known Christ after the flesh, yet now henceforth know we *him* no more," from which it follows that the body of sinful flesh is left behind forever, and that man (see 2 Cor. v. 17) through Christ is a new creature; for Christ will never bring back the body of sinful flesh with which he was clothed in the labors of the redemption.

Under such conditions as these the justification of man becomes a surety, but the philosophy of Eliphaz, Bildad, and Zophar comprehended nothing of it; for with them, no Redeemer, no redemption; but basing everything upon the Law, they swept the creature away forever and gave his place to another.

That Job was enlightened in regard to many features of the redemption is manifest from his speeches, but the light shed abroad to-day is far in excess of that which existed in the Third Age of Man; for then Job, with the eye of faith, looked forward to the advent of his Redeemer, but now the advent of the Redeemer is a matter of the past. Whose faith, therefore, is the stronger, that of Job? or that of man of the present day? Job continues his speech concerning the wicked man,—

XXVII. 18-23. "He buildeth his house as a moth, and as a booth *that* the keeper maketh.

"The rich man shall lie down, but he shall not be gathered: he openeth his eyes, and he *is* not.

"Terrors take hold on him as waters, a tempest stealeth him away in the night.

"The east wind carrieth him away, and he departeth: and as a storm hurleth him out of his place.

"For *God* shall cast upon him, and not spare: he would fain flee out of his hand.

"*Men* shall clap their hands at him, and shall hiss him out of his place."

The indications are clear that, by Job's reasoning, the wicked man that perishes is one from whom every good thing is taken away. Job indirectly yet positively indicated his need of a Redeemer. If he needed a Redeemer then he must have been a transgressor; if a transgressor, then he came under the condemnation of the Law; if under the condemnation of the Law, where can he draw the line between his own transgression and that of another that he should be redeemed and that the other should perish? He could not; therefore it follows that the wicked must be set upon their own base, and that the good be set upon their base; then, when such division shall have been accomplished, the wicked will meet the fate depicted for them by Job, while the good will enter into their new life. Job continues,—

XXVIII. 1. " Surely there is a vein for the silver, and a place for gold *where* they fine *it*."

If there is a vein for the silver why should not a place be found in the creature wherein dwelt the good? And if there is a place for gold where they fine it why should there not be a place wherein the good that dwells within the creature may be separated from the base elements that compass it? As, therefore,—

XXVIII. 2. " Iron is taken out of the earth, and brass *is* molten *out of* the stone,"—

So will the good be separated from the evil; and as—

XXVIII. 3. " He setteth an end to darkness, and searcheth out all perfection: the stones of darkness, and the shadow of death,"—

So the gold will be searched out wherever it may be found, and an end will be made to death; that is, the stones of darkness, which indicate absolute death, and the shadow of death, which indicates the semblance of death, shall be as though they never had been, and as though no cause had ever existed for their having been. Job continues,—

XXVIII. 4. " The flood breaketh out from the inhabitant; *even the waters* forgotten of the foot: they are dried up, they are gone away from men."

Thus the great flood of evil (see Rev. xii. 15-17) that was poured out of the mouth of the serpent will be dried up; they will be gone away from men forever, they will also be forgotten, and never more will they be. Job continues,—

XXVIII. 5. "*As for* the earth, out of it cometh bread: and under it is turned up as it were fire."

This verse points to the priesthood of man. Job continues,—

XXVIII. 6. "The stones of it *are* the place of sapphires: and it hath dust of gold."

This verse (see Deut. xxxiii. 13-17) points to great and precious hosts that shall be raised up to praise the name of their Redeemer and Restorer. Job continues,—

XXVIII. 7, 8. "*There is* a path which no fowl knoweth, and which the vulture's eye hath not seen:

"The lion's whelps have not trodden it, nor the fierce lion passed by it."

These verses point to the great mystery of the redemption that was hidden (see Col. i. 23-29) from ages and generations, but which (see also Rom. xvi. 25, 26) is now made manifest to his saints. Job continues,—

XXVIII. 9. "He putteth forth his hand upon the rock; he overturneth the mountains by the roots."

The rock is the Law, and the mountains indicate the Power of Evil; hence by the Law the Power of Evil will be overturned to the very roots. This verse also points (see Deut. xii. 1-3; Isa. lxv. 17) to the destruction of the earth that all remembrance of evil may pass away forever. Job continues,—

XXVIII. 10, 11. "He cutteth out rivers among the rocks; and his eye seeth every precious thing.

"He bindeth the floods from overflowing: and *the thing that is* hid bringeth he forth to light."

Thus the precious that was or shall be separated from the vile will be hidden, cared for, and brought again to light; and will rejoice in the light after evil shall have been overturned forever. Job continues,—

XXVIII. 12. "But where shall wisdom be found? and where *is* the place of understanding?"

Truly, where shall wisdom be found? and where is the place of understanding? Who can grasp the wonderful purpose that was purposed (see Isa. xiv. 24–27) in all its details? and who can comprehend the mystery of the redemption in all its fulness? Can man? Never; for—

XXVIII. 13. "Man knoweth not the price thereof; neither is it found in the land of the living."

Of wisdom Job continues,—

XXVIII. 14, 15. "The depth saith, It *is* not in me: and the sea saith, *It is* not with me.

"It cannot be gotten for gold, neither shall silver be weighed *for* the price thereof."

Thus this wisdom is found neither in the depths of the earth nor in the depths of the sea; it is priceless, so much so that—

XXVIII. 16–19. "It cannot be valued with the gold of Ophir, with the precious onyx, or the sapphire.

"The gold and the crystal cannot equal it: and the exchange of it *shall not be for* jewels of fine gold.

"No mention shall be made of coral, or of pearls: for the price of wisdom *is* above rubies.

"The topaz of Ethiopia shall not equal it, neither shall it be valued with pure gold."

Who then can hope ever to possess wisdom since the richest gems cannot purchase it? If through purchase, none. The text continues,—

XXVIII. 20, 21. "Whence then cometh wisdom? and where *is* the place of understanding?

"Seeing it is hid from the eyes of all living, and kept close from the fowls of the air."

Wisdom is hidden with the Almighty, and the place of understanding is with him. The eyes of all living are made blind to the working of the great purpose that it may reach fulfilment as preconceived and laid down. The apparent overthrow and demolition of the creature, from the bursting of the planet that still sends its fragments whirling round about the source of light to the crushing of a molecule, are foreseen incidents, not weak points in a general plan that corrects itself as exigency requires; yet,—

XXVIII. 22. "Destruction and death say, We have heard the fame thereof with our ears."

To destruction and death perceptible overthrow and demolition possess more weight than any fame to the contrary that may have reached their ears; if not, why do not destruction and death cease their labors? They are blind to wisdom. Why? Because—

XXVIII. 23–27. "God understandeth the way thereof, and he knoweth the place thereof.

"For he looketh to the ends of the earth, *and* seeth under the whole heaven;

"To make the weight for the winds; and he weigheth the waters by measure.

"When he made a decree for the rain, and a way for the lightning of the thunder;

"Then did he see it, and declare it; he prepared it, yea, and searched it out."

Thus from the beginning the whole work was foreknown, foreseen, prepared, declared, and searched out. This embodies wisdom as an infinitely great magnitude, and hence it is hidden from the eyes of all living; but the text continues,—

XXVIII. 28. "And unto man he said, Behold, the fear of the Lord, that *is* wisdom; and to depart from evil *is* understanding."

This summary certainly points to great wisdom and understanding, and, moreover, is comprehensible by man; therefore, by following this teaching man will become possessed of that which is priceless, and which cannot be purchased with sapphires, pearls, or rubies.

XXIX. 1–7. "Moreover Job continued his parable, and said,

"Oh that I were as *in* months past, as *in* the days *when* God preserved me;

"When his candle shined upon my head, *and when* by his light I walked *through* darkness;

"As I was in the days of my youth, when the secret of God *was* upon my tabernacle;

"When the Almighty *was* yet with me, *when* my children *were* about me;

"When I washed my steps with butter, and the rock poured me out rivers of oil;

"When I went out to the gate through the city, *when I prepared my seat in the street!*"

These verses point to the days when Job, as the Adam and progenitor of the Third Race, dwelt in Eden free from sin and transgression, even as the Adam and progenitor of the Fourth Race (see Gen. ii. 7–25) dwelt in Eden free from sin and transgression. Job continues,—

XXIX. 8. "The young men saw me, and hid themselves: and the aged arose, *and* stood up."

This verse points to the overlap of the Second and Third Races of Men; the aged indicating and representing the Second, while the young men represent the Third Race. Job continues,—

XXIX. 9, 10. "The princes refrained talking, and laid *their* hand on their mouth.

"The nobles held their peace, and their tongue cleaved to the roof of their mouth."

These verses indicate the respect in which Job was held by those around him before transgression marred the beauty of his existence. The protection of the Almighty was about him, and kept him pure as he had been created; for (see Rom. vii. 9; Gen. ii. 7–17) man was alive without the Law once; but when the commandment or Law came sin revived, and man died; hence in the earlier days of his life Job (see ii. 3) was a perfect and an upright man, one that feared God and eschewed evil. The great nation that peopled the earth at the time of the calling of Job was on the eve of destruction; they were (see Isa. iii. 1–11; Jer. v. 1–18; Ezek. xi. 1–12) overwhelmed in sin, and their days had nearly run out; wherefore there was none in the earth like unto Job before transgression brought him low. Job continues,—

XXIX. 11-13. "When the ear heard *me*, then it blessed me; and when the eye saw *me*, it gave witness to me:

"Because I delivered the poor that cried, and the fatherless, and *him that had* none to help him.

"The blessing of him that was ready to perish came upon me: and I caused the widow's heart to sing for joy."

In the fallen nation around him Job had an ample field in which to exercise the noble qualities with which he was endowed; and that he made good use of them is indicated by the text, for up to this time the Law had not entered to him, or, at least, he had not as yet fallen into transgression, and hence he was (see i. 9, 12; xxix. 2-5) under the special protection of the Almighty. Job continues,—

XXIX. 14. "I put on righteousness, and it clothed me: my judgment *was* as a robe and a diadem."

This verse indicates that the Law has now entered in as a ruling principle for the government of Job. With the entering in of the Law the special protection of the Almighty is taken away from Job, and, as a free agent, he stands upon his own righteousness and judgment. Such being the situation, Satan (see i. 13), as a free agent also under the Law, can make aggression upon him in numberless ways; but if the righteousness that Job puts on shall prove strong enough, and if his judgment shall be correct enough, then Satan cannot touch him for harm. Job continues,—

XXIX. 15-18. "I was eyes to the blind, and feet *was* I to the lame.

"I *was* a father to the poor: and the cause *which* I knew not I searched out.

"And I brake the jaws of the wicked, and plucked the spoil out of his teeth.

"Then I said, I shall die in my nest, and I shall multiply *my* days as the sand."

Thus under the Law Job as a free agent did many acts of mercy and justice; but what followed? Why his heart was lifted up, and he thought to multiply his days as the sand, thereby driving the possibility of death into the remote future. Job undoubtedly thought to establish life through righteousness by works; for he continues,—

XXIX. 19-25. "My root *was* spread out by the waters, and the dew lay all night upon my branch.

"My glory *was* fresh in me, and my bow was renewed in my hand.

"Unto me *men* gave ear, and waited, and kept silence at my counsel.

"After my words they spake not again; and my speech dropped upon them.

"And they waited for me as for the rain; and they opened their mouth wide *as* for the latter rain.

"*If* I laughed on them, they believed *it* not: and the light of my countenance they cast not down.

"I chose out their way, and sat chief, and dwelt as a king in the army, as one *that* comforteth the mourners."

In these verses Job describes the eminence of his position, but through the eminence of his position the insidious Serpent was undermining the vitality of Job's reverence for his Maker. How so? Why should Job proclaim that his righteousness through free agency or his righteousness by works would multiply his days beyond all thought of time, and fix his dying hour as far beyond his natal day as the hidden focus of the proud aspiring parabola lies beyond the known, what further need would he have of a Creator or of a Protector, or of any power beyond himself? By the text Job's righteous works as a free agent under the Law led him into the fatal error of imagining that he had established life through righteousness by works, and, hence, of saying (verse 18), " I shall multiply *my* days as the sand ;" which in itself, as coming from a creature, is a transgression ; for the creature (see Isa. xiv. 12–14) cannot be like the Most High. What followed this transgression ? Job implies the answer,—

XXX. 1. " But now *they that are* younger than I have me in derision, whose fathers I would have disdained to have set with the dogs of my flock."

This verse indicates that through transgression Job has fallen into the power of the Evil Kingdom, and has become their sport; which indication Job confirms as follows :

XXX. 2. " Yea, whereto *might* the strength of their hands *profit* me, in whom old age was perished?"

In this verse Job no more lays claim to length of days, to days multiplied as the sand ; on the contrary, old age was perished from him. Why? Because of his transgression. If, therefore, Job recognizes the shortening of his days, then the indication clears up as to why he exclaimed (xix. 23-27), "Oh that my words were now written ! oh that they were printed in a book !

"That they were graven with an iron pen and lead in the rock forever!

"For I know *that* my Redeemer liveth, and *that* he shall stand at the latter *day* upon the earth:

"And *though* after my skin *worms* destroy this *body*, yet in my flesh shall I see God:

"Whom I shall see for myself, and mine eyes shall behold, and not another; *though* my reins be consumed within me;" which words furnish the key to Job's philosophy. Job continues of those deriding him,—

XXX. 3-11. "For want and famine *they were* solitary; fleeing into the wilderness in former time desolate and waste:

"Who cut up mallows by the bushes, and juniper roots *for* their meat.

"They were driven forth from among *men*, (they cried after them as *after* a thief,)

"To dwell in the cliffs of the valleys, *in* caves of the earth, and *in* the rocks.

"Among the bushes they brayed; under the nettles they were gathered together.

"*They were* children of fools, yea, children of base men: they were viler than the earth.

"And now am I their song, yea, I am their byword.

"They abhor me, they flee far from me, and spare not to spit in my face.

"Because he hath loosed my cord, and afflicted me, they have also let loose the bridle before me."

Those deriding Job that are younger than he are, very probably, the later generations of the Second Race; hence their fathers existed as transgressors at the time Job dwelt in Eden as "a perfect and an upright man;" wherefore he, at that time, would have disdained or hesitated to have set them even with the dogs of his flock. As the fathers, so the children; both deride and persecute Job, who, although a transgressor, still strives to do right. Job continues,—

XXX. 12-14. "Upon *my* right *hand* rise the youth; they push away my feet, and they raise up against me the ways of their destruction.

"They mar my path, they set forward my calamity, they have no helper.

"They came *upon me* as a wide breaking in *of waters:* in the desolation they rolled themselves *upon me*."

The youth of which Job now speaks probably are his descendants, the people of the Third Age, that have fallen into and taken up with the evil devices of the Second Race, even as later (see Gen. vi. 1-5) the people of the Fourth Race took up with the evil devices of the Third.

From indications otherwise given the near approach of the destruction of the Second Race has been set forth, and, as the youth of the Third Race have taken up with their devices, so when destruction shall come upon the Second, no helper will be found for them, even as (see Gen. vi. 1-7) the youth of the Fourth Race were swept away in the Deluge that overwhelmed the Third when the days of the Third had run out. Job continues,—

XXX. 15-19. "Terrors are turned upon me: they pursue my soul as the wind: and my welfare passeth away as a cloud.

"And now my soul is poured out upon me; the days of affliction have taken hold upon me.

"My bones are pierced in me in the night season: and my sinews take no rest.

"By the great force *of my disease* is my garment changed: it bindeth me about as the collar of my coat.

"He hath cast me into the mire, and I am become like dust and ashes."

These verses point to the great Famine that swept away the Second Race; and this affliction is now about Job; hence terrors meet him on every hand, and pursue after him; his welfare disappears in the great Drought that went hand in hand with the Famine; his flesh is shrivelled up upon his body and binds him as the collar of a coat binds the wearer; he is truly cast into the mire, and he truly has become like the dust and ashes; for Job's is a great family, and Job's family, together with the Second Race, pass away, and (see verses 12-14) raise up against him, personally, the ways of their destruction. Job continues,—

XXX. 20-24. "I cry unto thee, and thou dost not hear me: I stand up, and thou regardest me *not*.

"Thou art become cruel to me: with thy strong hand thou opposest thyself against me.

"Thou liftest me up to the wind; thou causest me to ride *upon it*, and dissolvest my substance.

"For I know *that* thou wilt bring me *to* death, and *to* the house appointed for all living.

"Howbeit he will not stretch out *his* hand to the grave, though they cry in his destruction."

This cry goes up from Job in the midst of the famine and desolation that surround him; but by the desolation and famine, as consequents of transgression, Job knows that he will be brought to the land of the shadow of death, and also to absolute darkness or death. Man, however, through his Redeemer (see **xix.** 25–27), will be brought back from absolute death, in that he dies with his Redeemer and rises again with his Redeemer; but the wicked will come back no more; for "he will not stretch out *his* hand to the grave, though they cry in his destruction." Job continues,—

XXX. 25. "Did not I weep for him that was in trouble? was *not* my soul grieved for the poor?"

In this verse Job expresses his righteous actions and motives, and therefore, under the Law, he looked for good for himself and his house; but he continues,—

XXX. 26–31. "When I looked for good, then evil came *unto me:* and when I waited for light, there came darkness.

"My bowels boiled, and rested not: the days of affliction prevented me.

"I went mourning without the sun: I stood up, *and* I cried in the congregation.

"I am a brother to dragons, and a companion to owls.

"My skin is black upon me, and my bones are burned with heat.

"My harp also is *turned* to mourning, and my organ into the voice of them that weep."

Thus, notwithstanding Job's righteous acts and righteous motives, transgression overtook him; yet it was through the unlooked-for result of seeking to establish life through free agency or through righteousness by works; and, hence, it was, at the time, transgression through ignorance; for what man under the ruling of the Law would not seek for the rich fruits that pertain to the Law? If there were no better beyond than the

Law, then Job would have been justified in his seeking to live in it; but inasmuch as the Law carries recognition of evil in order to condemn it; and inasmuch as the creature that was pronounced good at the first will certainly fall into evil, the indication follows that, from the infinite wisdom and perfection of the Almighty, a way of life can be and will be prepared for the creature that is not of the Law; hence (see xxix. 14) the judgment with which Job was clothed, and which was as a diadem to him, was defective, erroneous; and, as such, caused him to transgress through ignorance; for (see Gal. iii. 21) "if there had been a law given which could have given life, verily righteousness should have been by the law;" but the law is not against the promises of God; which promises embody a means of life that is not of the Law. Later, however, Job comprehended the true life-conferring source, and, in the charge to the people of the Third Age (see Rev. iii. 1–6), his eyes were enlightened to the greatness of the promises of God. Job continues,—

XXXI. 1, 2. "I made a covenant with mine eyes; why then should I think upon a maid?

"For what portion of God *is there* from above? and *what* inheritance of the Almighty from on high?"

The covenant made with the eyes evidently is righteousness by works under the Law as a free agent; hence under such conditions, even as Job implies, what portion of God is there from above? or what inheritance of the Almighty is there from on high, that the Law should not rule for the time being as an absolute monarch? In essentiality, nothing; for Job continues,—

XXXI. 3. "*Is* not destruction to the wicked? and a strange *punishment* to the workers of iniquity?"

The Law entered that the offence might abound, and the Law entered bearing with it an ordination to life; hence by its rulings free agency can and must exist independent of any portion of God from above as regards the penalty of transgression and the ordination to life; wherefore Job continues,—

XXXI. 4. "Doth not he see my ways, and count all my steps?"

As the Almighty sees all the ways of Job, and counts all his steps, so will the Law take cognizance of the same, and render reward to the good, and recompense to the evil; for the ordination to life preserves the good, while the ministration of death condemns the evil. Job continues,—

XXXI. 5, 6. "If I have walked with vanity, or if my foot hath hasted to deceit;

"Let me be weighed in an even balance, that God may know mine integrity."

Hence, whatever may be the sum of Job's transgression, he requests that his integrity be made manifest also. If, however, as the reasoning of Eliphaz, Bildad, and Zophar implies, there is no separation of the good from the evil, but that, because of transgression, the good must be overwhelmed forever by the evil, why make integrity manifest? From Job's stand-point integrity is made manifest as proof of faith in a Redeemer, or of faith in the advent of one that shall redeem him from the evil that environs him. If a man has no integrity then no proof exists of his faith in righteousness; hence let such, as with Job, be weighed in an even balance, and a just weight will be established, both as regards Job with the proofs of his faith about him, and as regards the evil-doer with no such proofs about him. Thus, while the Law judges both the good and the evil, it cannot separate them, and while they are united in the one individuality the Law is powerless to fulfil the judgment rendered; but should the evil be separated from the good, then (see 1 Sam. xv. 9) it, the evil, could and will be utterly destroyed. Job continues,—

XXXI. 7, 8. "If my step hath turned out of the way, and mine heart walked after mine eyes, and if any blot hath cleaved to mine hands;

"*Then* let me sow, and let another eat; yea, let my offspring be rooted out."

These verses indicate the remarkable integrity and pureness of Job's life; and yet, notwithstanding his integrity, great and terrible afflictions came upon him for transgression through ignorance. In the context Job indicates the heinousness of the crime pertaining to the house that sought the overthrow and downfall of man. Job continues,—

XXXI. 9–15. "If mine heart have been deceived by a woman, or *if* I have laid wait at my neighbour's door;

"*Then* let my wife grind unto another, and let others bow down upon her.

"For this *is* a heinous crime; yea, it *is* an iniquity *to be punished by* the judges.

"For it *is* a fire *that* consumeth to destruction, and would root out all mine increase.

"If I did despise the cause of my manservant or of my maidservant, when they contended with me;

"What then shall I do when God riseth up? and when he visiteth, what shall I answer him?

"Did not he that made me in the womb make him? and did not one fashion us in the womb?"

Thus, while Job still brings forward his integrity, he also points to his transgression, should God rise up and judge him.

If Job was suddenly created as the Adam and progenitor of the Third Race, how is it that he was made in the womb? Job himself indicates the reply when he asks, "And did not one fashion us in the womb?" thus pointing to a bringing forth that was not from the womb; but the result was as though it thus had been brought forth, even as (see Gen. ii. 7; v. 1–3) Adam was as one that was fashioned in the womb, the proof being witnessed in the similitude of Seth his son, who was after his likeness and image; moreover, the figure of birth as applied to the newly-created is fully indicated (Rev. xii.). Job continues,—

XXXI. 16–18. "If I have withheld the poor from *their* desire, or have caused the eyes of the widow to fail;

"Or have eaten my morsel myself alone, and the fatherless hath not eaten thereof;

"(For from my youth he was brought up with me, as *with* a father, and I have guided her from my mother's womb.)"

Thus from his youth Job was as a father, as a provider, and as a counsellor, which conditions clearly fulfil in the light that Job is the Adam and progenitor of one of the races of men suddenly brought into existence, yet perfect, both physically and mentally, as man. If, however, the youth of Job be but a step above infancy, then the interpolation of the text (verse 18) becomes weak in comparison, for how can Job guide the widow, even from his mother's womb? Job continues,—

XXXI. 19-23. "If I have seen any perish for want of clothing, or any poor without covering;

"If his loins have not blessed me, and *if* he were *not* warmed with the fleece of my sheep;

"If I have lifted up my hand against the fatherless, when I saw my help in the gate:

"*Then* let mine arm fall from my shoulder blade, and mine arm be broken from the bone.

"For destruction *from* God *was* a terror to me, and by reason of his highness I could not endure."

In these verses the great integrity of Job as a free agent is further made manifest; but, at the same time, Job's fear of destruction from God in case of failure was one incentive to righteousness, while his sense of the highness and perfection of the Almighty was another, although the probability is strong in every way that Job took an individual delight in well-doing from the noble qualities with which he, as a creature, was endowed. Job continues,—

XXXI. 24-28. "If I have made gold my hope, or have said to the fine gold, *Thou art* my confidence;

"If I have rejoiced because my wealth *was* great, and because mine hand had gotten much;

"If I beheld the sun when it shined, or the moon walking *in* brightness;

"And my heart hath been secretly enticed, or my mouth hath kissed my hand:

"This also *were* an iniquity *to be punished by* the judge: for I should have denied the God *that is* above."

Now while Job continues the enumeration of righteous pertainings he brings himself into condemnation, in that his mouth hath kissed his hand; that is, he said (xxix. 18), "I shall die in my nest, and I shall multiply *my* days as the sand." It follows that if Job, through free agency under the Law, through righteousness by works, or through self-righteousness, thought to prolong his days indefinitely, that such thought would carry with it a denial of any need for a God, for a Protector, or for a Redeemer; and, hence, such thought is transgressive, punishable by the judge or Law. Job, however, committed this trespass through ignorance. Job continues,—

XXXI. 29-31. "If I rejoiced at the destruction of him that hated me, or lifted up myself when evil found him;

"(Neither have I suffered my mouth to sin by wishing a curse to his soul.)

"If the men of my tabernacle said not, Oh that we had of his flesh! we cannot be satisfied."

Who are the men of his tabernacle? They evidently are those who persecute him, the host of evil that pertains to the army of Satan; for (see ii. 4–7) Job's flesh was put in the hands of Satan. Job continues,—

XXXI. 32-34. "The stranger did not lodge in the street: *but* I opened my doors to the traveller.

"If I covered my transgressions as Adam, by hiding mine iniquity in my bosom:

"Did I fear a great multitude, or did the contempt of families terrify me, that I kept silence, *and* went not out of the door?"

If Job is the first man, or the progenitor of the Third Race, who is the Adam of whom he speaks? The indications are that the Adam spoken of by Job (see Gen. v. 2) is the progenitor of the race of men that preceded him, and whose children find a representative in the stranger (see verse 32) that did not lodge in the street, and representatives (see xxx. 1, 2) in the children of those who derided him, whose fathers were transgressors when (see ii. 1–3) he stood a perfect and an upright man before the Almighty.

Did Job in his first integrity fear the great multitude of transgressors that made up the Second Race that existed contemporary with him? or did the contempt of these families terrify him that he kept silence, and went not out among them? The indications are that Job kept himself aloof not from fear or from any expression of contempt that might fall from them, but because he took no delight in their evil ways, and shared not their transgressive desires. Job continues,—

XXXI. 35–37. "Oh that one would hear me! behold, my desire *is, that* the Almighty would answer me, and *that* mine adversary had written a book.

"Surely I would take it upon my shoulder, *and* bind it *as* a crown to me.

"I would declare unto him the number of my steps; as a prince would I go near unto him."

Thus Job expresses his desire that the Almighty would answer him, and, also, that his adversary had written a book. Who is Job's adversary? He is (see i. 12; ii. 4–7) Satan, King of Evil. Had Satan written a book, what kind of a book would it have been? It would have been the acme of subtlety and plausibility.

Job, however, possessed as he is with such great light and faith, fears neither plausibility nor subtlety with all their varied array of masks. Job continues,—

XXXI. 38–40. "If my land cry against me, or that the furrows likewise thereof complain;

"If I have eaten the fruits thereof without money, or have caused the owners thereof to lose their life:

"Let thistles grow instead of wheat, and cockle instead of barley. The words of Job are ended."

Here again Job sets forth his righteous dealings. Why should he have been thus particular in setting forth his righteousness? The indications are that it was to show the utter futility of establishing life through free agency or of establishing life through works. Who among men was more righteous than Job? whose life among men was more rigidly searched than that of Job? whose trials among men exceeded those of Job? where, among men, can another than Job be found through whom the hopelessness of establishing life through works can be more fully shown? If Job with all his righteousness failed to secure it, then the utter impossibility of any creature, through his own will and pleasure, controlling the life-conferring source is indicated. Job's three friends, however, do not say that man can reach such a lofty eminence; but they indicate by their reasonings that righteousness by works may secure to the creature the full number of his prescribed days, and that, when these days shall have been fulfilled, they shall come (see v. 26) to the "grave in a full age, like as a shock of corn cometh in in his season." Miserable philosophy that snatches the ripened fruit from the possessor's mouth! How can it stand the test of Job's strong words? It cannot; the spirit of man rejects the false position, and flings it headlong into darkness as a hideous, deformed, improbable possibility. Within his inmost soul man grasps the floats that buoy up the chain of existence, and so from point to point hopes to progress into the unknown that lies so far beyond his vision; but below, deeper in the sea that marks the handiwork of the Almighty Power, the chain itself, perfect in every detail, forms an unbroken pathway, each link of which contains a key unlocking ciphers of the next, so that none whose faith is firm need ever meet a yawning chasm, unbridged abyss, or dizzy height to strike dismay as he advances.

XXXII. 1–3. "So these three men ceased to answer Job, because he *was* righteous in his own eyes.

"Then was kindled the wrath of Elihu the son of Barachel the Buzite, of the kindred of Ram: against Job was his wrath kindled, because he justified himself rather than God.

"Also against his three friends was his wrath kindled, because they had found no answer, and *yet* had condemned Job."

Thus Job's righteous acts under the Law could not be gainsaid by his friends; he invited research into his doings; but, from the stand-point of human judgment, they really could not point to a single action on the part of Job wherein he had transgressed; even Elihu accords this. It is no wonder, therefore, that, under the circumstances, Job was righteous in his own eyes.

Indications were strongly marked that Job's friends based their accusations and charges against him because of the tribulations that befell him, and not because they were eye-witnesses or possessed proof otherwise of his transgression; hence Elihu's wrath was kindled against them because, while they condemned Job, they could not answer him by proving the charges which they had preferred. If Job were perfectly upright and righteous under the Law, then it is evident that he would justify himself rather than God; for wherein should God justify him were all his thoughts and deeds perfect under the Law? hence, where Job sets forth his righteousness, a tendency appears to exist that Job, even as Elihu states, seeks to justify himself under the Law; but is it so in reality? Not at all; for Job acknowledges that he is a transgressor, in that (see xix. 25) his Redeemer liveth. If Job's Redeemer lives, then he, Job, must be redeemed; but if he is not a transgressor, wherein should he be redeemed? and why should he need a Redeemer? The indications are that Job needs a Redeemer because of transgression through ignorance; for what man possesses perfect judgment in all things? Not one; hence the enumeration of Job's righteous acts under the Law is not set forth that he may justify himself, but that the utter impossibility of establishing life through righteousness by works, free agency, or self-righteousness under the Law may be clearly set forth; Paul confirming the indication where he states (Gal. iii. 21), "if there had been a law given which could have given life, verily righteousness should have been by the law."

Job's righteous acts were fulfilled in themselves as a proof of his faith in the promises of redemption; but, as already set forth, they cannot confer life upon him.

The indication now follows that Elihu's wrath against Job is not well founded, but that, on the contrary, great exception may be taken to it.

XXXII. 4, 5. "Now Elihu had waited till Job had spoken, because they *were* elder than he.

"When Elihu saw that *there was* no answer in the mouth of *these* three men, then his wrath was kindled."

Who is Elihu that he should thus condemn not only Job, but Eliphaz, Bildad, and Zophar also? Indications arise and become marked that Elihu (see 2 Cor. xi. 14) is Satan in disguise, or Satan transformed as an angel of light. Who was it that sought the destruction of Job's children? Satan. Who was it that brought such great personal affliction upon Job? Satan. Why did Satan bring these things about? He brought them about that Job might transgress. But inasmuch as Job, from a human stand-point, was upright and righteous, so much so that even his three friends could not gainsay him, what wonder that Satan should be filled with wrath not only against Job, but against his three friends also? None at all. If, therefore, Satan is thus wrathful, and Elihu is thus wrathful, what prevents the transformation of Satan as Elihu that such transformation should not be or find place? more especially since Job (see xxxi. 35) desired that his adversary had written a book.

XXXII. 6, 7. "And Elihu the son of Barachel the Buzite answered and said, I *am* young, and ye *are* very old; wherefore I was afraid, and durst not shew you mine opinion.

"I said, Days should speak, and multitude of years should teach wisdom."

The days of which Elihu speaks, and the years of which Elihu speaks, point to the days and years from the calling of man in the First Age. What do they say? The grave; the grave; the grave: as with the past, so with the future. This is the wisdom that Elihu wishes to teach in part, yet not as an absolute necessary ruling, while it embodies the wisdom with which Eliphaz, Bildad, and Zophar sought to overwhelm the arguments of Job. Elihu continues,—

XXXII. 8, 9. "But *there is* a spirit in man: and the inspiration of the Almighty giveth them understanding.

"Great men are not *always* wise: neither do the aged understand judgment."

Thus, through the spirit that is in man, understanding is given them as free agents under the Law; but as free agents under the Law great men are not always wise; neither under the Law do the aged understand judgment. Such is a brief description of man as substantially given by Elihu. Elihu continues,—

XXXII. 10–13. "Therefore I said, Hearken to me; I also will shew mine opinion.

"Behold, I waited for your words; I gave ear to your reasons, whilst ye searched out what to say.

"Yea, I attended unto you, and, behold, *there was* none of you that convinced Job, *or* that answered his words:

"Lest ye should say, We have found out wisdom: God thrusteth him down, not man."

Thus Elihu carefully attended the arguments of the three men, lest they should say, "We have found out wisdom; God thrusteth him down, not man;" by which free agency under the Law would be discarded. The indications are clear, however, that all hosts are free agents under the Law that the offence and condemnation may abound independent of the judgment of the Almighty, so that none can say of the condemned transgressor, "God thrusteth him down, not man;" for man, even though the Almighty instituted the Law, condemns himself through his transgression as a free agent under the Law. Elihu also reaffirms his opinion that Job's three friends failed to answer or confute the words of Job. Elihu continues,—

XXXII. 14. "Now he hath not directed *his* words against me: neither will I answer him with your speeches."

Inasmuch, therefore, as the reasoning of Eliphaz, Bildad, and Zophar failed to convince Job or to answer his words, Elihu will advance other arguments with which to overwhelm Job, and to throw down his hopes of redemption and life.

XXXII. 15. "They were amazed, they answered no more: they left off speaking."

This verse relates to the three friends of Job. Elihu continues,—

XXXII. 16–22. "When I had waited, (for they spake not, but stood still, *and* answered no more,)

"*I said,* I will answer also my part; I also will shew mine opinion.

"For I am full of matter; the spirit within me constraineth me.

"Behold, my belly *is* as wine *which* hath no vent; it is ready to burst like new bottles.

"I will speak, that I may be refreshed: I will open my lips and answer.

"Let me not, I pray you, accept any man's person; neither let me give flattering titles unto man.

"For I know not to give flattering titles; *in so doing* my Maker would soon take me away."

Thus Elihu, as the Adversary of Job, stands ready to define his position, to support it, and to answer the arguments of Job. Elihu continues,—

XXXIII. 1–3. "Wherefore, Job, I pray thee, hear my speeches, and hearken to all my words.

"Behold, now I have opened my mouth, my tongue hath spoken in my mouth.

"My words *shall be of* the uprightness of my heart: and my lips shall utter knowledge clearly."

If Elihu be Satan then his words must be measured by his character, that is defined as follows (St. John viii. 44): "He" (the devil) "was a murderer from the beginning, and abode not in the truth, because there is no truth in him. When he speaketh a lie, he speaketh of his own: for he is a liar, and the father of it." Such is the character drawn of the one that now says, "My words *shall be of* the uprightness of my heart: and my lips shall utter knowledge clearly." Elihu continues,—

XXXIII. 4, 5. "The Spirit of God hath made me, and the breath of the Almighty hath given me life.

"If thou canst answer me, set *thy words* in order before me, stand up."

Did the Spirit of God make Satan, and did the breath of the Almighty give him life? If so, why (see St. John viii. 44) should God create a murderer in the beginning? The indications are, from the unlimited perfection of his attributes, that the Almighty did not make Satan, and did not breathe into him the breath of life; moreover (see Rev. iii. 14–21; Col. i. 13–17), Jesus Christ is the beginning of the creation of God, and the first-born of every creature; hence the claim of Satan that he is God's creature is set forth as a baseless fabrication. Elihu continues,—

XXXIII. 6. "Behold, I *am* according to thy wish in God's stead: I also am formed out of the clay."

Here again Satan claims to be a creature; and if a creature, how could he place himself in God's stead without authority? besides, Job did not wish that another would place himself in God's stead, but he said (xxxi. 35), "Oh that one would hear me! behold, my desire *is, that* the Almighty would answer me, and *that* mine adversary had written a book." Satan heard Job's desire, but instead of answering in God's stead he speaks for himself; which is more in accordance with Job's expressed desire "and *that* mine adversary had written a book." Elihu continues,—

XXXIII. 7–11. "Behold, my terror shall not make thee afraid, neither shall my hand be heavy upon thee.

"Surely thou hast spoken in mine hearing, and I have heard the voice of *thy* words, *saying,*

"I am clean without transgression, I *am* innocent; neither *is there* iniquity in me.

"Behold, he findeth occasions against me, he counteth me for his enemy;

"He putteth my feet in the stocks, he marketh all my paths."

Job is subject to both the kingdom of good and the kingdom of evil; hence, inasmuch as Job once lived a perfect and an upright man, the records of which are found in i. 8; ii. 3, the indications are that such transgressions as might pertain to Job were due (see Rom. iii. 20) to a knowledge of sin by and under the Law. Separate this knowledge from Job and put it upon its own base, and show wherein Job's actions would have varied from those recorded in the general text. If Job transgressed through ignorance, he could not at the time of such transgression tell where he could have amended his ways; hence he felt the innocence that he expressed, and the freedom from transgression implied by his words. Elihu continues,—

XXXIII. 12. "Behold, *in* this thou art not just: I will answer thee, that God is greater than man."

This answer, taken simply, implies that because of greater power than man, God's action, whether right or wrong, should not be questioned, which is fallacious reasoning; for Satan is a power far greater than man, and should not his acts be questioned?

The unquestionability of God's acts are set at rest by the infinite perfection of his attributes, hence faith in God casts aside all question; but faith in Satan, where is it? The indication also arises that Elihu's statement, "that God is greater than man," is intended to take cognizance of God as a universal Ruler, in order that perfect supervision may have place; for the indication follows that no creature is endowed with omnipresence, omniscience, and omnipotence, that he should not fail in his care for the remote and unseen. Elihu continues,—

XXXIII. 13. "Why dost thou strive against him? for he giveth not account of any of his matters."

Who will agree with this saying? for God does give account of many of his matters by revealing purposes and plans, the uses thereof, their combinations and resultants. God's revealed justification of his acts brings comfort to his creatures, who, in their tribulation and sorrow, would otherwise be blind; while such justification or account points to the true cause of many marring influences and sources of discomfort. Elihu continues,—

XXXIII. 14-17. "For God speaketh once, yea twice, *yet man* perceiveth it not.

"In a dream, in a vision of the night, when deep sleep falleth upon men, in slumberings upon the bed;

"Then he openeth the ears of men, and sealeth their instruction,

"That he may withdraw man *from his* purpose, and hide pride from man."

It is true that many records are given in the Scriptures of instruction by visions and by dreams, but Satan implies that these are given to hide pride from man. If such be the case, then an existing power attacks the creature from which special protection is needed; if special protection is needed, then a fall is an imminent probability; if a fall, then a Redeemer would be necessary, or the creature would become prey forever to the non-creative power that caused his fall; which position will not hold good, for it is evident that the creative is greater than the non-creative. Wherein, then, do the words of Elihu answer those of Job that they should confute the necessity for a Redeemer? Thus far they fail, even as the words of Eliphaz or Bildad or Zophar failed. Elihu continues,—

XXXIII. 18. "He keepeth back his soul from the pit, and his life from perishing by the sword."

This saying evidently relates to the perfect and upright man (see i. 9, 10) that is hedged about on every side by the protection of the Almighty. Elihu continues,—

XXXIII. 19-22. "He is chastened also with pain upon his bed, and the multitude of his bones with strong *pain:*

"So that his life abhorreth bread, and his soul dainty meat.

"His flesh is consumed away, that it cannot be seen; and his bones *that* were not seen stick out.

"Yea, his soul draweth near unto the grave, and his life to the destroyers."

These verses relate to the creature after his fall as a free agent, and are consequents that follow transgression, by which the transgressor draws near unto the grave, and his life to the destroyers. The claim of Satan (see verse 4), that he is made of God, tends to deceive the creature that is under bondage to him into the belief that he, Satan, although a transgressor, does not, of necessity, lose his life because of his transgressions; for the beginning of the days of Satan are not traceable, while he still exists, apparently as powerful as ever, and apparently as far from death as ever; but nevertheless by the Law the transgressor shall not only draw near unto the grave, but (see Gen. ii. 16, 17) he shall surely die. Elihu continues,—

XXXIII. 23-26. "If there be a messenger with him, an interpreter, one among a thousand, to shew unto man his uprightness;

"Then he is gracious unto him, and saith, Deliver him from going down to the pit: I have found a ransom.

"His flesh shall be fresher than a child's: he shall return to the days of his youth:

"He shall pray unto God, and he will be favourable unto him: and he shall see his face with joy: for he will render unto man his righteousness."

These verses indicate that, of necessity, the transgressor need not go down to the pit,—which pit doubtless is the grave,—but rather that the uprightness dwelling with the transgressor will ransom him. The Law, however, regarding transgression is irrevocable; wherefore no system of ransoming can deliver the transgressor from death; he will surely die. If he die not, then the Law is unstable, unreliable, and the words of Elihu would be fruitful with truth. If, however, the Law is immutable, then the words of Elihu are specious and tend to deceive. Elihu continues,—

XXXIII. 27, 28. "He looketh upon men, and *if any* say, I have sinned, and perverted *that which was* right, and it profited me not;

"He will deliver his soul from going into the pit, and his life shall see the light."

Here, again, by the words of Elihu the Law is set aside through repentance, and the transgressor, for the time being, is delivered from death; which, under the Law, cannot be. Elihu further continues,—

XXXIII. 29, 30. "Lo, all these *things* worketh God oftentimes with man,

"To bring back his soul from the pit, to be enlightened with the light of the living."

What kind of a ransom is it that Elihu brings forward that man should be delivered from death, and that he should be enlightened with the light of the living? Simply the self-righteousness and repentance which make the sum of his uprightness. In this summary the Law is ignored, and a combination of good and evil holds the creature; through which condition transgression and repentance, threatened death and promised life, alternately blasts or softens the creature's continued existence or natural life. The words of Elihu neither throw down the Kingdom of Evil nor establish the supremacy of the Kingdom of Righteousness; they provide no way for the separation of the good from the evil, and, therefore, do not call for any Redeemer; hence the position set forth by Elihu is far short of that of Job, both in strength and excellence. Eliphaz, Bildad, and Zophar accorded man the full complement of his years, or the years of the natural life that pertained to him should he fulfil the Law; but that after these years should have expired he would pass away forever. Elihu accords indefinite length of life to the creature (not to all, however, for there are more sin-tinctured hosts of creatures than man of Adam's race) through repentance; but the creature will, during such life, be subject to both good and evil influences. Job, however, looks forward to a life after the years of the natural life shall have expired; he looks forward to the separation of the good from the evil; he looks forward to a Redeemer; and will not base his hopes on his own righteousness or free agency; for with free agency or self-righteousness as an existing condition the presence of an aggressive enemy is indicated.

The presence of Evil calls for the continuity of the Law, and the Law calls for free agency; but the fulfilment of the Law will sweep away the transgressor; hence when every transgressor shall have been swept away, then the Law will have waxed old, the Kingdom of Evil will have been overthrown, and the Kingdom of Righteousness will stand established forever without a rival; wherefore, thenceforth and forever, there will be no transgression, no repentance, no tribulation, no oblivion to the fathers, no forgetfulness for the children, while the righteous Kingdom will be peopled with a host as the stars of heaven for multitude and as the sand that is by the sea-shore for number.

Through death the Law is fulfilled upon the transgressor, through death the good is separated from the evil, and through death the resurrection can follow that will bring the redeemed creature back to life freed from transgression, and fitted forever to enjoy the immortality that crowns the subjects of the Righteous King. Elihu continues,—

XXXIII. 31–33. "Mark well, O Job, hearken unto me: hold thy peace, and I will speak.

"If thou hast any thing to say, answer me: speak, for I desire to justify thee.

"If not, hearken unto me: hold thy peace, and I shall teach thee wisdom."

The position of Job has already been set forth to some extent, but whether the wisdom claimed by Elihu will exceed that of Job remains to be seen.

XXXIV. 1–6. "Furthermore Elihu answered and said,

"Hear my words, O ye wise *men;* and give ear unto me, ye that have knowledge.

"For the ear trieth words, as the mouth tasteth meat.

"Let us choose to us judgment: let us know among ourselves what *is* good.

"For Job hath said, I am righteous: and God hath taken away my judgment.

"Should I lie against my right? my wound *is* incurable without transgression."

What is Job's right? Job's right is his first estate; Job's right is that of a perfect and an upright man; he entered upon this right from the first day of his creation, and it was his. He was (see Gen. i. 31) pronounced very good by his Creator, and, hence, he was good; wherefore, as Elihu said, "Let us know among ourselves what *is* good," so the thing that is good is unmistakably brought before him in the person of Job as he stood in his right in the garden of Eden.

Why should Job's wound be incurable without transgression? It is because of the utter impossibility of the creature in his own strength to withstand the wiles of the Adversary, and to fulfil the Law in all its requirements. A perfect fulfilment of the Law would require infinite judgment; hence transgression through ignorance would certainly follow the judgment of the creature, whether man or angel; wherefore transgression may be sin, but not, of necessity, crime or heinous iniquity. Elihu continues,—

XXXIV. 7-9. "What man *is* like Job, *who* drinketh up scorning like water?

"Which goeth in company with the workers of iniquity, and walketh with wicked men.

"For he hath said, It profiteth a man nothing that he should delight himself with God."

Why should Job have given utterance to such an expression? It was to show the absolute futility of establishing life through free agency or righteousness by works under the Law; for as far as righteous works which spring from delight with God are concerned, they cannot redeem the transgressor from the penalty that surely rests upon him; neither, because of righteous works, can the creature claim perfect judgment in all things. The expression of Job does not condemn him, but, on the contrary, it stamps the immutability of the Law that was given for the government of all hosts. What construction does Elihu put upon Job's words? The context replies,—

XXXIV. 10-12. "Therefore hearken unto me, ye men of understanding: far be it from God, *that he should do* wickedness; and *from* the Almighty, *that he should commit* iniquity.

"For the work of a man shall he render unto him, and cause every man to find according to *his* ways.

"Yea, surely God will not do wickedly, neither will the Almighty pervert judgment."

Elihu clearly indicated (see xxxiii. 27, 28) that God would hear the repentant man; wherefore from Elihu's stand-point the inference is manifest that it doth profit a man should he delight himself with God; hence Elihu condemns the utterance of Job as a scornful expression, and, as being such, that God will not pervert his judgment by clearing Job or by sustaining him in his utterance. Elihu's statement, however (see xxxiii. 23-28), which substantially sets forth the claim that

God delivers the repentant from death because of his repentance, is contrary to the Law; for repentance cannot redeem the transgressor from death, but repentance may become one proof of the transgressor's faith in a Redeemer: of a Redeemer, however, Elihu says nothing. Repentance profits a man nothing so far as redemption itself is concerned, for nothing can take the place of the Redeemer; hence of the two Job's expression is the more justifiable, but that of Elihu is open to great question. The judgment and justice of the Almighty will not be perverted should Job obtain renewed life; for Job stated (xix. 26, 27), "And *though* after my skin *worms* destroy this *body*, yet in my flesh shall I see God: whom I shall see for myself, and mine eyes shall behold, and not another; *though* my reins be consumed within me,"—which unquestionably implies that death will have covered him in fulfilment of the Law before his participation in this renewed life. Of the Almighty Elihu continues,—

XXXIV. 13–15. "Who hath given him a charge over the earth? or who hath disposed the whole world?

"If he set his heart upon man, *if* he gather unto himself his spirit and his breath;

"All flesh shall perish together, and man shall turn again unto dust."

By these statements Elihu indicates no return of the spirit of man to his tabernacle after death, even as in the philosophy of Eliphaz death seals the sum of existence for the creature; hence once dead, forever dead. Elihu continues,—

XXXIV. 16, 17. "If now *thou hast* understanding, hear this: hearken to the voice of my words.

"Shall even he that hateth right govern? and wilt thou condemn him that is most just?"

Now, although Job is a transgressor, yet, through faith, he believes that his Redeemer lives, and, hence, that through his Redeemer he shall live. From Elihu's stand-point the intelligence that is once dead through transgression is dead forever; for the Law killeth, but does not make alive; wherefore, considering the immutability of the Law, and that Job is a transgressor, Elihu's question, "Shall even he that hateth right govern?" from his own stand-point, is pertinent as far as appearance goes, for Job as a transgressor cannot govern, but the answer does not, of necessity, cast down Job or make void the basis of his faith; for the Redeemer does not redeem the transgressor through his power, simply, but through the absolute fulfilment of the Law in the body of sinful flesh that pertained to the transgressor, and which he took upon himself through the body that had been previously prepared for that purpose. In this light, therefore, Job said (ix. 22), "He destroyeth the perfect and the wicked," from which, evidently, Elihu accredits Job with condemning him (see text) that is most just. From Job's position, the just, the upright, the righteous, the innocent One must be condemned that the transgressor may live through his death. Elihu's questions do not unsettle or weaken Job's position in the least, although they are set forth with great plausibility. Elihu continues,—

XXXIV. 18, 19. "*Is it fit* to say to a king, *Thou art* wicked? *and* to princes, *Ye are* ungodly?

"*How much less to him* that accepteth not the persons

of princes, nor regardeth the rich more than the poor? for they all *are* the work of his hands."

In these verses Elihu sets forth the improbability of any redeemer arising to redeem the transgressor, for from his stand-point death through the Law has hold upon the transgressor only; hence Elihu essentially asks, How can the Redeemer die except he be a transgressor himself? The answer to this question finds solution through the priesthood of Melchizedek; by which the spirit of man is and was regenerated or born into the body of the Redeemer that was prepared for him suitable for this purpose. The indication now is clear that as the reasoning of Eliphaz, Bildad, and Zophar discarded all probability of the advent of the Redeemer, so also the reasoning of Elihu discards it, and, hence, with it the wonderful working of that most wonderful priesthood, the priesthood of Melchizedek. Elihu continues,—

XXXIV. 20–22. "In a moment shall they die, and the people shall be troubled at midnight, and pass away: and the mighty shall be taken away without hand.

"For his eyes *are* upon the ways of man, and he seeth all his goings.

"*There is* no darkness, nor shadow of death, where the workers of iniquity may hide themselves."

Thus by Elihu's reasoning death is annihilation; there is no shadow of death where the transgressor may hide himself; but Job holds to the shadow of death, to the semblance of death in a land of darkness wherein the transgressor may hide himself and bide the time of his Redeemer. Moreover, man being a compound of good and evil, the indication is clear that the Law cannot fulfil absolute, eternal death upon the transgressor because of the good that dwells within him, without bringing condemnation upon itself; hence there must be a shadow of death, that the transgressor under tribulation may find rest until one shall arise that shall separate the good from the evil. Elihu continues,—

XXXIV. 23. "For he will not lay upon man more *than right;* that he should enter into judgment with God."

By this verse Elihu, from his stand-point, brings to notice the compensation that may fall (see xxxiii. 23–28) to the transgressor through repentance. What is this compensation? It is (see xxxiii. 27, 28) a lengthening of the days of the repentant transgressor, that none may accuse God with injustice or with not rewarding a righteous act. By this system of reasoning, alternate transgression and repentance would make void the penalty of transgression; but this penalty must be considered; hence, when considered, the indications point to the sure fulfilment of the Law upon the transgressor notwithstanding his repentance. Elihu continues,—

XXXIV. 24–28. "He shall break in pieces mighty men without number, and set others in their stead.

"Therefore he knoweth their works, and he overturneth *them* in the night, so that they are destroyed.

"He striketh them as wicked men in the open sight of others;

"Because they turned back from him, and would not consider any of his ways: .

"So that they cause the cry of the poor to come unto him, and he heareth the cry of the afflicted."

The mighty men that are broken, according to the reasoning of Elihu, are those who repent not that their lives may be prolonged; when, therefore, such shall have been cut off, others will be set up in their stead, as witnessed in the apparent destruction of the races of men whose places became occupied (see Isa. xlviii.) by others newly created.

By this philosophy the Evil Kingdom will have an aggressive field of operation indefinite in extent, and all creatures will be in continual dread for fear their lives shall be taken away because of their transgression, while no means are hinted at whereby the creature may be redeemed from this dreadful bondage except it be by descent into actual and eternal death. This particular reasoning is also advanced by Bildad (see xviii. 16–20), and is to be classed with the miserable comfort with which he and his friends sought to console Job.

If Elihu is Satan transformed as man or as an angel of light, then his specious arguments fall with great weight upon the ears of his hearers, irrespective of host; for his great length of days as a transgressor gives strength and plausibility to his words, that the transgressor, irrespective of host, need not, of necessity, die because of his transgression; and that (see verse 27), should they turn back to the Almighty and consider his ways (see xxxiii. 27, 28), the Almighty would prolong their days. Elihu continues,—

XXXIV. 29, 30. "When he giveth quietness, who then can make trouble? and when he hideth *his* face, who then can behold him? whether *it be done* against a nation, or against a man only :

"That the hypocrite reign not, lest the people be ensnared."

These remarks are plausible; but can the transgressor look for quietness under the Law? Not at all; for the Law, with the penalties thereof, cannot be set aside from their rulings; hence a transgressor at ease does not indicate freedom from penalty; wherefore trouble can be made, and, under the ruling of the Law, during the natural life of the creature, trouble will be made.

The Law entered that the offence might abound, and not that sin should not be imputed; hence no justification from sin can be looked for by or through the Law. Moreover, the Law unquestionably condemns the transgressor to death ; wherefore from this immutable decree there is no escape, be the transgression small or great. It is true that when God gives quietness none can give trouble, but the words of Elihu are intended to apply to the transgressor in his transgression, whereby he may obtain ease or remission of sin through repentance; and that without repentance the transgressor will be banished forever from the face of the Almighty; whence it follows that Elihu's words are fallacious, tending rather to deceive the transgressor than to lead him into the true path of life.

Such being the case, the philosophy of Eliphaz, Bildad, Zophar, and Elihu fails to meet the reasoning of Job that goes far beyond the valley of the shadow of death, even to the beyond of the region of absolute death itself; for his immortal postulate, "I know *that* my Redeemer liveth," is the great key that unlocks the hidden and reveals to some extent (see Rom. xi. 33) "the depth of the riches both of the wisdom and knowledge of God," whereby quietness can be given and trouble can be averted; for none can arise from absolute death that can give trouble. Elihu continues,—

XXXIV. 31, 32. "Surely it is meet to be said unto God, I have borne *chastisement*, I will not offend *any more:*

"*That which* I see not teach thou me: if I have done iniquity, I will do no more."

Through these verses Elihu indicates a system of rewards and punishments during the natural life of the creature, irrespective of host; but the indication is clear that punishment or chastisement cannot redeem the creature from the ministration of death that pertains to the Law; for the overthrow of the Evil Kingdom depends upon the absolute immutability of the ministration of death pertaining to the Law; hence, although the creature shall surely die because of his transgression, yet his redemption, his absolute death, and his resurrection from absolute death, are made entirely possible through his Redeemer. The reasoning is weak that carries not the creature beyond the region of absolute death, while the light of to-day seeks to bridge the chasm left by the philosophy of Eliphaz, Bildad, Zophar, and Elihu. Elihu continues,—

XXXIV. 33. "*Should it be* according to thy mind? he will recompense it, whether thou refuse, or whether thou choose; and not I: therefore speak what thou knowest."

The words of Elihu indicate that the system of rewards and punishments comes from the Almighty and not from the Evil Kingdom. Which or how is it? The indications are that the Almighty established the Law for the punishment of the transgressor. It follows therefore that, inasmuch as the Almighty instituted the Law for this purpose, he himself is not the source of transgression, neither is the Law the source of transgression; hence the Law, not the Almighty, judges and recompenses the transgressor. If the Almighty is not the source of transgression, whence is it? or is transgression a sourceless abounding? To analyze an effect and say there is no cause seems to be a very curious deduction; so also to behold transgression and then to deny any source of transgression would seem to be very curious also; wherefore to deny the cause is to deny the effect, and to deny the source of transgression is to deny the transgression. If, however, the fire scorch, then a cause is evident, and if a transgression occur, then a source of transgression must exist, even though it be infinitely distant.

If the Law entered that the offence might abound, then the Law will recompense, and not the Evil Kingdom. To whom will the Law render recompense? To the transgressor. Who is the transgressor? He is one under the bondage of the Source of Transgression; hence the recompense that falls to the lot of the transgressor because of his transgression will fall also upon the Source of Transgression; whence it follows that, although the Law judges and the Almighty compensates through the Law, the necessity for such compensation really is brought about through the devices of the Evil Kingdom,—that is, through the devices of the Source of Transgression; hence the statement of

Elihu, "He will recompense it, whether thou refuse, or whether thou choose; and not I," is misleading; for, as already implied, compensation is brought about through the devices of Satan, in that he caused man to transgress; which compensation is death, although Elihu implies that it may be a system of chastisement during the natural life indefinitely lengthened because of repentance. Elihu continues,—

XXXIV. 34, 35. "Let men of understanding tell me, and let a wise man hearken unto me.

"Job hath spoken without knowledge, and his words *were* without wisdom."

In what way does Elihu consider that Job's words were without wisdom? He evidently considers that Job's words were without wisdom in that, notwithstanding his transgression, he looks forward to redemption from the absolute death that shall surely follow transgression; while from Elihu's stand-point chastisement and a lengthening of days during the natural life due to repentance are all that man can hope for. Elihu continues,—

XXXIV. 36, 37. "My desire *is that* Job may be tried unto the end, because of *his* answers for wicked men.

"For he addeth rebellion unto his sin, he clappeth *his hands* among us, and multiplieth his words against God."

Thus Satan, not satisfied with the tribulations that have already befallen Job, desires that he may be tried unto the end. Why? Elihu says, "Because of *his* answers for wicked men." Job's answers for wicked men, however, embody the hopes of the transgressor for his redemption from the absolute death that follows through the Law; they are answers overflowing with comfort for the creature that suffers tribulation and sorrow during his natural life, but at the same time they overwhelm the Kingdom of Evil till it stands tottering on the eve of its eternal downfall.

Are Job's answers rebellion against God? are they a multiplicity of words against the Almighty? Far from it; but, on the contrary, they are based upon the promises that were revealed later unto Abraham that (see Gen. xxii. 16-18) " in thy seed shall all the nations of the earth be blessed ;" which seed (see Gal. iii. 16) is Christ.

XXXV. 1-3. "Elihu spake moreover, and said,

"Thinkest thou this to be right, *that* thou saidst, My righteousness *is* more than God's?

"For thou saidst, What advantage will it be unto thee? *and*, What profit shall I have, *if I be cleansed from my sin?*"

The words which Elihu credits Job with having spoken were (see xxi. 14, 15) substantially uttered by him; but Job was then describing a prosperous wicked man, while at the same time (see xxi. 16) he repudiated their counsel. Now, although Job was under transgression, he was not prosperous; no, on the contrary, he was overwhelmed with affliction; hence the words of Job do not apply to Job. The prosperous wicked man did not claim for himself even righteousness, still less that he was more righteous than God. Elihu, however, construes the words of Job against him, in that he is a transgressor, and that, as such, he comes under his own definition of what a wicked man really is. Job clearly states (ix. 20), "If I justify myself, mine own mouth shall condemn me: *if I say*, I *am* perfect, it shall also prove me perverse." Wherefore, then, the construction given by Elihu? more especially since Job said (ix. 30, 31), "If I wash myself with snow water, and make my hands never so clean; yet shalt thou plunge me in the ditch, and mine own clothes shall abhor me." The indication is clear that, under the Law, the service of the creature to his God cannot redeem him from transgression; which view is taken by Job; but this view does not imply that Job is more righteous than God, or that Job stands in no need of a Redeemer, or that Job feels in any degree the measure of happiness of the Almighty as the Supreme Unity. Elihu continues,—

XXXV. 4-7. "I will answer thee, and thy companions with thee.

"Look unto the heavens, and see; and behold the clouds *which* are higher than thou.

"If thou sinnest, what doest thou against him? or *if* thy transgressions be multiplied, what doest thou unto him?

"If thou be righteous, what givest thou him? or what receiveth he of thine hand?"

The creature was not brought forth to increase the pleasure or happiness of the Almighty; he was already perfect in every particular and needed nothing to complete his perfection; hence the creature was brought forth that it might enter into this happiness and enjoy the gifts showered upon him by the beneficent Provider. Wherefore it follows that the Almighty cannot derive profit, advantage, pleasure, pain, or any such thing in his being from any source outside of his own excellence as the Supreme Unity. As a Person of the Trinity, however, conditions may arise in which God can enter into the work, pleasures, and pains of his creatures, can make himself visible unto them, and can derive both advantage and profit from his labors; but the philosophy that indiscriminately condemns the creature to absolute death at the end of his natural life, and from which no recall is possible, sweeps one of the brightest jewels from the King's great crown, and leaves the setting but a hiding-place for dross. Elihu continues,—

XXXV. 8. "Thy wickedness *may hurt* a man as thou *art;* and thy righteousness *may profit* the son of man."

This answer of Elihu indicates that the wickedness of man may hurt a man such as Job, and that the righteousness of man may profit the son of man; but that the wickedness and righteousness of man can add neither advantage nor profit to the Almighty as the Most High God; which in itself may be, and probably is, absolute truth; but through the triunity of the Most High the creature may be, and is, brought into a close relationship with the Almighty that carries with it, as a result, a Kingdom of Righteousness filled with intelligent souls that rejoice in the light, life, and gifts with which they are and will be endowed. The indication is strongly marked that Elihu discards or ignores the three Persons of the Trinity, and that, like Eliphaz, Bildad, and Zophar, he holds to the one God only, and hence that there is no Redeemer as the Second Person of the Trinity.

What profit, then, is it for man to deny himself and be righteous? From the stand-point of Eliphaz, the prescribed days of his natural life (see v. 18–26) will be accorded him for his righteousness; from Elihu's stand-point (see xxx. 23–29), righteousness, even though coupled with transgression, will, through the power of the Almighty, preserve the creature's life indefinitely; but, from Job's stand-point, righteousness is a proof of faith in the advent of One that shall redeem the creature from unrighteousness through the separation of the good from the evil, whereby an unblemished and eternal life may be secured to the creature. The proof of a matter may be considered as establishing the essence thereof; hence, as the proof is righteousness, so the kingdom to which Job looks forward will be the Kingdom of Righteousness.

The philosophy of Eliphaz terminates in oblivion for the creature; the philosophy of Elihu points to an indefinite length of days, but which will hold the creature subject to both good and evil; should the creature die, however, then that death would be absolute with no possibility of recall; Job's philosophy sets forth and confirms the absolute death of each and every creature under the Law that the Law may meet with absolute fulfilment upon each and every transgressor, irrespective of host. Through absolute death the good will be separated from the evil; for the Law does not condemn the good; hence, should the good be recalled, the Law could not say unto it, what doest thou here? but, should evil rise again from the dead, the ministration of death pertaining to the law could and would say unto it, what doest thou here? but if not, then the penalty of the Law would have been a vain entering, in that it could not retain evil in the pit of absolute death. By Job's philosophy the separation of the good from the evil is accomplished by the Redeemer, not by man himself, but by the Redeemer, by One that is without blemish, by One upon whom the Law has no hold; but if Job looked forward to no Redeemer, then his philosophy would possess little more strength than that of Eliphaz, of Bildad, or of Zophar. Elihu continues,—

XXXV. 9-11. "By reason of the multitude of oppressions they make *the oppressed* to cry: they cry out by reason of the arm of the mighty.

"But none saith, Where *is* God my maker, who giveth songs in the night:

"Who teacheth us more than the beasts of the earth, and maketh us wiser than the fowls of heaven?"

The arm of the mighty evidently is the Law; and by transgression under the Law oppressors find in the creature an aggressive field of operation. The oppressed, therefore, according to Elihu, cry out by reason of the Law, but none seek unto God their Maker for relief. Why should Elihu advance this position? It is, doubtless, because of the eminence of the Law as the ruling principle; and also that the profit pertaining to repentance may be brought into notice. Elihu continues,—

XXXV. 12. "There they cry, but none giveth answer, because of the pride of evil men."

The oppressed can find no relief from the Law in the Law. Why? Because of their transgression the Law cannot turn from its immutable penalty; moreover, the pride of evil men keeps the Law continually active, in that from Elihu's stand-point they will not repent. Elihu continues,—

XXXV. 13, 14. "Surely God will not hear vanity, neither will the Almighty regard it.

"Although thou sayest thou shalt not see him, *yet* judgment *is* before him; therefore trust thou in him."

By these verses Elihu indicates that the Almighty will not regard the transgressor who pays no heed to him, and that judgment is before such transgressor; Elihu therefore enjoins Job to trust in the Almighty. Why should Elihu enjoin Job to trust in the Almighty? It is that, through repentance, Job as a transgressor may have the days of his natural life indefinitely lengthened. Elihu continues,—

XXXV. 15, 16. "But now, because *it is* not *so*, he hath visited in his anger; yet he knoweth *it* not in great extremity:

"Therefore doth Job open his mouth in vain; he multiplieth words without knowledge."

Here Elihu indicates that the anger of the Almighty is visited against Job because of transgression, and that because he heeds not the system of repentance set forth by Elihu that the extreme penalty of the Law will be fulfilled upon him, which penalty from Elihu's stand-point is absolute, eternal death. Job, however, believes in a resurrection after absolute death through his Redeemer; hence, to Elihu Job's words are vain and without knowledge.

XXXVI. 1-4. "Elihu also proceeded, and said,

"Suffer me a little, and I will shew thee that *I have* yet to speak on God's behalf.

"I will fetch my knowledge from afar, and will ascribe righteousness to my Maker.

"For truly my words *shall* not *be* false: he that is perfect in knowledge *is* with thee."

If Elihu be Satan transformed, then the words of Elihu become the words of Satan; and if Elihu be Satan, then the indications which he advances pointing to the Almighty as being his Maker become weak, for Satan (see St. John viii. 44), although a murderer from the beginning, was not (see Rev. iii. 14) the beginning of the creation of God; hence the words of Elihu as Satan are unreliable, untrustworthy, a mixture of probabilities and improbabilities plausibly set forth, even as indicated by the text where Elihu implies that the Almighty is his Maker. Elihu continues,—

XXXVI. 5–12. "Behold, God *is* mighty, and despiseth not *any:* he *is* mighty in strength *and* wisdom.

"He preserveth not the life of the wicked: but giveth right to the poor.

"He withdraweth not his eyes from the righteous: but with kings *are they* on the throne; yea, he doth establish them for ever, and they are exalted.

"And if *they be* bound in fetters, *and* be holden in cords of affliction;

"Then he sheweth them their work, and their transgressions that they have exceeded.

"He openeth also their ear to discipline, and commandeth that they return from iniquity.

"If they obey and serve *him*, they shall spend their days in prosperity, and their years in pleasures.

"But if they obey not, they shall perish by the sword, and they shall die without knowledge."

It is true that God is mighty, that he is no respecter of persons, that he is mighty in strength and wisdom, that he preserveth not the life of the wicked, that he withdraweth not his eyes from the righteous; but who are the righteous that they, as Elihu claims, shall be exalted and established for ever? From Elihu's standpoint, the righteous are those who turn from their transgressions to obey the commandments of God, and to serve him, for by so doing (see verse 11) "they shall spend their days in prosperity, and their years in pleasures," while those obeying not "shall die without knowledge."

From the position as thus set forth no Redeemer would be required to establish length of days to the transgressor; for from Elihu's stand-point length of days is established through repentance; but the Law absolutely requires a consideration of the penalties carried with it, hence Job holds fast to his belief that a Redeemer is necessary to relieve man from the penalty that environs him through transgression. Wherefore the position of Job is the stronger of the two, in that he does consider the penalty without respect to person. Elihu, however, allows that the unrepentant transgressor shall die; but it follows that the death of the worst of the transgressors and the preservation of the better class of sin-tinctured beings will never abolish the Evil Kingdom or break down its vitality. Elihu continues,—

XXXVI. 13-15. "But the hypocrites in heart heap up wrath: they cry not when he bindeth them.

"They die in youth, and their life *is* among the unclean.

" He delivereth the poor in his affliction, and openeth their ears in oppression."

Elihu evidently intends these words for Job personally, for he continues,—

XXXVI. 16, 17. "Even so would he have removed thee out of the strait *into* a broad place, where *there is* no straitness; and that which should be set on thy table *should be* full of fatness.

" But thou hast fulfilled the judgment of the wicked : judgment and justice take hold *on thee*."

Job's integrity is his faith in his Redeemer, and as he will not give up his belief in redemption Elihu argues that he transgresses, in that he goes beyond the Law that was given for the government of all hosts. If, however, the Law were all, then Job's faith would be baseless; but the charges to the Four Ages of Man (see Rev. ii., iii.) point to more than repentance and reformation that life may be indefinitely conferred upon the transgressor. The indication is clear that repentance and reformation cannot redeem the transgressor and make void the Law, neither will the words of Job (see xxvii. 5) justify his friends through righteousness by works.

The tribulations that have come upon Job are no measure of the extent of his transgression; but they point to the immutability of the Law that environs the transgressor without regard to extent of transgression; hence Elihu's words, as the words of Satan, tend to deceive his hearers, whoever they may be, while, by their significance, the fear of death constantly strikes dismay in every soul that heeds them; wherefore Elihu's words convey the idea of absolute death without hope, but those of Job indicate absolute death with hope of renewed life through his Redeemer. Elihu continues,—

XXXVI. 18, 19. "Because *there is* wrath, *beware* lest he take thee away with *his* stroke: then a great ransom cannot deliver thee.

"Will he esteem thy riches? *no*, not gold, nor all the forces of strength."

Thus Elihu implies that when the penalty of transgression shall have been fulfilled upon the transgressor, even upon such a one as Job, that nothing can deliver him; "*no*, not gold, nor all the forces of strength;" hence, from Elihu's stand-point, absolute death is absolute, eternal annihilation.

Moreover, with Eliphaz, Bildad, and Zophar, also, death is an absolute eternal environment; there is, with them, no valley of the shadow of death in which the transgressor such as Job may hide and bide the day of his Redeemer. Descent into the valley of the shadow of death does not, however, relieve the transgressor from the penalty of transgression; but this penalty is paid by the absolute death of the Redeemer, into whose body man was and is born or regenerated through (see St. Mark xiv. 22) the communion or eating thereof. Elihu continues,—

XXXVI. 20, 21. "Desire not the night, when people are cut off in their place.

"Take heed, regard not iniquity: for this hast thou chosen rather than affliction."

Elihu accuses Job of transgression rather than righteousness; but he bases his charge (see verse 17) upon Job's afflictions rather than upon any heinous iniquity to which he can point; or, in other words, he bases his charge upon an effect rather than upon the cause.

The expression, "Desire not the night, when people are cut off in their place," indicates or points to Job's desire to rest awhile in the valley of the shadow of death; but from Elihu's stand-point the valley of the shadow of death is identical with absolute death; wherefore should the transgressor once enter therein he would be cut off in his place thenceforth forever; hence Elihu counsels Job to accept life with affliction rather than descend into the valley of the shadow of death with his hopes of returning from thence. Elihu continues,—

XXXVI. 22–25. "Behold, God exalteth by his power: who teacheth like him?

"Who hath enjoined him his way? or who can say, Thou hast wrought iniquity?

"Remember that thou magnify his work, which men behold.

"Every man may see it; man may behold *it* afar off."

In these verses Elihu points to God's rule over his creatures in their natural lives, but in no way does he imply the redemption of the transgressor through the assumption of the creature's iniquity by the Redeemer. Elihu continues,—

XXXVI. 26–28. "Behold, God *is* great, and we know *him* not, neither can the number of his years be searched out.

"For he maketh small the drops of water: they pour down rain according to the vapour thereof;

"Which the clouds do drop *and* distil upon man abundantly."

These verses point to the littleness of the creature in comparison with the greatness of the Almighty, and also that the creature's judgment is as his comparative magnitude. Elihu continues,—

XXXVI. 29, 30. "Also can *any* understand the spreadings of the clouds, *or* the noise of his tabernacle?

"Behold, he spreadeth his light upon it, and covereth the bottom of the sea."

These verses point to the hidden mystery connected with the calling of the creature, and also the mystery involved in the general purpose of the Almighty. Elihu continues,—

XXXVI. 31–33. "For by them judgeth he the people; he giveth meat in abundance.

"With clouds he covereth the light; and commandeth it *not to shine* by *the cloud* that cometh betwixt.

"The noise thereof sheweth concerning it, the cattle also concerning the vapour."

These verses still bear upon the mystery of the calling of man, and the mystery involved in the purpose of the Almighty. These verses also point to judgments and rulings that are brought upon the people in their natural lives (for Elihu recognizes no other than the natural life, be it one year or a myriad of years) through the agency of encompassing elements, of which one— viz., water—is particularly indicated. Elihu continues,—

XXXVII. 1–4. "At this also my heart trembleth, and is moved out of his place.

"Hear attentively the noise of his voice, and the sound *that* goeth out of his mouth.

"He directeth it under the whole heaven, and his lightning unto the ends of the earth.

"After it a voice roareth: he thundereth with the voice of his excellency; and he will not stay them when the voice is heard."

These verses point to the limitless extent and absolute supremacy of God's rule. Elihu continues,—

XXXVII. 5-13. "God thundereth marvellously with his voice; great things doeth he, which we cannot comprehend.

"For he saith to the snow, Be thou *on* the earth; likewise to the small rain, and to the great rain of his strength.

"He sealeth up the hand of every man; that all men may know his work.

"Then the beasts go into dens, and remain in their places.

"Out of the south cometh the whirlwind: and cold out of the north.

"By the breath of God frost is given: and the breadth of the waters is straitened.

"Also by watering he wearieth the thick cloud: he scattereth his bright cloud:

"And it is turned round about by his counsels: that they may do whatsoever he commandeth them upon the face of the world in the earth.

"He causeth it to come, whether for correction, or for his land, or for mercy."

In these verses Elihu continues his description of the wonderful power of God; all of which tends to convey the idea that he, Elihu, counsels Job with the best of intentions, and also that his plausible statements may possess greater weight with those cognizant of them; but at the same time he does not lose sight of his point that the elements encompassing the people are also for their correction; and if for correction, that they may turn from iniquity, and repent that a lengthening of days may fall to them.

Should the creature, because of his transgression, be blotted out of existence at once or at the time of his transgression, the Adversary would have no field of aggression; hence the reasoning of Elihu acknowledges the supreme power and leniency of the Almighty, and apparently harmonizes with the Law, yet it also preserves an aggressive field of operation for Satan's host. Elihu continues,—

XXXVII. 14-20. "Hearken unto this, O Job: stand still, and consider the wondrous works of God.

"Dost thou know when God disposed them, and caused the light of his cloud to shine?

"Dost thou know the balancings of the clouds, the wondrous works of him which is perfect in knowledge?

"How thy garments *are* warm, when he quieteth the earth by the south *wind?*

"Hast thou with him spread out the sky, *which is* strong, *and* as a molten lookingglass?

"Teach us what we shall say unto him; *for* we cannot order *our speech* by reason of darkness.

"Shall it be told him that I speak? if a man speak, surely he shall be swallowed up."

In these verses Elihu still points to the wondrous knowledge and power of the Almighty, and that he rules with a personal supervision over all things. The indications are well marked, however, that the Almighty as the Supreme Unity did not rest from his labors, and hence from his personal supervision, until after Job's day, or until after the creation of the Adam of the Fourth Race of Man. Elihu continues,—

XXXVII. 21-24. "And now *men* see not the bright light which *is* in the clouds: but the wind passeth, and cleanseth them.

"Fair weather cometh out of the north: with God *is* terrible majesty.

"*Touching* the Almighty, we cannot find him out: *he is* excellent in power, and in judgment, and in plenty of justice: he will not afflict.

"Men do therefore fear him: he respecteth not any *that are* wise of heart."

In these verses Elihu continues his record of the attributes of the Most High; but not a single word is to be found in his remarks that points to the advent of a Redeemer, or that points to any means whereby the transgressor may be delivered from the absolute death that shall cover him through the fatal ministration pertaining to the Law. Elihu said (xxxiii. 3), "My lips shall utter knowledge clearly," and he said (xxxiii. 33), "I shall teach thee wisdom." Wherein, then, lies the wisdom of Elihu? or where has Elihu shown true wisdom? He admits that the Almighty is the Creator, and he indicates that after the Almighty has exercised his creative power the creature is left to battle with a power far stronger than himself, and that, should he be overcome, tribulation will certainly fall to his lot; also that in many cases, even if not in all eventually, death will claim them forever as his own. Is this real and true wisdom? Would the Almighty thus bring forth multitudes to become the sport and prey of a rival power, with no possibility of redemption? Job utterly rejects the position, and refuses (see xvi. 1–4) to call such reasoning wisdom.

The words of Elihu seem to be directed more particularly to the Gentile Host that is under bondage to him, the host (see Heb. ii. 14, 15) which, through fear of death, "were all their lifetime subject to bondage." The Gentiles may be endowed with great length of days, so that the statements of Elihu would, to them, appear to carry great weight; for repentance for transgression might be construed as the reason why the penalty of transgression was not at once fulfilled upon the transgressor, or as the reason why the natural life of the creature was extended; hence Satan preaches righteousness, or is transformed (see 2 Cor. xi. 13, 14) as an angel of light, that, through his assumed righteousness and his plausibility, great hosts may be misled and an aggressive field thus kept before him.

Should, however, from Elihu's stand-point, the penalty of transgression be fully carried out at once, then the ante-creative situation would become re-established, and the plans of the Almighty for the happiness of creature intelligencies would have been planned in vain. Is, therefore, the situation thus indicated the result of far-reaching wisdom? does it embody the end and aim of the Almighty King of Glory? Wherein is essential Evil vitally touched by it? Wherein is the earth, and every living thing that moves upon the face thereof, subjugated by it? The indications are that the deductions and teachings of Elihu are almost wholly at variance with the plan of the Almighty for the overthrow of Evil, and for the redemption of the Fallen; and, hence, are deductions and teachings that do not answer Job, or throw down his great postulate, "I know *that* my Redeemer liveth."

XXXVIII. 1, 2. "Then the Lord answered Job out of the whirlwind, and said,

"Who *is* this that darkeneth counsel by words without knowledge?"

This record evidently applies to Elihu, and it condemns the words of Elihu as darkening counsel by defective deduction and by teachings that tend to mislead the hearer away from the true light.

XXXVIII. 3, 4. "Gird up now thy loins like a man; for I will demand of thee, and answer thou me.

"Where wast thou when I laid the foundations of the earth? declare, if thou hast understanding."

At the time the foundations of the earth were laid Job was (see Rōm. viii. 28–30) already foreknown; and those whom the Almighty foreknew he predestinated to be conformed to the image of the Son. The Son is the Word, or the Assenting Power of the Infinite Majesty or of the Supreme Unity, and, hence (see St. John i. 1, 2), was in the beginning with God, and, in the infinite beyond, was God. For the Word a body (see Heb. x. 5; Ps. xl. 7) was prepared, which body (see Col. i. 15; Rev. iii. 14) was the first-born of every creature, and the beginning of the creation of God. When the Word invested this body it became (see Rev. xii. 1–4; Ps. xxii. 10) the only begotten Son, and, consequently, as such was God. This body, therefore, that is a creature, and the first-born of all creatures, is the body to which man by predestination is to be conformed; wherefore it follows that he is not made conformable to that wherein the Word of God dwelt previous to his advent as the Son. This body really appears to be the foundation of the earth,—the indestructible body that is without blemish, the chief corner-stone (see Eph. ii. 20–22), upon which all the light and life of the creature world is supported and borne up; hence, although Job was the Adam and progenitor of the Third Race of Men, yet (see 2 Cor. v. 1, 2) the building of God, the house not made with hands, eternal in the heavens, was in Job's day an actual presence as the body that was prepared for the Son that he might do the will of God; hence, again, Job was not in existence when the great foundation of the earth was laid; but Job's material body was formed from the earth or matter otherwise that was created later. The Lord answers Job,—

XXXVIII. 5–7. "Who hath laid the measures thereof, if thou knowest? or who hath stretched the line upon it?

"Whereupon are the foundations thereof fastened? or who laid the corner stone thereof;

"When the morning stars sang together, and all the sons of God shouted for joy?"

The great Foundation, the Chief Corner-Stone, having been indicated and brought into notice, who can lay a measure upon the building thereof, or who (see Zech. ii. 1–5) can stretch a line upon it? None; for "Jerusalem shall be inhabited *as* towns without walls for the multitude of men and cattle therein;" hence the material foundations of the earth are fastened upon the body that was previously prepared for the Son; for (see Zech. ii. 5), "For I, saith the Lord, . . . will be the glory in the midst of her" (Jerusalem), and (see Rev. xxi.) "the Lamb is the light thereof." Is it any wonder, therefore, that the morning stars sang together and the sons of God shouted for joy when they comprehended the indestructibility of the Foundation upon which they were builded? Not at all; wherefore the indications follow that the foundations of the earth are fastened upon the immutable will of the Supreme Unity which gave his Word, in the Person of the only begotten Son, for the Chief Corner-Stone that the immutable will be performed. The Lord further questions Job,—

XXXVIII. 8–11. "Or *who* shut up the sea with doors, when it brake forth, *as if* it had issued out of the womb?

"When I made the cloud the garment thereof, and thick darkness a swaddling band for it,

"And brake up for it my decreed *place*, and set bars and doors,

"And said, Hitherto shalt thou come, but no further: and here shall thy proud waves be stayed?"

The sea evidently shadows the Evil Kingdom which (see Rev. xii. 13–17) sought to overwhelm man with its destructive flood; but as the earth opened her mouth and swallowed up the flood, so the place is decreed and opened for the Evil Kingdom that it shall go thus far and no farther; hence the bars and doors that stay the proud waves thereof are the Ages or Times, the bounds of which are set beyond all change, they (see Acts xvii.

26; Deut. xxxii. 8) having been before appointed and set by the Most High.

The cloud-garment points to the valley of the shadow of death that shall envelop the sin-tinctured creature, but the thick darkness indicates the absolute death that shall cover all (see ix. 22), both the perfect and the wicked. The Lord further questions Job,—

XXXVIII. 12, 13. "Hast thou commanded the morning since thy days; *and* caused the dayspring to know his place;

"That it might take hold of the ends of the earth, that the wicked might be shaken out of it?"

The dayspring (see St. Luke i. 78, 79) is the Messiah; the Messiah is the Son; and the Son is the Word, for whom a body was prepared that he might do the will of God; which will (see St. Luke i. 78, 79) is that, through the dayspring, light may shine upon them that sit in darkness and in the shadow of death, and also (see text) that the wicked might be shaken out of the earth. The text continues,—

XXXVIII. 14, 15. "It is turned as clay *to* the seal; and they stand as a garment.

"And from the wicked their light is withholden, and the high arm shall be broken."

Thus the earth in the hand of the Almighty is as the clay to the seal; and, hence, the earth, in the hand of the Almighty, points to instrumentality in the sure overthrow of the wicked. The Lord further questions Job,—

XXXVIII. 16. "Hast thou entered into the springs of the sea? or hast thou walked in the search of the depth?"

Who can point to the source of evil and say, Here is the beginning and here is the fountain-head thereof? Who can search out the depth of evil and say, I know whence it comes? Not one; for evil dwells not with the Almighty, neither was it brought forth by the Most High; wherefore it follows, even as the text implies, that the source of evil existed throughout the infinite past. This verse may also point to the fulness of the Supreme Unity. The Lord further questions Job,—

XXXVIII. 17. "Have the gates of death been opened unto thee? or hast thou seen the doors of the shadow of death?"

The indications are that Job comprehended to some extent both absolute death and the shadow or semblance of death; the two great and wonderful conditions of darkness that befall all creatures, the perfect as well as wicked. Job's belief in these two conditions is clearly set forth, while his faith in his Redeemer is unmistakably made manifest. In his own person Job has not seen the doors of the shadow of death, neither have the gates of absolute death been opened unto him; yet his reasoning and his utterances are far beyond those of his friends, who could find no better fate for the creature than absolute death after the years of the natural life had been fulfilled. The Lord further questions Job,—

XXXVIII. 18. "Hast thou perceived the breadth of the earth? declare if thou knowest it all."

The breadth of the earth (see Gen. i. 1–7) takes in and includes all matter, from the great spheroid on which man dwells and has his home to the most distant invisibility, not one atom of which can proclaim an independent existence; for far-reaching ties bind it to the mass that nothing be amiss, and that no promise, whether for good or for evil, shall fail to seal it. The Lord further questions Job,—

XXXVIII. 19–21. "Where *is* the way *where* light dwelleth? and *as for* darkness, where *is* the place thereof,

"That thou shouldest take it to the bound thereof, and that thou shouldest know the paths *to* the house thereof?

"Knowest thou *it*, because thou wast then born? or *because* the number of thy days *is* great?"

Thus neither the source of light nor the source of darkness, the source of good nor the source of evil, can be traced: they existed far beyond the call of the creature as independent conditions or attributes pertaining to separate and independent Powers; hence no creature can trace the way of light to its utmost bound, be his days ever so great; neither can he discern the house wherein evil first realized vitality. The Lord further questions Job,—

XXXVIII. 22, 23. "Hast thou entered into the treasures of the snow? or hast thou seen the treasures of the hail,

"Which I have reserved against the time of trouble, against the day of battle and war?"

These verses point to the Judgmental Era, during which time (see Rev. xvi. 17–21) great tribulation will come upon the Evil Host for their transgression, and at which time great signs and wonders will be wrought among them. The Lord further questions Job,—

XXXVIII. 24. "By what way is the light parted, *which* scattereth the east wind upon the earth?"

Job pertains to the Third Age, and the east points to the Second, the people of which are on the eve of destruction; wherefore, by what way is the light parted, or by what way is the good separated from the evil that pertains to the people of the Second Age? This question involves consideration of the plan for the redemption of man; and that such a plan exists Job certifies where he states, "I know *that* my Redeemer liveth." By this plan the people of the Second Age are redeemed from their bondage to death through Job's Redeemer, who, later, in his body separated the good from the evil, paid the penalty of their transgression, and rose again from the dead, bringing them back with him clothed with the perfect body into which they had been regenerated. The Lord further questions Job,—

XXXVIII. 25–27. "Who hath divided a watercourse for the overflowing of waters, or a way for the lightning of thunder;

"To cause it to rain on the earth, *where* no man *is; on* the wilderness, wherein *there is* no man;

"To satisfy the desolate and waste *ground;* and to cause the bud of the tender herb to spring forth?"

These verses point to the plan of redemption in which others than man of Adam's race are concerned. The watercourse indicates the flow of Living Water (see Ezek. xlvii. 1–9) that shall bring healing whithersoever the river cometh. This watercourse is prepared by the Almighty in his wonderful plan for the redemption of his creatures, and he alone has directed its way. Through the flow of Living Water the desolate and waste places will be rebuilt and filled with rejoicing. The Lord further questions Job,—

XXXVIII. 28–30. "Hath the rain a father? or who hath begotten the drops of dew?

"Out of whose womb came the ice? and the hoary frost of heaven, who hath gendered it?

"The waters are hid as *with* a stone, and the face of the deep is frozen."

Thus reward for the good, and compensation for the evil, is comprehended in the great plan of the Almighty for the overthrow of Evil, and for the establishment of the Kingdom of Righteousness in which no evil thought or action can ever find place. Job's attention is also called to the Almighty as the Creator. The Lord further questions Job,—

XXXVIII. 31, 32. "Canst thou bind the sweet influences of Pleiades, or loose the bands of Orion?

"Canst thou bring forth Mazzaroth in his season? or canst thou guide Arcturus with his sons?"

In consideration of the day in which Job lived, it is quite probable that the four constellations mentioned in the text are those which grace the heavens with a line of glory, commencing with Pleiades and ending with Sirius and his surrounding lesser lights; however, be Mazzaroth the same with the signs of the zodiac instead of Taurus, and be the Arcturus of Job the same with the Arcturus of to-day, the indications remain that, inasmuch as the times and orbits of these constellations cannot be changed, influenced, or bound, they are under the absolute government of a mighty Power that is infinitely supreme; hence by the order of their march the inanimate bear witness of their Maker and

Governor, not conqueror; while at the same time free agency is established in the animate and intelligent that the qualities of both good and evil may be proved, and also that the fitness or unfitness of the creature as a self-governing intelligence worthy of life may be fully demonstrated. Free agency under the Law was also established that the offence might abound and judgment be rendered against all evil-doers, irrespective of host, so that eventually evil could be wholly blotted out never to return. The Lord further questions Job,—

XXXVIII. 33–35. "Knowest thou the ordinances of heaven? canst thou set the dominion thereof in the earth?

"Canst thou lift up thy voice to the clouds, that abundance of waters may cover thee?

"Canst thou send lightnings, that they may go, and say unto thee, Here we *are?*"

The indications are perfectly clear that neither Job nor any creature can grasp all the ordinances of heaven that they should be obedient unto him. In the drought he is powerless, and in the flood he is without strength. How, then, can man, the creature man, hope, either now or in the indefinite future, to rise above the heavens that they should obey him? How can he hope to bind the flood, to stay the drought, to check the fire, that they should acknowledge him their master? The Lord further questions Job,—

XXXVIII. 36–38. "Who hath put wisdom in the inward parts? or who hath given understanding to the heart?

"Who can number the clouds in wisdom? or who can stay the bottles of heaven,

"When the dust groweth into hardness, and the clods cleave fast together?"

Even though the elements were obedient to Job, where would he find wisdom enough, where would he gain understanding enough, that no error of judgment bring suffering upon the innocent? Would such perfection develop of itself? If so, what would prevent a corresponding development of evil in its own line? Nothing; hence it follows that the separation of the good from the evil through development, simply, would be a vain measure; for evil, as an independent energy, could sting the good, however great the excellency thereof might be (see xx. 4-7), quite as readily as the cobra's deadly fang stings its victim. The Lord further questions Job,—

XXXVIII. 39-41. "Wilt thou hunt the prey for the lion? or fill the appetite of the young lions,

"When they couch in *their* dens, *and* abide in the covert to lie in wait?

"Who provideth for the raven his food? when his young ones cry unto God, they wander for lack of meat."

Here the insufficiency of Job as a provider is indicated and set forth. How, then, can man hope to be filled with wisdom so that none go hungry or that none lack for meat? He cannot; for countless myriads of creatures daily wait the food which only infinite wisdom can supply; yet Job, in his blindness and righteousness under the Law (see xxix. 14-25), thought to have sat as chief among men, and to have dwelt as a king in the army; he thought to have gained life, and to have filled the mission of man as subjugator, provider, and counsellor. The Lord further questions Job,—

XXXIX. 1–4. "Knowest thou the time when the wild goats of the rock bring forth? *or* canst thou mark when the hinds do calve?

"Canst thou number the months *that* they fulfil? or knowest thou the time when they bring forth?

"They bow themselves, they bring forth their young ones, they cast out their sorrows.

"Their young ones are in good liking, they grow up with corn; they go forth, and return not unto them."

If Job knows not when the wild goats bring forth, or if he knows not when the hinds calve, how can he be a watchful guardian over the interests of the creature? The indication is clear that he cannot. What then? is there no head to rule and govern these things? and will no head ever exist except it be in the indefinite future? The order and regularity observable and calculable in the movements of the inanimate creature (see xxxiii. 31–35) carry proof that there is a head that rules and governs; which head the Scriptures reveal as the Sublime Unity, the Living God, the Infinite Majesty, that is perfect, upright, and just in all his attributes. The Lord further questions Job,—

XXXIX. 5–8. "Who hath sent out the wild ass free? or who hath loosed the bands of the wild ass?

"Whose house I have made the wilderness, and the barren land his dwellings.

"He scorneth the multitude of the city, neither regardeth he the crying of the driver.

"The range of the mountains *is* his pasture, and he searcheth after every green thing."

These verses, as allegory, appear to shadow the calling and mission of the creature. Can Job hope thus to bring forth? The Lord further questions Job,—

XXXIX. 9–12. "Will the unicorn be willing to serve thee, or abide by thy crib?

"Canst thou bind the unicorn with his band in the furrow? or will he harrow the valleys after thee?

"Wilt thou trust him, because his strength *is* great? or wilt thou leave thy labour to him?

"Wilt thou believe him, that he will bring home thy seed, and gather *it into* thy barn?"

Through the unicorn the Adversary is indicated; will, therefore (see remarks of Elihu), the Adversary gather Job's seed into Job's barn? The indications are that he will not; for after causing Job excessive tribulation he said (see xxxiv. 36), "My desire *is that* Job may be tried unto the end;" hence Job cannot trust in him, neither can he bind him nor bring him into servitude. The Lord further questions Job,—

XXXIX. 13–18. "*Gavest thou* the goodly wings unto the peacocks? or wings and feathers unto the ostrich?

"Which leaveth her eggs in the earth, and warmeth them in the dust,

"And forgetteth that the foot may crush them, or that the wild beast may break them.

"She is hardened against her young ones, as though *they were* not hers: her labour is in vain without fear;

"Because God hath deprived her of wisdom, neither hath he imparted to her understanding.

"What time she lifteth up herself on high, she scorneth the horse and his rider."

Through the ostrich a host other than man of Adam's race appears to be indicated, while the horse and rider (see Rev. vi. 1–8) point to man of Adam's race. It will be seen from the text that the young ostrich must have a protector and a provider, for the parent bird cares nothing for it; hence the host shadowed by the ostrich, be it what or which it may, is sintinctured, and, hence, is a compound of both good and evil. The Lord further questions Job,—

XXXIX. 19–25. "Hast thou given the horse strength? hast thou clothed his neck with thunder?

"Canst thou make him afraid as a grasshopper? the glory of his nostrils *is* terrible.

"He paweth in the valley, and rejoiceth in *his* strength: he goeth on to meet the armed men.

"He mocketh at fear, and is not affrighted; neither turneth he back from the sword.

"The quiver rattleth against him, the glittering spear and the shield.

"He swalloweth the ground with fierceness and rage: neither believeth he that *it is* the sound of the trumpet.

"He saith among the trumpets, Ha, ha! and he smelleth the battle afar off, the thunder of the captains, and the shouting."

The horse (see Rev. vi. 1–8) is indicative of man of Adam's race, and man of Adam's race (see Gen. i. 27, 28) was called as an instrumentality for the subjugation of the earth, and of every living thing that moved upon it; hence as Satan (see Gen. iii.) was present in the earth with man, so he, as the Adversary and Enemy of God, was to be subjugated also. Thus man of Adam's race from the first was called forth (see also 2 Sam. i. 25–27) as "a weapon of war" in the great battle for the overthrow of Evil. In this battle fell Saul and Jonathan, both marvellous horses of war, of whom it is said (2 Sam. i. 21–27), "Ye mountains of Gilboa, *let there be* no dew, neither *let there be* rain, upon you, nor fields of offerings: for there the shield of the mighty is vilely cast away, the shield of Saul, *as though he had* not *been* anointed with oil. From the blood of the slain, from the fat of the mighty, the bow of Jonathan turned not back, and the sword of Saul returned not empty. . . . How are the mighty fallen in the midst of the battle! . . . How are the mighty fallen, and the weapons of war perished!" The Lord further questions Job,—

XXXIX. 26–30. "Doth the hawk fly by thy wisdom, *and* stretch her wings toward the south?

"Doth the eagle mount up at thy command, and make her nest on high?

"She dwelleth and abideth on the rock, upon the crag of the rock, and the strong place.

"From thence she seeketh the prey, *and* her eyes behold afar off.

"Her young ones also suck up blood: and where the slain *are*, there *is* she."

Now although man is called as a weapon of war in the great battle for the overthrow of Evil, yet inasmuch as the hawk does not fly by the wisdom of man, nor does the eagle mount up at his command, so the indication is given that man, in himself, cannot subjugate the powerful Adversary that roams the earth (see i. 7; ii. 2) at his will.

XL. 1, 2. "Moreover the Lord answered Job, and said,

"Shall he that contendeth with the Almighty instruct *him?* he that reproveth God, let him answer it."

How can a man contend with the Almighty that he should instruct him? Man can contend with the Almighty in this,—viz., that he, man, should seek to secure eternal life through his own free agency as a perfect and an upright man, or to secure eternal life through righteousness by works. Such a one reproves God in that untold multitudes of God's creatures under transgression (see philosophy of Eliphaz, Bildad, and Zophar) would perish without a single ray of hope leading to deliverance. Should one creature be strong enough to obtain eternal life through the Law, then all creatures might ask why did he not create us strong enough also that we might live? hence indications come out clearly that no law (see Gal. iii. 21) was given that could develop perfect righteousness in the creature.

XL. 3-5. "Then Job answered the Lord, and said,

"Behold, I am vile; what shall I answer thee? I will lay mine hand upon my mouth.

"Once have I spoken; but I will not answer: yea, twice; but I will proceed no further."

Thus Job will bring forward his righteousness no more; he will not answer the Almighty with his righteousness that he should reprove him; on the contrary, he now acknowledges that he is vile; for the words of the Lord have shown him the utter inability of the creature to create, govern, order, subdue, provide, protect, or to deliver, when such magnitudes are or shall be called for.

XL. 6-8. "Then answered the Lord unto Job out of the whirlwind, and said,

"Gird up thy loins now like a man: I will demand of thee, and declare thou unto me.

"Wilt thou also disannul my judgment? wilt thou condemn me, that thou mayest be righteous?"

Job claimed for himself (see xxix. 14-25), because of his righteousness, days multiplied as the sand; but now the indication becomes manifest that this claim disannuls the judgment of the Lord, in that eternal life is obtainable independent of the Lord; whereas eternal life is a free gift of the Almighty; none being able in themselves to reach the standard of excellence and perfection that can and will confer it. The Lord further questions Job,—

XL. 9-14. "Hast thou an arm like God? or canst thou thunder with a voice like him?

"Deck thyself now *with* majesty and excellency; and array thyself with glory and beauty.

"Cast abroad the rage of thy wrath: and behold every one *that is* proud, and abase him.

"Look on every one *that is* proud, *and* bring him low; and tread down the wicked in their place.

"Hide them in the dust together; *and* bind their faces in secret.

"Then will I also confess unto thee that thine own right hand can save thee."

If Job is, in himself, perfect and upright enough to be endowed with eternal life, then, even as the text demands, let him arise from his dust and sackcloth, and deck himself in excellence, glory, and beauty. The indications are clear enough that he cannot; therefore he is not righteous enough in himself to grasp and wear the crown of eternal life. Even though he were righteous enough to obtain eternal life through his own works, yet the great command (see Gen. i. 28) given for the subjugation of Evil would remain unfulfilled; wherefore through this unfulfilment Job, although righteous as far as his own actions were concerned, would fail to obtain the crown of life; hence it follows that he only who is perfectly upright and righteous, who can cast down evil in all its ramifications, who can govern, order, subdue, provide, protect, and deliver, whenever and wherever such magnitudes may be called for, shall win and wear the crown of eternal life. The Lord further answers Job,—

XL. 15–24. "Behold now behemoth, which I made with thee; he eateth grass as an ox.

"Lo now, his strength *is* in his loins, and his force *is* in the navel of his belly.

"He moveth his tail like a cedar: the sinews of his stones are wrapped together.

"His bones *are as* strong pieces of brass; his bones *are* like bars of iron.

"He *is* the chief of the ways of God: he that made him can make his sword to approach *unto him*.

"Surely the mountains bring him forth food, where all the beasts of the field play.

"He lieth under the shady trees, in the covert of the reed, and fens.

"The shady trees cover him *with* their shadow; the willows of the brook compass him about.

"Behold, he drinketh up a river, *and* hasteth not: he trusteth that he can draw up Jordan in his mouth.

"He taketh it with his eyes: *his* nose pierceth through snares."

The behemoth of the text seems to shadow the locomotive engine as it existed in the day of Job; not that it was the conception of Job, but, rather, that it was the conception of the Second or Hiddekelic race, which, for a time, was contemporary with Job. This wonderful machine—fitted as it was with bones of brass and with bones of iron; that consumed the wood of the mountain and the coal of the valley; that madly dashed across the well-marked plain or loitered where the reed and fens and willows of the brook encompassed it; whose thirsty mouth drained the bountiful supply of water that glittered here and there in its pathway—became lost to sight and had passed entirely out of remembrance when the Adam of the Fourth race was called into existence. The endowments, however, which developed from the inanimate this wonderful semblance of life came from the Almighty; whereby the indication is strongly marked that God's purposes are frequently carried out through instrumentalities, and that the creature, as an instrumentality, finds pleasure, employment, and profit in fulfilling the ways of God; hence (see 1 Cor. xii. 4) "there are diversities of gifts, but the same Spirit," that the purposes of God may be fulfilled, and the creature be made happy in the gifts with which he is endowed. The Lord further questions Job,—

XLI. 1–11. "Canst thou draw out leviathan with a hook? or his tongue with a cord *which* thou lettest down?

"Canst thou put a hook into his nose? or bore his jaw through with a thorn?

"Will he make many supplications unto thee? will he speak soft *words* unto thee?

"Will he make a covenant with thee? wilt thou take him for a servant for ever?

"Wilt thou play with him as *with* a bird? or wilt thou bind him for thy maidens?

"Shall the companions make a banquet of him? shall they part him among the merchants?

"Canst thou fill his skin with barbed irons? or his head with fish spears?

"Lay thine hand upon him, remember the battle, do no more.

"Behold, the hope of him is in vain: shall not *one* be cast down even at the sight of him?

"None *is* so fierce that dare stir him up: who then is able to stand before me?

"Who hath prevented me, that I should repay *him?* whatsoever *is* under the whole heaven is mine."

Under the guise of some great sea-monster the iron-clad war-vessel is now shadowed forth. The leviathan as a vessel of war was also developed by the creature through the endowments with which he was gifted. Who, therefore, among men can stand up against such a ponderous exhibition of strength? much less can one stand up against the Source and Giver of such marvellous skill. The context continues with a description of this wondrous embodiment of genius, as follows:

XLI. 12-34. "I will not conceal his parts, nor his power, nor his comely proportion.

" Who can discover the face of his garment? *or* who can come *to him* with his double bridle?

" Who can open the doors of his face? his teeth *are* terrible round about.

" *His* scales *are his* pride, shut up together *as with* a close seal.

" One is so near to another, that no air can come between them.

" They are joined one to another, they stick together, that they cannot be sundered.

" By his neesings a light doth shine, and his eyes *are* like the eyelids of the morning.

" Out of his mouth go burning lamps, *and* sparks of fire leap out.

" Out of his nostrils goeth smoke, as *out* of a seething pot or caldron.

" His breath kindleth coals, and a flame goeth out of his mouth.

" In his neck remaineth strength, and sorrow is turned into joy before him.

" The flakes of his flesh are joined together: they are firm in themselves; they cannot be moved.

" His heart is as firm as a stone; yea, as hard as a piece of the nether *millstone.*

" When he raiseth up himself, the mighty are afraid: by reason of breakings they purify themselves.

" The sword of him that layeth at him cannot hold: the spear, the dart, nor the habergeon.

" He esteemeth iron as straw, *and* brass as rotten wood.

" The arrow cannot make him flee: sling stones are turned with him into stubble.

"Darts are counted as stubble: he laugheth at the shaking of a spear.

"Sharp stones *are* under him: he spreadeth sharp pointed things upon the mire.

"He maketh the deep to boil like a pot: he maketh the sea like a pot of ointment.

"He maketh a path to shine after him; *one* would think the deep *to be* hoary.

"Upon earth there is not his like, who is made without fear.

"He beholdeth all high *things:* he *is* a king over all the children of pride."

Such is the description of the leviathan, and such a description fits the huge ironclad war-vessel of modern times, in whose neck as a great floating ram (see verse 22) remaineth strength. Thus in the day of Job, many years before the Adam of the Fourth Race was brought forth, high art and science were developed to a degree of excellence that is not surpassed even by the standard that exists to-day. All this excellent attainment, however, passed out of remembrance; it became lost to sight in the depopulation of the earth that took place in the day of Job, at which time the wise and learned Hiddekels were swept away because of their transgression and failure of mission. That such excellence did exist before the day of Solomon is confirmed as follows (Eccl. i. 9–11): "The thing that hath been, it *is that* which shall be; and that which is done *is* that which shall be done: and *there is* no new *thing* under the sun. Is there *any* thing whereof it may be said, See, this *is* new? it hath been already of old time, which was before us. *There is* no remembrance of former *things;* neither shall there be *any* remembrance of *things* that are to come with *those* that shall come after." Wherefore it follows that art and science were as far advanced in the day of Job as they are at the present time. The ironclad vessel of war and the locomotive engine, with its sweeping train, are marked specimens of the mechanical and scientific attainments of the Second or Hiddekelic race of men; the race with which Job was for a time contemporary; for Job, as the Adam and progenitor of the Third Race, was created before the destruction of the Second was fulfilled.

The description of the ironclad is so perfect that it must have been given by inspiration; for no indications are apparent that such conceptions were developed into accomplished facts prior to the advent of the present century. But if they did exist in the day of Job, then the day of Job must find place previous to the creation of the fourth Adam; and if previous to the creation of the fourth Adam, then the record (Eccl. vi. 10), "That which hath been is named already, and it is known that it *is* man: neither may he" (see Job xl. 2–5) "contend with him that is mightier than he," will apply to Job as the Adam of the Third Race of Men.

XLII. 1–3. "Then Job answered the Lord, and said,

"I know that thou canst do every *thing,* and *that* no thought can be withholden from thee.

"Who *is* he that hideth counsel without knowledge? therefore have I uttered that I understood not; things too wonderful for me, which I knew not."

In these verses Job acknowledges the infinite knowledge of the Almighty, and, hence, accords the infinite perfection of the Almighty as a Governor of all things that he alone should order, subdue, provide, protect, and deliver, whenever and wherever such may or might be called for.

The one that hideth counsel without knowledge is Satan, the powerful King of Evil; hence Job uttered things that he understood not, and so fell into transgression. It must be remembered that Job (see xxix. 14–25) thought to multiply his days as the sand through self-righteousness or righteousness by works; but the words of the Almighty opened his eyes to the greatness of those who shall be considered worthy of eternal life through their own works; for not only righteous thought and action are called for, but the casting down and the complete overthrow of every wicked thing is called for also. Inasmuch, however, as Job did not fully recognize or know the one that hid counsel without knowledge, evidently Elihu, he was not able, from his own statement, to subdue Evil in all its indefinite reach. Job continues,—

XLII. 4–6. "Hear, I beseech thee, and I will speak: I will demand of thee, and declare thou unto me.

"I have heard of thee by the hearing of the ear; but now mine eye seeth thee:

"Wherefore I abhor *myself*, and repent in dust and ashes."

Thus Job now more fully comprehends the greatness of the one that shall be the Subjugator and Ruler; wherefore, throwing aside all thought of obtaining life through free agency or righteousness by works, he abhors himself for his misapplied righteousness and repents in dust and ashes. It must be kept in mind, however, that Job, after his transgression and when evil had befallen him, did acknowledge and proclaim that his Redeemer lived, and that eventually, even after death, he should behold him; by which the attributes of God are preserved free from all blemish, in that the Lord separated the good from the evil, thus redeeming the creature because of the good that dwelt within him.

XLII. 7–9. "And it was so, that after the Lord had spoken these words unto Job, the Lord said to Eliphaz the Temanite, My wrath is kindled against thee, and against thy two friends: for ye have not spoken of me *the thing that is* right, as my servant Job hath..

"Therefore take unto you now seven bullocks and seven rams, and go to my servant Job, and offer up for yourselves a burnt offering; and my servant Job shall pray for you: for him will I accept: lest I deal with you *after your* folly, in that ye have not spoken of me *the thing which is* right, like my servant Job.

"So Eliphaz the Temanite and Bildad the Shuhite *and* Zophar the Naamathite went, and did according as the Lord commanded them: the Lord also accepted Job."

Thus Job's three friends are commanded by the Lord to offer for themselves a burnt-offering, but Elihu is left out entirely, even though Eliphaz, Bildad, and Zophar did not speak of the Lord the thing that was right as Job spoke it. From these indications it follows that Job's three friends were conscientious although mistaken in their views, but that Elihu was not so, and, hence, that he spoke with the intention to mislead his hearers. His denunciation of Job was bitter, and he desired (see xxxiv. 36) that Job might be tried to the end; but this desire was not granted, for it is stated,—

XLII. 10–15. "And the Lord turned the captivity of Job, when he prayed for his friends: also the Lord gave Job twice as much as he had before.

"Then came there unto him all his brethren, and all his sisters, and all they that had been of his acquaintance before, and did eat bread with him in his house: and they bemoaned him, and comforted him over all the evil that the Lord had brought upon him: every man also gave him a piece of money, and every one an earring of gold.

"So the Lord blessed the latter end of Job more than his beginning: for he had fourteen thousand sheep, and six thousand camels, and a thousand yoke of oxen, and a thousand she asses.

"He had also seven sons and three daughters.

"And he called the name of the first, Jemima; and the name of the second, Kezia; and the name of the third, Keren-happuch.

"And in all the land were no women found *so* fair as the daughters of Job: and their father gave them inheritance among their brethren."

By these verses the house of Job increased and multiplied; from which the indication follows (see also Gen. ix. 1, 2) that this replenishment took place after the destruction of the Hiddekelic or Second race in the great Hiddekelic Famine or Drought.

The doubling of Job's sheep, camels, oxen, and asses

contains a clear indication pointing to the division of time in Job's day,—that is, the first count indicates the first two Ages of Man, while the second count covers the first two Ages and also the two remaining Ages.

XLII. 16, 17. "After this lived Job a hundred and forty years, and saw his sons, and his sons' sons, *even* four generations.

"So Job died, *being* old and full of days."

By indications otherwise given Job, as the Adam and progenitor of the Third Race, was created about the year B.C. 13,465, and the Hiddekelic Race was destroyed about the year B.C. 12,098; wherefore at the time of this destruction Job would have been thirteen hundred and sixty-seven years old. Now, if to this the hundred and forty years that remained to Job be added, then the lifetime of Job would cover fifteen hundred and seven years; which period is still short of that during which the Messiah walked in the flesh as man. The indications are, however, that the years the Messiah walked in the flesh as man—viz., eighteen hundred and sixty—established the maximum limits of man's age,—that is, man of Adam's race.

THE END.

www.ingramcontent.com/pod-product-compliance
Lightning Source LLC
Chambersburg PA
CBHW031329230426
4367OCB000O6B/289